TWILIGHT OF THE CELTIC GODS

TWILIGHT OF THE CELTIC GODS

An Exploration of Britain's Hidden Pagan Traditions

David Clarke

with
Andy Roberts

Foreword by Dr Anne Ross

BLANDFORD

First published in the UK 1996 by Blandford

A Cassell Imprint

CASSELL PLC
Wellington House
125 Strand
London WC2R 0BB

Distributed in the United States by Sterling Publishing Co., Inc.
387 Park Avenue South, New York, NY 10016-8810

Distributed in Australia by Capricorn Link (Australia) Pty Ltd
2/13 Carrington Road, Castle Hill, NSW 2154

**A Cataloguing-in-Publication Data entry for this title is
available from the British Library**

ISBN 0-7137-2522-2

Typeset by Litho Link Ltd, Welshpool, Powys, Wales

Printed and bound in Great Britain by The Bath Press

This book is dedicated to
Guy Ragland Phillips (1909–1988)

ACKNOWLEDGEMENTS

MANY dozens of people have provided material, help and encouragement in the inspiration, preparation and writing of this book. My biggest thanks must go to my contributing author, Andy Roberts, and his wife, Helen, who have provided the main touchstone to bounce ideas to and from. Andy especially for practical help, insight, photos and lots of coffee.

The book could not have been written without the help of numerous friends, contacts and informants, many of whom have provided valuable references and allowed me to use material or memories. Special thanks must go in particular to Dr Anne Ross and Dick Feachem; John Taylor Broadbent; Alan and Griselda Garner; Pat Ellison, Fran Skinner, William Dyson, Robert Woodward, Glynis Reeve, John Davies, Neville Slack, Anthony Myers Ward, Eric Richards, and Richard Litchfield; Martin Petch and Dr John Prag of Manchester University Museum; Julia Smith, Paul Devereux, Brian Slade, John Billingsley, Mike Harding, Richard Holland; Michael Bishop and Buxton Museum; Alan Chattwood, Doug Pickford, Margaret Bellhouse, Paul Screeton, Phil Rickman, and Martin Dowland; Lynn Fade and the Kendal Museum; Ken Smith of the Peak National Park Authority; Justin and Alison at the Weston Park Museum in Sheffield; the Yorkshire Archaeological Society; John Widdowson and everyone at the Centre for English Cultural Tradition and Language at Sheffield University; Melanie Dodd for the horse; and Stuart Booth at Cassell for having faith in the idea when all hope had gone. The Invocation by Robin Williamson appears courtesy of Warlock Music Ltd/Polygram Music Publishing Ltd.

Also thanks to Craig Chapman for providing the drawings of Celtic subjects featured in this book. Craig is an artist and contemporary sculptor of Celtic iconography.

The authors have made every attempt to trace the holders of copyright materials used in this book and apologize to anyone whom we may have neglected to thank in the list of acknowledgements.

CONTENTS

FOREWORD

IT is sometimes said that the history of our land is enshrined in our churches. To that I would add 'and in our landscape'. It lies deep in our ancient monuments; in place-names; in medieval deserted villages, such as Wharren Percy, Yorkshire, with roots in the Iron Age and a full flowering in the medieval period; and in this context especially, perhaps, in the voices of the people who, for generation after generation, have taken their living from the soil.

Change of every kind has altered the face of Britain's landscape. The industrial revolution erupted with a grimy violence over many rural areas, destroying for ever the surrounding countryside and the pattern of rural life with its roots in the distant past – medieval, Iron Age perhaps, even Bronze Age and ultimately Neolithic. The pace of the undisturbed country is not fast; change is slow to be accepted, or was until the technological revolution of industry. Two world wars, separated by a mere twenty years or so, decimated the young men who traditionally kept the old calendar customs and festivals alive. Ever-improving communications gave a new mobility to rural folk who had for generations remained virtually rooted in their own small area of countryside. Latterly, television and tourism have taken a heavy toll of the traditional way of life on the land.

Is it too late to salvage any part of the testimony of the countryfolk of the British Isles, with their roots stretching back, ultimately, to the Celtic past? Have the archaic beliefs and customs, superstitions and calendar celebrations entirely died out? Is there, perhaps, yet time to record vestiges of genuine folk tradition and traces of ancient, perhaps pre-Christian belief before these precious unwritten records of our own past as a distinctive people are irrevocably destroyed and lost for ever? I do not myself believe that it is yet too late, but there is little time left.

This fascinating book demonstrates how, with dedication and single-minded purpose – and especially by relying to a great extent on fieldwork to augment and verify the written sources – there is still a wealth of traditional lore to be gleaned from our countryside where people still farm the land tilled by their forebears; and look to old remedies for healing, archaic sayings for guidance and comfort, and remember something of the simple pastimes and seasonal festivals of long ago. In Ireland there is a splendid collection of archaic lore enshrined in a great compilation known as *Dindshenchas* ('Tales of Eminent Places'). This is aptly known as 'the mythological geography of early Ireland'. England, Scotland and Wales cannot boast anything quite comparable to this great compilation, but the history of the landscape and past heroes and deities can still be glimpsed in the names of places and rivers, and in certain archaeological monuments which often demonstrate the length and strength of certain traditions and legends. Now is the time to start collecting the last remnants of our ancient and inspiring past and fieldwork is the best way to carry this out. *Twilight of the Celtic Gods* has just such a message. It not only informs us about certain areas and traditions but also stresses the need for field studies and folklore collection. It has achieved much; may its example help us all to achieve more before it is too late and our folklore and practice die out leaving little trace.

Anne Ross,
Aberystwyth

INTRODUCTION

'. . . all things begin and end on Albion's druid
rocky shore . . .'

William Blake, 'Jerusalem'

THE CELTIC REVIVALS

'Many a beautiful thing had the people who are gone, in tales and histories, invocations and prayers, hymns and songs, runes and lays, sweet beautiful and soft. The good people of that day lived not on senseless babbling, they disdained gossip and scandal and conversed about the state of the world and about the changes in the weather, about the moon and the sun, about the ebbing and flowing of the sea and about life in the depths of the ocean. Oh, my dear one, it would be such talk, such noble talk, the like of which you will not hear today . . .'[1]

This passage is taken from a conversation between 'an old Highlander' and Alexander Carmichael, a scholar who collected traditional lore in Scotland at the turn of the century. In those days there was a feeling that the old ways, beliefs and superstitions which had been kept alive around the fireside and hearth and passed from one generation to another by word of mouth were disappearing, along with a way of life lived close to the earth and the seasons.

Modern technology and communications reached some of the more isolated areas of the British Isles, which had remained largely untouched by the industrial revolution, only within living memory. Many islands, hill villages and remote valleys remained self-sufficient and isolated, even in the heart of England, until the early years of this century. Continuity in both landscape and people was a vital factor and often families could trace their relationship with the land they farmed back many generations. In those days outsiders were few and eyed with suspicion. But things have changed.

The industrial revolution was the biggest jolt to the traditional way of life, which was based on agriculture and livestock farming. The old ways were further eroded by the human vacuum left by the two terrible world wars, which stripped many areas of their young men and brought much that was left over from the past to an end.

This book is about those traditions which have survived until recent times in a few special places in the British Isles; places where a tribal, Celtic past has lingered to a surprising degree, both within the people themselves and within the landscape they inhabit. These are old traditions passed down through families and communities, and continue to have a private significance and meaning today which have been lost in many other places and are not easy to describe in written form. It is perhaps summed up best by Peter Outram, a resident of the Peak District village of Castleton, which every year on 29 May holds an ancient Garland ceremony whose origins are often said to be 'lost in the mists of time'.

In 1995, the eighth year he has carried the beehive-shaped garland of flowers and foliage upon his shoulders during a horseback procession lasting almost two hours, he said: 'I'm the only man in the world doing this today. It's something very special, and still sends tingles down people's spines.'[2]

We have spent many years in the field exploring these beautiful landscapes and speaking to those guardians of the living past who have been kind enough

1 Alexander Carmichael, quoted in Mairi MacDonald, *Old Highland Folk Beliefs* (West Highland Publications, Oban, 1983)

2 Stephen McClarence, 'Crowning Glory' (*Sheffield Telegraph*, 2 June 1995)

to share their memories and knowledge with us. The tradition we have found in Britain today is rooted in stories about the unseen world which earlier writers claimed was exclusively the property of a Celtic race living on the furthest western fringes of Britain. It is a body of belief similar to that which the Irish called the lore of the *sidh* or 'people of the hills'. This lore includes everything from belief in the old Celtic deities, the veneration of nature in the form of water, trees and stones to omens of death, strange rituals and customs and a variety of experiences with the supernatural Otherworld.

Subjects like these are often categorized as being characteristically 'Celtic' – and confined to those areas like Ireland, Cornwall, Wales, Scotland and Brittany which earlier writers believed shared a common racial identity. The inhabitants of these lands, they claimed, were all that remained of the Celtic-speaking Britons who were forced westwards in the wake of the Anglo-Saxons, who 'destroyed' Romano-British culture. This narrow definition continues even today, and has undergone a recent revival in the writings of the New Age movement, to whom the word 'Celtic' has become a buzzword, representing anything mystical, strange or different from the Anglo-Saxon norm.

In fact, this recent revival of everything Celtic is only the latest in a series of attempts to reinvent old myths and manipulate them to suit contemporary needs – a process which can be traced back to the medieval era, when monks first wrote down the old tales and legends and English kings revived the romantic Arthurian tradition for a new audience.

In Victorian England there was another equally influential movement which became known as the Celtic Twilight, which is actually the origin of much of what we believe about our Celtic ancestors today. This movement saw the spiritual world of the Celtic fringe through rosy spectacles as all that remained of a people who once lived a 'pure' native existence closer to nature, the earth and the seasons.

Castleton Garland Day is held every year on 29 May (unless this falls on a Sunday) in the once isolated village below Mam Tor in the Derbyshire Peak District. The Garland King is a man on horseback who carries a garland of spring flowers. At the end of the procession, the garland is hung upon the tower of the parish church.

Early folklorists like Alexander Carmichael, along with contemporaries such as Lady Gregory and W. Y. Evans-Wentz, had been inspired by the writings of the Irishmen William Butler Yeats, author of *Celtic Twilight* (published in 1902) and 'AE' (George Russell). These collectors of oral tradition found in what Yeats called 'the desolate places', away from the intrusion of the car and the wireless, beliefs and traditions which seemed to preserve elements of an earlier, pagan nature-based religion. Evans-Wentz, a scholar who went on to rediscover Tibetan mysticism, set out from Oxford University in 1907 on a tour of the Celtic west to record stories and lore of the fairy Otherworld. He later developed his view of the world as a living entity with animals, plants and humans all interlinked, a theory which has resurfaced recently for a modern audience in the works of scientist James Lovelock.

To writers at the turn of the century this endangered world view – protected and preserved through past adversity by the surviving Celtic languages – was rapidly approaching its twilight. It was vanishing, forced ever more westwards and into extinction by the forces of progress and communication. This in turn went hand in hand with the theory, developed by Sir James Frazer and his followers, that calendar customs and curious beliefs and traditions which survived in remote country areas were actually survivals of pagan fertility rites which 1,500 years of Chrisitianity had failed to snuff out.

Contemporary historians contributed to this concept, suggesting the British inhabitants of these islands had been enslaved by the Anglo-Saxons, destroying Celtic tribal culture and creating the England we know today. This neatly explained the almost complete absence of Celtic language and place-names from the south and east of the islands. Nearly a century later, our knowledge of this period of prehistory and history has changed out of all recognition, but the general perception of the legacy of the Celts and what is 'Celtic' remains highly emotive and nebulous. Facts are few, and belief and romanticism have clouded what we really know about our past.

What can be said with certainty is that the concept of a Celtic heritage, rather than being an undisputed historical fact, is something which has been re-created in modern times as a tool to connect people with their past in times of change and uncertainty. The 'Celtic twilight' movement was spawned during a time of great tension at the turn of the century, and the deep and emotional appeal of all things Celtic has resurfaced again during the great social upheavals of the 1960s. It continues to this day of the New Age and Earth Mysteries movements.

In the late twentieth century more and more people, disillusioned with religion and society in the West, are seeking to rediscover ancient and lost wisdom. They are studying a variety of sources: Celtic, Eastern, native American – often a mixture of all three – modernized, repackaged and re-exported in a form acceptable to our own society. Mysticism and paganism are part and parcel of this view of the Celts, with the druids seen as the guardians of their ancient wisdom, and the enigmatic standing stones and other megalithic monuments their pagan temples.

To cater for the demand, a whole vast publishing genre has geared itself to re-create and redefine for new generations what we mean by 'Celtic religion', using a variety of sources, ancient and modern. These books confidently tell us about what Celtic religion was and is, the gods and goddesses, the festivals, the rituals . . . But how can we really be so sure what the Celts believed when they left so little unambiguous evidence? And who were the Celts anyway? As J. R. R. Tolkien so perceptively concluded, 'Celtic' is actually a magic bag 'into which anything may be put, and almost anything may come . . .'[3]

To think of the Celtic peoples in purely ethnic terms is now seen as misguided, and attempts to trace the origins of a Celtic 'race' have been unsuccessful. However, it is often been said that Celtic 'culture' grew out of the Bronze Age in central Europe during the first millennium BC and at its greatest extent stretched from Galatia in Asia Minor to the western shores of Ireland. Subsequently, the Iron Age tribes and the Celtic languages spoken by their peoples were effectively destroyed by the growth of the Roman empire and the upheavals and migrations which followed its collapse in the fifth century AD.

Much confusion and myth-making followed the end of the empire, and those who seek Celtic continuity naturally look westwards, away from Rome and in particular to Ireland, Insula Sacra, never conquered by the legions, for their view of what is truly Celtic. Professor Colin Renfrew, in *The Archaeology of Language*, found that the word 'Celtic' actually has eight widely different definitions, including the Roman definition of the Celts – that of the people who called themselves Celts – a language group, an archaeological complex, a later medieval art style and a catch-all term for the medieval 'Celtic church'.[4]

All that can be said for certain in the midst of this confusion is that there plainly was a Celtic language grouping, apparently itself just a branch of a larger group of Indo-European languages which spread across Europe alongside the movement of farming technology. This Celtic language was undoubtedly spoken by many different tribes and peoples in northwestern Europe at the time of the Roman empire, many of whom seem to have shared a common cultural and religious perception. Two forms of the Celtic language survive in Europe today, the Brythonic or 'P' Celtic group, which includes Welsh, Breton, Cornish and old British, and the Goidelic or 'Q' Celtic group, spoken in Ireland, Scotland the Isle of Man. This division is made purely on the basis of simple pronunciation, and does not imply any racial difference between the speakers.

It is clear that a variation of this language was once spoken in England, but the disappearance of Celtic language there does not necessarily mean that those who spoke it were exterminated by Latin-speaking Romans and later English-speaking Anglo-Saxons. Rather, it seems the Celtic population adopted the language of their new kings and leaders, which was after all the language of the law and the rent collector. Archaeology demonstrates how the native Britons intermarried with their new masters, and very soon identities became blurred.

But at the same time it is also plain that although there was substantial Anglo-Saxon settlement across large areas of southern and eastern Britain, this did not occur at the same time and to the same degree everywhere. While the lowlands were more vulnerable to invasion, settlement and outside influence, in conservative uplands the English element may never have constituted a majority of the population, creating the conditions where old tribal ways and traditions could survive with minimal interruption.

3 Quoted in Malcolm Chapman, *The Celts: The Construction of a Myth* (Macmillan, 1992)

4 Colin Renfrew, *The Archaeology of Language* (London, 1987)

The Celtic Regions of the British Isles

The map opposite shows the traditional 'Celtic fringe' of Britain with the names of the major tribes which the Romans found inhabiting the islands. Ireland is shown split into the four ancient provinces.

In these areas, archaeology and folk tradition suggest the population of the highlands was able to preserve some form of identity and semi-independence until a quite recent historical period. The idea of a geographical distinction was recognized by Sir Cyril Fox in an essay published in 1932 called 'The Personality of Britain'. Using archaeological data, Fox divided Britain into highland and lowland zones, basically a division which corresponded to northwest and southwest. In his highland zone, Fox included not just the conventional Celtic fringe of Wales and Scotland but also Devon and Cornwall, the Derbyshire Peak District and the Pennines of northern England. It was in areas such as these that a continuity of both population and religion could be found.

The second and most important characteristic of these upland areas was the concept of the continuity of the landscape's human population. There is evidence, for example, in some areas of West Yorkshire and the Pennines that a substantial British or Celtic population survived long after areas further south had become incorporated into Anglo-Saxon kingdoms. In fact, a concentration of native British place-names, customs and traditions in this region coincides with the kingdom of Elmet, which survived as an independent Celtic kingdom as late as the seventh century AD.

In regions like these, evidence of human continuity is very strong. In one Pennine valley we have studied, most of the family surnames common today were equally common in the seventeenth century, and many can be traced even further back into medieval times in the Duchy of Lancaster Court Rolls and Pleas of the Royal Forest of the Peak. In this case, even the upheavals of the industrial revolution failed to put an end to the old traditions, whose twilight lingered until the beginning of the space age.

THE LIVING TRADITION IN BRITAIN

Clearly much nonsense has been written about who the Celts were and what constitutes Celtic religion and belief. This book may well be seen by some as just another addition to this long and tired genre. We like to see it not as another journey into Celtic myth-making but as an exploration of genuine archaic and *living* traditions we have found in Britain today. Although we will use the word 'Celtic' in this book, we are using it as term of convenience rather than a classification of 'a people' or 'a race'. As one of our informants points out, when we talk of Celtic beliefs, customs and traditions what we really mean is the survival of very archaic beliefs which point back into prehistory and *may* have been exhibited by the historial Celts. A few are alive and well, others are teetering on the brink of extinction, most are already gone. One of the most

Traditional Celtic lands

CALEDONIAN
Grampian Mts.
TRIBES

North
Sea

Antonine
Wall
Firth of Forth
DUM- NONII
R.Clyde
SELGOVAE
VOTADINI

NOVANTAE

Hadrian's
Wall
R.Tyne
Solway Firth
Cumbrian
Mts.
Lake District
B R I G A N T E S
R.Tees

ULSTER

ISLE of MAN
The
Dales
R.Wharfe
R.Derwent
PARISI

CONNAUGHT

R.Boyne

LEINSTER

Peak

District
R.Humber

ANGLESEY

DECEANGLI
ORDO-
CORNOVII
VICES
Cambrian Mts.

CORITANI

ICENI

MUNSTER

DEMETAE
R.Severn

CATUVELLAUNI

TRINOVANTES

SILURES
DOBUNNI
ATREBATES

Miles
20 0   40   80   120

DUROTRIGES
R.Thames
CANTIUM

DUMNONII
Dartmoor
West
Penwith
ISLE of
WIGHT

English Channel

Contemporary Celtic artist Craig Chapman with some of the archaic-style heads he has carved from local stone.

surprising features is where we find them; not, as expected, in the 'Celtic fringe' but in the heart of Old England itself.

These traditions, which may or may not be regarded as 'Celtic', are not too different from those found by W. Y. Evans-Wentz and others who toured Scotland and Ireland at the turn of the century. What can be said is that they all come from similar landscapes or mindscapes – often isolated valleys hemmed in by high mountains, which have helped to preserve continuity of both people and custom. Two of the strongest archaic traditions featured in this book come from areas not commonly associated with the old perception of what constituted the Celtic heartlands: the Peak District of the English Midlands and the Yorkshire Dales of northern England, both identified by Fox's survey as centres of cultural continuity but long overlooked by ethnologists.

One of them is located in a collection of mill towns and farming villages barely 32 kilometres (20 miles) from the centre of one of England's largest and most densely populated cities – hardly the place anthropologists would go looking for pockets of surviving pagan Celtic tribes! This is particularly surprising because these traditions appear to have been so strong and deep-rooted in the identity of communities that they have survived literally thousands of years of social change and settlement, and latterly the upheavals of industrialization which are said to have destroyed them completely elsewhere.

'Tradition' can be defined as the accumulated personal experiences, beliefs and attitudes of people in a particular group or society that have been held for a long time and passed from generation to generation within families and communities. The major mode for the transmission of the material in our study is oral tradition, which was itself the only means the pre-literate tribes the Romans found in the British Isles had of communicating their culture from one generation to the next. Two thousand years ago Caesar described how the druids in Gaul had a taboo about committing their tradition to writing; instead they were skilled in the transmission of sacred knowledge by complex methods of oral recitation.

In many parts of the British Isles, oral tradition is still a living thing, long after the eclipse of the historical Celts. It continues to change and to grow, and every day, every year, something is added or taken away. By their very nature, folk memories of this kind are vulnerable and easily destroyed if a vital link in the chain of their transmission to a new generation is broken. Much has been distorted and lost, but there are still important truths to be found if only the centuries of fable can be peeled away. By its very nature, a living tradition is difficult to isolate and investigate if one does not wish to expose it to unwelcome outside attention and push it still further towards extinction. Hence we tread carefully, confident that what we discuss is done in safety, mainly because our informants feel that some portions of their tradition have truly reached their twilight and can therefore be discussed.

Although real places and landscapes will be featured in this book, great care has been taken to protect the identities of individuals involved in our stories. Places described in this book do exist and can be visited, though we would ask visitors to treat all ancient monuments and landscapes with the respect they deserve. During the course of our fieldwork, informants have often volunteered information of a highly sensitive and personal nature and we have used only what we have been given permission for, or information that is already on the record, having been used on radio, TV or in books and articles.

The living archaic traditions featured in this book we have found in certain parts of Derbyshire, Yorkshire, Devon and elsewhere where it was once believed the Anglo-Saxons settlers had displaced all previous lore and language. Here the pagan forces are not merely vague memories but are still feared and if not openly worshipped, then certainly acknowledged. And these deeply held and sincere beliefs, which are closely guarded by sensitive communities, have nothing to do with witchcraft or New Age revivals.

One of the first academic works to take seriously the notion of the continuity of Celtic tradition was *Pagan Celtic Britain*, published in 1967. The author, Dr Anne Ross, was born and bred in the Celtic heartlands; her mother's family came from central Perthshire and her father's people from the Grampians. She has spent much of her life conducting fieldwork in both her own country, Ireland and wherever else a living tradition has continued.

Continuity of tradition has always been the central theme in Dr Ross's work and this theme has been recognized by us and by many other fieldworkers in whose footsteps we followed, like the late Guy Ragland Phillips and Sidney Jackson. We have looked for clues to, and teased out strands of the living tradition, and tried to trace them in the landscape and folk tradition of the areas we have studied. While we have used archaeological evidence where necessary to support our findings, we have concentrated mainly upon the vernacular tradition and used primary source materials wherever possible.

Anne Ross was fully aware of the existence of one strong tradition in the High Peak of Derbyshire from the 1970s, when her fieldwork originally brought her into contact with a spokeswoman, or 'guardian' as she was dubbed. Along with TV producer Roy Davies, Dr Ross was astonished to discover how strongly archaic beliefs and attitudes had survived in small industrial towns so close to huge conurbations like Manchester and Leeds. And after a visit to a display of carved stone heads organized in Bradford, she described the Pennine valleys as being a 'treasure house of continuity', adding, 'I had always imagined the West Riding to be an industrial hotchpotch in which all traces of past cultures would have been obliterated. I had failed to realize that each mill town and village was, almost to this day, largely cut off from the others and isolated.'[5]

In the text which follows the primary sources of information about the living Celtic tradition have come from five main informants. Three of them no longer live in the areas they are discussing, and only two have any knowledge of the existence of each other. The texts in italics which constitute some of the chapters here, or are included in the body of others, are extracts from letters to the authors from an informant born in one Yorkshire valley. They were sent in response to a questionnaire on his family traditions. We have called this person the 'Dalesman'.

5 Guy Ragland Phillips,
Brigantia:
A Mysteriography
(Routledge & Kegan
Paul, 1976)

1

CELTIC BELIEF

'The most meaningful connections and
happenings really are wordless. I'm aware of
influences, some of them extremely subtle, but
the most meaningful of them I think go beyond
words . . . It's not something that's entered
through books, it's something that you feel
through the soles of your feet and through the
top of your head and your fingertips and
it's wordless . . .'

Anonymous, from *The Call of the Celts*, BBC Radio 4,
Hallowe'en, 1986

THE GUARDIAN

My name is not really important, but I think the story I have to tell is. Although I now live in north London, I spent my childhood and most of my adult life in the Wharfe valley area of Yorkshire, where I and a group of families I am related to originate. I come from an old tradition, a very old tradition if the learning passed down through our families is to be believed, a way of understanding the world which transcends, yet encompasses the mundanity of much of life. It's really a way of looking at the universe which includes human beings as a fundamental part of the whole process. Notice that I say tradition rather than religion, because I suppose that's what it is. We don't really worship, in essence because we ourselves are part of the very thing we would have to worship, and so instead we revere, and stand in awe of, the powers that create and sustain us and the world.

I was always told that my family and its various branches and offshoots have lived in this part of the world since time began. This was the exact term we used, 'since time began', and we have worked with and on the land as farmers, craftsmen and in related professions, at least up until the 1960s, when things began to change and fragment. At that time the last of the older generation died and many if not most of the younger ones moved away – in some cases emigrating to America – and generally lost interest in what most of them had come to see as just an old family tradition which had less and less relevance to the 'modern world'. For my part, I think what I have been shown and taught have increased relevance in these times, but I have my own theories on these aspects of things, as you'll see. Yes, I suppose we are 'pagans' – but only in the sense that the world of paganism originally meant the beliefs and practices of those in the countryside.

From my early childhood onwards I was schooled in the family tradition – we actually called it 'the learning' – and rather than a formal teaching such as exists in the Christian tradition, our teaching took a much more relaxed yet somehow intense form. Instruction was the responsibility of older family members, who held no position or title as such, other than the respect we accorded them because of their knowledge and experience. They had lived, we hadn't – yet. They were, I suppose, our 'tribal elders' and I am one such now, or would be if there was anyone young or interested enough left in the families to pass my knowledge on to.

At the time of my 'awakening', as we called it, my maternal grandmother was responsible for passing on the teachings – it was initially passed on from grandparent to child, female to male or male to female – and this at first took the form of what might be called 'nature walks' – remember, I was only seven at the time – in which we would walk for miles in all weathers, at all times of year and at all times of day and night. This was quite frightening, as I was often in unfamiliar territory and we initially walked in total silence. If I tried to speak or ask questions, I was hushed with a 'just look and listen' or something similar. Gradually I became accustomed to these regular excursions and after a few months or so, when I could walk quickly and silently across most forms of terrain, my grandmother started the instruction proper. I suppose to most people, even now, it wouldn't seem very much, just a boy and his grandmother out for a walk, albeit at some peculiar times.

She instructed me well and slowly I began to realize just what I was being taught. Slowly from being a series of roads, paths, fields and hills, I began to see the general topography of the area in which I lived in a very different way altogether. There were no physical barriers to us and we would roam freely, paying little attention to the recognized rights of way or easy ways across the countryside, but instead paying total attention to the land and how it was formed, its shapes, textures and hidden places. Instead of land to be swiftly passed through on the way to somewhere else, it was revealed to me as part of the body of a living thing whose mysteries were accessible if you looked in the right way, at the right time. And as we walked, she would point out and name certain landscape features which were important to the learning, and I came to know them by those names. She would tell me stories about them and the powers that inhabited and protected them. Giants, fairy-folk, spirits and more subtle forces and powers were everywhere, and what to me had once been, say, a hill was now a place full of possibilities, a hive of life and death both physically and non-physically, all of which were necessary for its continued existence and significance within our leaning.

My grandmother explained to me what I see now was a simplistic form of ecology: that the earth was a living, breathing entity and everything was interrelated. Nowadays, that's a widely held idea, but held, I think, more from an intellectual point of view. To us it was the experience that mattered and formed our ideas. I was taught to look at anything from a hill to a stream to a leaf and in looking correctly to see both the physical processes and the higher meanings. It's not easy to explain really, it has to be experienced.

The result of all this teaching and experiencing was what I came to know. And as a small child I didn't need too much persuading to enter this new awareness, this new form of consciousness. Everything pulsated with life and mystery at that age anyway and so the idea that the world – and more importantly for me at that time, my part of it – was alive on many levels was truly incredible but yet somehow familiar. It just seemed right, like there could be no other way. Like coming home.

With hindsight I can see now that the time of 'awakening' was carefully timed to just catch the young ones at a time when their processes of discrimination and intelligence were developing and could be harnessed without much trouble. Too early and the child would be too young to understand what was being taught and perhaps be put off later, too late and the capacity for awe and wonder would be already dulled by the world's complications and distractions. That was one significant part of our learning: it enables the awe and mystery inherent in the world as a child to be kept for life and used as a basis for everything which followed.

After a while I was fully conversant with the Wharfe valley from the town of Ilkley up to its source in the high Dales and I happily accepted it as an embodiment of the power from which all life comes. Occasionally my elder brother or some male cousins would come out with us, but they were already at the end of their instruction in the tradition and practising alone or with their families. But it was fun and we would test each other on the landscape names, retell the stories and legends of the area and continue to absorb the awesome mystery that we had so suddenly found ourselves part of.

During this process my grandmother also began teaching me about the workings of the natural world, which at school was limited to walks and nature tables, in itself far removed from the knowledge most of us country kids already had. But her instruction went deeper still. I had to learn all, and I mean all, the names – local names that is – for every single plant, tree, type of stone, animal, bird, insect, fish and so on. I had to know where they could all be found, what they looked like at any given time of the year and what, if any, their uses were – medicinal, practical or whatever.

This was no mere book-learning, it was 'out in the field' work: touching, tasting, sitting and watching, until I could distinguish between a beech and an alder twig by feel alone in the middle of the night – in a snowstorm if necessary! I had to be able to correctly identify a heron's cry and feather, tell just by sense of smell where a fox had crossed the path and so on. This was deep learning. I was taught about specific times of the year, month and day and what they meant and could be used for and how the weather and its patterns indicated certain things to come with crops and animals. The sun, moon and night sky too became a different place, populated with heroes and villains, gods and goddesses. So far away yet still a part of the one power I was being slowly exposed to.

It didn't seem to matter to her that I didn't actually use much of this information, but she had to be satisfied that I knew it in a far deeper sense than just, say, repetition or lip-service, and she knew when I didn't.

During those first few years of instruction in the natural world I was also eased into the fundamental belief of our tradition – that the land is sacred. And to that end we thought of ourselves as stewards, guardians of the areas where members of our family dwelt, people who could be of some use to others who had forgotten or never knew what we still held on to. It seemed as though we did too, because farmers, stockmen, gamekeepers and many ordinary countryfolk all knew of our knowledge of plants and animals, and certain members of the family would help them with natural and herbal remedies for both animal and human problems alike. This just seemed to be accepted and expected. Nor were we considered out of the ordinary for holding these beliefs and knowledge. It was as though it was once widely held and accepted but was now the province of only a few.

None of this seemed particularly strange to me, and as things were revealed it all just seemed to slip into place and become a part of me, and I in turn felt a part of it, together with a renewed sense of community with members of my family wherever they were scattered. I suppose it was a tribal thing really . . . That's the best way of putting it, tribal.

Did we worship? No, not really. To us being alive and part of the body of the mother was worship for us – staying true to the tradition and marking the special times, being open to the natural powers was enough. The powers that we held in awe were locked inside the landscape, inherent in the power of the weather and manifest in the cycle of the changing of the seasons, and in the end they in turn ran through us. It was nothing complicated, nothing supernatural, and to me, at least, the way people are supposed to live.

As I grew older and read widely in mythology, legend and history, I came to realize that many of the things I had been taught, and which had subsequently become a part of me, had also been understood and practised by my ancestors, possibly for many thousands of years. Even back to prehistoric times. I wouldn't go so far as to say we are specifically 'Celtic', or indeed any other race or culture. That sort of thing is for others to work out. We are just – as some Indian tribes call themselves, I believe – the people of the land, and this was the reason, I think now, why we didn't see ourselves as special or different in any way. I also came to the realization that all the learning and specific ways of looking and seeing we had were a form of initiation into the true mystery of life.

Why am I telling you these things? Well, I suppose that even though I've been aware for some time that our learning was not solely confined to the area I come from, it was only when I read about other traditions in Derbyshire and elsewhere that I realized just how widespread and similar our beliefs were across the whole country. At one time I think it's feasible to suggest that everyone thought in this way and that time and progress have eroded the knowledge into small pockets of belief carried on in small communities, families and individuals who can still find some use and value in what they have been taught, and who can't forget.

Like yourselves, I share the feeling that we are at the end of something that may never be rekindled. I think the time has come when it needs sharing beyond the boundaries we have always kept to in my lifetime and learning. I don't think I'm giving away any secrets for the simple reason that there are none! Mystery, yes, but secrets, no. It's an open book if you are prepared to read it correctly. To me it was all obvious, and anyway I believe that you can reveal matters of this nature to people but in the end reading a book won't change anything in itself. It's a start but it has to be taken further, you have to experience, know and ultimately understand – in that order – these things, and I think the time has come now when we have to understand them quickly, before it really is too late.[1]

THE VALLEY

'That what we shall call the tradition was never, in my experience anyway, a body of doctrine but a milieu in which one grew up. It is analogous to the milieu in which Laurie Lee grew up, in Slad, as described in *Cider with Rosie*. We were born just in time to catch the tail end of the old world and the old ways and, through them, to touch the long and living past. How can it be passed on? That world in which that was a living tradition is gone. The gods are real enough – they canot be reduced to metaphors – but I don't know who can make them immanent for modern man . . .'

A former resident of Longdendale valley, Derbyshire Peak District

Head eastwards from Manchester's busy city centre and after 24 kilometres (15 miles) the concrete jungle slowly changes into a fundamentally different landscape. Travel along the main A628 trans-Pennine road away from the metropolis, and the twentieth-century hustle and bustle gradually gives way to bleak moorland scenery when the village of Mottram-in-Longdendale is reached.

From here, the visitor can climb a steep stairway into the blustery graveyard which surrounds the gaunt parish church of St Michael and All Angels. The fourteenth-century church, built of rough blackened moor stone, stands on a prominent hilltop sacred from prehistory, its stark appearance enhanced by the stony gaze of fearsome stone heads which glare northwards from the tower and window dripstones.

1 Pers. comm., 1994

Stretching away in the distance to the north and east is a stunning vista of harsh mountain scenery encompassing Longdendale valley, the Derbyshire mill town of Glossop and, behind it, the long, dark, brooding expanse of high gritstone moorland known as Bleaklow. As the name suggests, Bleaklow is a vast boggy plateau divided only by the valley of the River Etherow, which drains westwards from the moors at Woodhead towards the coast.

Longdendale valley is a special place. Parts of it have a brooding atmosphere, enhanced by the uncompromising weather which batters walkers on the Pennine Way, a long-distance footpath which crosses the high moors north to south. Beauty remains here, despite the rape of the valley's natural resources over the past two centuries. First, it was the channelling of the river to provide water power for cotton mills, then came the reservoirs and a railway for thirsty city-dwellers and lastly there came a string of ugly electricity pylons along the valley bottom.

Despite the industrial depression, traces of a different time linger to a surprising degree. Even with the encroachment of the twentieth-century, this trans-Pennine valley has one foot planted firmly in the timeless past. Among its older residents there continues a feeling of continuity, both in family and in landscape, and a sense of 'identity' which has bred a distinctive personality found elsewhere in the Pennines and Celtic west.

As one of the central characters in our story says, it doesn't matter how long you have lived in Longdendale, you can become part of it if you have the

The Longdendale valley. Only a short distance from one of Britain's largest cities, the valley of the River Etherow is one of the last bastions of genuine Celtic tradition.

right kind of disposition, the right sort of inclinations and the right sort of beliefs. It is a place that gets a very deep hold on people: 'They only live here for a few years and they remember it for the rest of their lives because they feel it, partly because we are enclosed by the hills and it sort of isolates you.'

Longdendale valley, like many others which branch westwards from the high Pennine chain of northern Britain – the Celtic Brigantia – is one location which has retained an authentic tradition with an unbroken link with the Celtic past. Here, clinging to the very rocks, are some of the last vestiges of an old tradition which is vanishing almost as quickly as you read these words.

Elsewhere in the Peak District there are more 'high-profile' reminders of the Celtic past: the Castleton Garland ceremony, Ashbourne's Shrovetide football game and the rapidly multiplying well-dressings, revived and adapted by many villagers in the limestone districts of the White Peak. Similar customs survive in the High Peak, but the tradition we are discussing is different and possibly as old as the hills, valleys and mountains themselves.

Visitors to this area will find few clues to the nature of the surviving tradition, and in the words of one informant, you can be certain that anyone who is willing to tell a stranger what they know, 'will by their very responding, give proof that they know nothing . . . It is in the blanks, the interstices, that you may find the pattern of the truth.'

Following this advice, the authors have spent many years slowly filling in those blanks. This book is part of the result of our quest. It really began in 1977, when one of the guardians who represents this surviving tradition in the Derbyshire Peak District first agreed to come forward and discuss the elements of her beliefs as part of a BBC TV documentary on the survival of Celtic customs. She was filmed in semi-darkness and TV producers went to some pains to protect her identity from the eyes of prying newsmen.

Even the name of the small Derbyshire town from which this woman came was not revealed, but it was said she represented 'a secret Peak District community which still practised a Celtic tradition with its origins rooted 2,000 years in the past'.[2]

This community, so the TV programme claimed, was made up of between 200 and 500 people on scattered farms and smallholdings in the High Peak district. They were 'ordinary farming families' who retained a belief in the earth, the Mother Goddess, the pagan gods and protected their secrets by means of 'guardians' whose exact role was never fully explained.

The survival of pockets of pagan belief – 'Celtic enclaves' – had long been suspected in this area of the Pennine foothills, where many British place-names have survived. But a whole 'community' which continued a tradition of belief which stretched back to Celtic times, nearly 2,000 years ago – surely this could not be genuine? Some authorities have concluded that the idea is so unbelievable, a more likely explanation is that the Derbyshire tradition is a revival or product of the 1960s New Age movement, which has spawned so much nonsense ever since.

After much careful investigation of the historical evidence, and many discussions with informants who are not connected with each other and have no axe to grind, we came to the conclusion that this tradition is indeed genuine –

2 'Twilight of the English Celts', *Chronicle*, BBC2, 27 October 1977

but certainly not unique in the British Isles. It is, or was, not a 'cult', 'religion' or 'belief system' separate from Christianity, which all of its adherents profess to follow, but more, in the words of one, 'an attitude, a way of perceiving things, a milieu which is ever more fragmenting, disintegrating . . .'

From our own enquiries, it seems what remains of this hidden tradition was 'discovered' almost by accident through the fieldwork of Anne Ross, who had visited the Derbyshire Peak District while researching the TV programme, which aimed to challenge the long-held theory that the Anglo-Saxons were the source of most English customs and beliefs.

After meeting representatives of this tradition, producer Roy Davies said, 'They are a very, very sensitive people and they have never been identified in public. This is the first time they have spoken. They believe in the old Celtic gods and goddesses and their religion is tied to the fertility of the earth. They have fertility rites in the sense that they practised in the past, rites which ensure the fertility of their crops. I could not get as close to them as I would have wanted. There was very much a clampdown on questions about their leaders, on where they met and on what they actually did when they met.'[3]

Why did the Longdendale guardian come forward to speak? She explained, 'Well, it wasn't something I wanted to do, but it seems to be a duty on me, because over the years some of the pride in the old things has rather got pushed out of the way and there are people who have done these things who perhaps now consider that they weren't right.'[4]

So, it seemed that the guardian, encouraged by her trust in the programme-makers, was taking what she saw as the right opportunity to give her people back respect in their traditional beliefs – using the very public medium of television. She told me later that during the 1960s and 1970s, people in her valley had begun to doubt the old ways, thinking that what they had done in the past was wrong and against the teachings of the Church. It was her memory of an old lady that finally drove her to speak out: her parson had told the old lady that the old ways were evil, that she would go to hell if she believed in them; this had made the old lady frightened of dying, the guardian said – a terrible situation for someone of that age.

The archaic Celtic tradition which has survived in these hills is now as near dead as it can be, but those who retain some knowledge are sensitive about their inheritance. They don't wish to be labelled cranks or have their beliefs held up to ridicule or sensationalized by outsiders. Their defensive attitude has been hardened in recent years by the activities of self-styled witches and Satanists who have desecrated the little chapel of Woodhead, near the head of the valley.

As local informants go to pains to point out, 'witchcraft' and 'New Age' are words which have no place in the local tradition, and as Rex Bellamy writes with characteristic local humour, 'any woman cavorting about Longdendale naked would swiftly find themselves in an intensive care unit.'[5] In the words of the guardian, 'It is a worship of God, not of pagan idols or anything funny like that, and it seemed we had to give them back their respectability to know that they were doing right. It just had to be done, so I did it.'

We have visited Longdendale many dozens of times and explored the hills, moors and lanes of the villages which cluster on the hillsides around the mill

3 'BBC Guards Secret of Peak District Pagan Worshippers' (*Sheffield Star*, 28 October 1977)

4 *Chronicle*, op. cit.

5 Rex Bellamy, *The Peak District Companion* (David & Charles, 1981)

town of Glossop, which lies at the foot of the Snake Pass road across Bleaklow. On one of these occasions we spent an October afternoon walking in a hidden valley near Woodhead, where rivulets of water from the moors eke a path westwards towards the reservoirs.

Our companion that day was a woman whose connections with the valley and the beliefs of those who have lived here goes back centuries into that timeless Celtic past. She is a native of the valley and can trace her family connections to the land back a number of generations on both sides. She has appeared on several television documentaries as a spokesperson for her tradition, as we will call it, but until recently was unwilling to be identified openly.

This lady is one of at least five guardians who have inherited beliefs and traditions from the archaic past of this valley, which today lies on the boundary between Derbyshire, Cheshire and Greater Manchester. It is a region of great contrasts, both physical and mental, and until very recently the majority of the inhabitants came from families who had lived in the valley for generation after generation.

On the afternoon of our visit to Woodhead, we traced the footsteps of the Irish navvies who had once worked on the underground railway tunnel whose three tracks were built at great cost to life and limb during the nineteenth century. At 5.4 kilometres (three miles 66 yards) in length, the Woodhead Tunnel is the longest of its kind in the world and is now used only for carrying freight. But the valley is still there, mysterious and insular as ever. The influx of Irish immigrants no doubt contributed to the native British stock, and it is interesting that a number of people who have come into the valley have been from a Celtic background, including one family from Cornwall.

'Until quite recently we were a farming area and people here were people who had been here for generations,' explained our companion. 'We think of ourselves as Celts, but how much of our actual tradition is Celtic I couldn't honestly say. Most of our beliefs fit in perfectly well with the normal way of life – there isn't anything odd about them.'[6]

But, she explained, when you begin talking about archaic beliefs in a country which is officially Christian, it sounds very strange and almost primitive. As a child, she said, you didn't really know what was going on, and it wasn't until you were a little older that the realization crept in that living in a place like this, some of the 'old ways' didn't just die out after all, but instead simply merged into everyday consciousness'.

The old ways were in effect survivals of what many people today would describe as a form of paganism: for instance, belief in certain Celtic deities and spirits, acknowledging the earth and the changing seasons through special festivals and giving thanks to the mother for the harvest. In essence, people brought up in these Pennine valleys saw it simply as a tremendous respect for the earth – 'She is your mother, she is what you live on.'

After following the track eastwards alongside the Woodhead reservoirs at the very head of the valley, near the border with Yorkshire, the path slowly turns right over a packhorse bridge and sweeps upwards and enters the mouth of a beautiful wooded glen – truly a lost world. Invisible to thundering traffic

6 *Chronicle*, op. cit.

on the busy Woodhead road a short distance above us, we climbed upwards past grouse butts and old shooting cabins into a dense deciduous wood beside a rushing and bubbling stream coming from Bleaklow Moor above us.

This was a very numinous place, and as we paused and sat down by the ruins of a stone cabin, she pointed out on the other side of the stream a striking stone boulder which looked for all the world like a face staring across at us. From every angle, the strange patter of indentations on the gritstone resolved itself into rough human features. Whether it was natural or man-made we couldn't say, but we have encountered guardian stones like this in numinous places before.

'The water coming from the moor when I was small was clear, was pure, and you could drink it, and the streams coming down to the river were something else,' she explained. 'They were beautiful – the spirit of the land coming out into the sunlight and seeing the daylight.' Pointing to the gritstone bedding planes that protruded upwards through the rushing springwater, these words about the Earth Mother took on a special significance: 'You can see her bones, you can see the water flowing which is the life of the earth.'

'We've always been here,' explained my guide. 'This is what we are – just ordinary people who have always been close to the earth and acknowledged it. There's nothing odd about that. There are some things that must go on, something as basic to life as belief in the earth and the good things of it, and thanking God you've got them. It's a peculiar thing to put into words, but until recently that was what we were – people who had been here almost for ever.'[7]

DREAMING ON THE EDGE

'I suspect the truth is that the Celts are still here and have always been here. In a way, before they arrived. What this land has the ability to do is not to be invaded, but to assume and consume the take unto itself and make its own. And, for me, the professional Celts who go out to the fringes and moan and wear tartans rather objectionably are really not Celtic. Because the true Celts, the ones who cared, stayed where they were and we're still here . . .'[8]

Alan Garner

7 Ibid., and 'The Isle is Full of Noises', *Everyman*, BBC1, November 1993

8 From transcript, copyright Alan Garner, 1993

Alderley Edge is a sheer sandstone cliff which rises like a whaleback from the flat Cheshire plain 32 kilometres (20 miles) south of Manchester in the heart of a beautiful landscape. From the top of the rocky sandstone outcrop known as Stormy Point or the Devil's Grave, the visitor can obtain some of the finest views in this part of the Midlands. Centuries ago, long before local landowners planted the Edge with trees, the views from the ancient beacon mound on the summit must have been breathtaking. Looking westwards there was nothing but Beeston Castle between the viewer and the hills of North Wales, and beyond the Celtic sea and Insula Sacra of Ireland. And a short distance to the northwest, on the road to Wilmslow, was the black pool of Lindow, a place of offerings and perhaps sacrifice in the Celtic past.

To award-winning writer Alan Garner, Alderley Edge was and continues to be the source of his inspiration – in his own words, 'my nuclear reactor'. Born into a family of craftsmen who lived and worked on the Edge for generations, he can trace the family name in records as far back as the 1590s. However, Garner suspects his ancestors' identification with the landscape of this area goes back far beyond the sixteenth century, back to the time when a tribe the Romans called the Cornovii lived there, and even beyond that.

'I think we have always been here,' he explains. 'And if you know where to look, you can go and pick up flint artefacts that have been lying and waiting for 8,000 years, and when I pick them up I know the DNA of whoever dropped that is shared by me. And then I feel at one with the land.'[9]

Like the others we have met in our quest, Garner's sense of his Celtic inheritance goes back to his childhood, his family or 'tribe', and an inherited oral tradition of great antiquity. It was around the woods, rocks and caves of the Edge that he played as a child, and listened to the local stories and folk-tales told by his grandfather, a smith. The rich body of lore and legend which characterizes the area surrounded him as he grew up to the extent that he eventually came to know 'every tree and the significance of every rock and folk-tale'. His sense of 'belonging' or symbiosis with the land and his ancestors he describes as 'a tribal matter', which can best be compared with the mindscape of traditional peoples like the Australian Aboriginals, who saw their land as sacred.

Speaking recently, he said, 'I know that the way I absorbed information from my family background was given to me as if I were being reminded of something that I had forgotten, but really knew . . .'[10] Furthermore, Garner was the first in his family to receive a university education, and in his later career as a writer he returned to his homeland and allowed himself to become a keen and willing channel for the stories and traditions of his childhood.

Several reviewers have compared Garner's role as a writer to that of the shaman as medium, bringing into being 'that which I can see but others can't'. Indeed, his first two adventure novels written for children, *The Weirdstone of Brisingamen*, first published in 1960, and its sequel, *The Moon of Gomrath*, are both rooted deeply in the magical landscape of the Edge and the immediate environment in which he grew up. *The Weirdstone* is a wonderful, exuberant fantasy about two ordinary children who are drawn into a supernatural battle between good and evil when they arrive to stay on the Edge with Gowther and Bess Mossock, who farm there. It is not long before they become involved in a series of strange and frightening events involving an Otherworld populated by witches, an evil hooded figure and cave-dwelling elves and dwarfs whose names are drawn from Celtic and Norse mythology.

Central to the plot is the wizard Cadellin, who takes the two children into the 'cave of the sleepers', Fundindelve, where 140 knights, all but one with a

9 Ibid.

10 *Everyman*, op. cit.

milk-white steed, lie in enchanted sleep in preparation for the final battle of good against evil. The wizard tells them that he has lost the magic stone Firefrost, which binds the spell, and fears it will be broken if the stone falls into the wrong hands. The fantasy is based upon elements drawn from a famous Cheshire folk-tale, 'The Wizard of Alderley', which Garner learned from his paternal grandfather before the Second World War, and which in the story Farmer Mossock repeats when the children ask him about the meaning of the Wizard's Well on Alderley Edge.

Alan Garner's fascination with myth, folklore and his family connection with the land is reflected in all of his writings, and the local dialect he uses in the stories can be traced back to the fourteenth-century Gawain poet, who lived and worked in the same region of northwest England. Garner is particularly effective in his reworking of traditional stories in a modern context, and this fusing of old and new has continued in three subsequent works *Elidor*, *The Owl Service* and *Red Shift*. The latter, an exciting multi-layed novel, features three central characters who live in different eras but are all linked together in time and space at Mow Cop, a numinous hilltop in Cheshire. All three also possesses for a time the same Neolithic stone axe-head which has a special significance for each character. In fact, the axe-head used in the novel is actually one Garner found buried beneath the Goldenstone, a standing stone he located and excavated on Alderley Edge – which also plays a part in the legend of the wizard.[11]

Although Alan Garner may not describe himself as a guardian of an ancient tradition in the way others we have met do, he nevertheless fulfils that role and is aware of both the responsibility this places upon him and the dilemmas it causes. Not wishing to see the loss of delicate and disintegrating local knowledge and recognizing the need for it to be recorded before the chain of memory is broken, he is also aware of the dangers of careless relevation to unprepared and unschooled minds. 'The ornithologist is particularly careful not to betray the nest of a rare bird and, for the same reason, I can't let what is my responsibility to keep alive become the museum specimen that all may visit at the expense of its extinction.'[12]

Garner's fears, shared by informants in other areas, are well founded. Today, Alderley Edge is a beauty spot owned by the National Trust and is much frequented by tourists on Sundays and Bank Holidays. But on Hallowe'en, the eve of the great Celtic feast of the dead, crowds of drunken revellers gather in the roads and woods of the Edge, wearing masks and robes, and, making considerable noise and causing great nuisance, stumble along the wooded cliffs and lanes in search of an occult force they have heard lurks there. Sensation-seekers from the big cities have been drawn here since the year 1962, when a newspaper carried pictures of a 'coven of witches' from Manchester dancing and cavorting on the Edge. They were clad in white ritual robes as they circled a bonfire, preparing to initiate a new member. Later, more pictures of a self-styled 'Queen of the Witches' were published, showing her holding a ceremonial knife as she looked out across the Cheshire plain towards Manchester and claimed her domain.[13]

Prior to these overblown and sensationalized events, there was actually no 'ancient' tradition of witchcraft associated with Alderley Edge. As elsewhere, a

11 Neil Philip, *A Fine Anger: A Critical Introduction to the Work of Alan Garner* (Collins, 1981)

12 Alan Garner, pers. comm., 1993

13 Doug Pickford, *Cheshire: Its Magic and Mystery* (Sigma Press, 1994)

little knowledge can become a dangerous thing. For although the Edge has continued to have an image as a strange and special place, these feelings come not from associations with 'witchcraft' or occult forces of any kind, but rather from a more ancient tradition which is *truly* connected with the mysteries of Britain's Celtic past.

Pilgrims who visit the Edge today first call at the Wizard restaurant and information centre and can then follow a well-worn path into the woods to the sandstone cliffs at Stormy Point. Other routes lead visitors to the dense woodland planted in the eighteenth century surrounding the Armada beacon, which stands upon one of the many prehistoric barrows in the area and features in one of Garner's stories as the home of the Wild Hunt.

Further west along the Edge, they can find a wishing well formed by a natural spring which emerges from a sandstone outcrop, the water collecting in a stone trough below. Above the spring a bearded face is carved in relief upon the rock, depicting the Wizard of Alderley, a Merlin-like figure. Below it is a crudely executed inscription, of later origin, which reads:

> . . . drink of this
> and take thy fill,
> for the water falls
> by the Wizhards will . . .

The Wizard's Well is actually a Victorian creation, carved over 100 years ago for the local landowners, the Stanleys and the Traffords, who revelled in revamping their romantic dreams of druids and ancient Britons during the Victorian revival of everything Celtic. It was this same era which spawned a rough ring of standing stones in another part of the woods on Alderley Edge which has become known as the Druid's Circle. Since the 1960s this place has become the target for modern visitors on Hallowe'en, and is now a centre of rituals of all kinds for New Age folk from the cities. However, as one writer has pointed out, the stone circle is actually nothing but a folly, a red herring.

Despite all the false trails laid by revivals and misinterpretations, there are a number of ancient traditions and legends associated with the Edge, most important of which is the story of the Wizard, which we have already mentioned. The feeling of strangeness or numinosity which many people detect when they visit the cliff and its woods may well stem from an authentic memory of an association with the Otherworld. Indeed, during the thirteenth century, a charter describes one part of the cliff, near Stormy Point (the Devil's Grave), as 'Elfgrenhoks', meaning 'the sandy ridge of the elves'.[14] These place-names suggest a connection with strange happenings which may have led early settlers to regard the area with superstitious awe.

Evidence of human occupation in this area actually goes back to the neolithic period. The sandstone rock which forms the escarpment itself is rich in minerals and the slopes are riddled with caves and old mineworkings, which have been in use since the late Bronze Age. The act of mining took something precious from the very body of the goddess, and was therefore surrounded with many propitiatory rituals. And it was in the Celtic Iron Age that some believe Alderley Edge may have become an important economic and religious

14 Alan Garner, 'Family Oral Tradition and Applied Archaeology in East Cheshire', lecture paper delivered to the Folklore Society, Manchester, 1977

centre for the Celtic tribe known as the Cornovii, who inhabited the forested border country of Cheshire and the Welsh marches.

Copper was the most important mineral mined on the Edge, but lead, cobalt and zinc were also sought by the prehistoric miners. A pigment containing some of them was identified in traces of paint upon the skin of an Iron Age body cut from the peat of Lindow Moss, to the northwest of the Edge, during the 1980s. The name Lindow seems to be derived from *llyn dhu*, Celtic for 'black pool'. Peat-cutting operations here have since turned up a human skull and the remains of a number of bodies of Iron Age and Romano-British date.

The best known of these is a young man in his twenties who has been christened 'Lindow Man'. He seems to have been the subject of a grisly triple death after eating a last ritual meal – perhaps as a druidic offering to a Celtic deity of the Underworld.

In their book on the mystery of Lindow Man, Anne Ross and Don Robins speculate that he may have met his end not at Lindow but at a sacred Celtic shrine nearby – possibly upon Alderley Edge itself, 'close to the well, on its highest point'.[15] Perhaps he also drank from one of the springs which emerge from the rocks on the slopes of Edge, some of which have been venerated for centuries. Indeed, several Bronze Age palstaves have been found to the northwest of the Edge, in circumstances which suggest they were deposited as offerings to springs or pools of water.

Alan Garner speaks of the landscape of Alderley Edge as a place of wonder for the Celts, a physical boundary between land and sky, but feels it is also significant as a boundary in consciousness – a place of dreaming, where the Otherworld could be accessed. He says of it, 'Alderley Edge is as full of significance and function as a modern cathedral but the difference is that it is a Celtic cosmos'.[16]

Both he and other local writers have suggested that for the tribes who settled and mined metals on the hill, the Edge, or one special part of it, may have been seen as an image of the great Mother Goddess whom they worshipped. An ancient wood of beech, oak and yew trees does exist to this day on one part of the ridge, around a spring which was undoubtedly sacred in pagan times. Oak and yew have very ancient connotations in Celtic myth, where they are associated with the druids and their secret rites. Druids were the wise men or shamen of the pagan Celtic tribes, and their memory seems to linger at Alderley in the form of the legend of the wizard.

Following a route through this sacred wood, the visitor joins a path which spirals clockwise towards two springs which emerge from the sandstone bedrock beneath a cliff. The first trickles into a stone trough and is known as the Holy Well, which once had a reputation for healing and fertility. A number of bent pins, thrown into the waters as votive offerings, were removed from the spring earlier this century and are now preserved in a museum, and at one time rags were tied to a sacred hawthorn tree close by. This is the only spot on the Edge where yew trees can be found, and has a special, magical atmosphere. Around the corner is a smaller trough into which water trickles from the rock above. This is known as the Wishing Well, behind which is a small cave in the rock cut a century ago by a metal prospector.

15 Anne Ross and Don Robins, *The Life and Death of a Druid Prince* (Rider, 1989)

16 *Chronicle*, op. cit.

Caves, caverns, wells and springs were all boundaries or gateways in Celtic lore, places where morals had the opportunity to access the Otherworld and communicate with the spirits and gods who dwelt there. The Otherworld was a form of dreaming and could be accessed at special times, boundaries like dawn and midnight – neither today nor tomorrow – and dates like Hallowe'en, which is neither summer nor winter. And following in that long tradition, Alan Garner says, in relation to the special places, the woods and the Holy Well, 'for me when I am sleeping I come here and try to share Arthur's dreams because Arthur is asleep under his mantle . . . and whoever is under Arthur's mantle can see all, but cannot himself be seen . . .'[17]

The Holy Well, coupled with the story of the Sleeper under the Edge and the wizard whose task it is to find a sacred white mare for the god under the earth is at the heart of the Celtic cosmos of Alderley Edge. The tradition of the wizard really is of truly ancient vintage, and has its origins in the Cheshire folk-tale which provided the inspiration for Alan Garner's first novel. As previously mentioned, Garner heard the story directly from the lips of his grandfather, and had he not listened and remembered the story it could well have ended its period of transmission there and then.

According to the first written version, in 1805, the folk-tale dates from the late seventeenth century and therefore pre-dates the Victorian era of myth-manufacturing, which almost rivals that of the New Age movement in the confusion its has sown. It was originally told by a parson called Shrigley, who was curate of Nether Alderley in 1753 and claimed it was a true account of events which had occurred 80 years before his time.

This is the story. A farmer had, one day 'at the end of October' – the end of summer – set out on his 'milk-white mare' from his home in Mobberley, with the intention of selling the animal at the market in Macclesfield, nearby. This route for some reason required the farmer to cross the Edge, and at dawn he had reached the spot known as Thieves' Hole. There he was startled by the appearance of an old man, 'tall and strangely clad in a deep, flowing garment.' He ordered the farmer to stop and immediately offered him a sum of money for the horse. When the sum was refused, the stranger said, 'Go then to Macclesfield, but mark my words, you will not sell the horse. Should you find my words come true, meet me this evening and I will buy your horse.' With this offer ringing in his ears, the farmer laughed and went on his way. But sure enough, he was nonplussed when no one at market wished to buy the horse, despite many compliments from admirers.

Night fell and as the apprehensive farmer approached Thieves' Hole once more, he spied the old man waiting for him. This time the farmer agreed to sell and the old man led him by a very specific route to a rock known as the Iron Gates, 'by the Seven Firs, the Golden Stone, by Stormy Point and Saddle Bole'. Just as the farmer was beginning to think he had gone far enough, he heard a horse neighing underground, and at this point the old man, stretching out one arm, touched a rock with a staff he held. Immediately the rock opened and a monstrous pair of iron gates inside a tunnel flew aside with a sound like 'a peal of thunder'. Turning to the petrified farmer, the old man said, 'Fear nothing and behold a sight which no mortal eye has ever looked upon.'

17 *Everyman*, op. cit.

Entering the cave behind the old man, the farmer was led through a succession of passages cut in the rock into a chamber where slept 140 warriors in bright armour and 139 milk-white horses all fast asleep. The old man explained that the farmer's horse was required to complete the number in the enchanted cave, and he pointed towards the inner sanctum where glistening treasure was piled. From the treasure, the old man bade the farmer to take his price for the mare, and said, 'Remember my words, there will come a day when these men and these horses, awakening from their enchanted slumber, will descend into the plain, decide the fate of a great battle and save their country.' With that, the farmer took his price and left behind the horse as the iron gates closed with a fearful crash behind him, leaving him alone and in darkness on the hill known as Stormy Point. From that day the farmer and others who were told the story by their fathers and grandfathers have looked for the iron gates and the entrance to that enchanted cave, but they have never been seen again.[18]

The 'old man' who is central to the legend was never identified in the early versions but by the Victorian era he had been transformed into Merlin, an intermediary figure who was himself inspired by the tales of ancient druid magicians. The king or god in the magical cave he is equipping is therefore Arthur, the once and future king. But both are really metaphors of deeper Celtic symbols, for Arthur is just one of the latest names for the Sleeper – the 'king beneath the hill' – an ancient legend which can be found in some of the earliest recorded mythology, not only in Celtic Britain but across the world. Every tribe has preserved stories about great leaders, heroes or gods who lie sleeping in caves or beneath hills, ready to arise when their country requires them. In England, Arthur lies sleeping not only beneath Alderley Edge but also in a cavern at Sewingshields on the Roman Wall, beneath the Eildon Hills in the Borders and in numerous locations in Cornwall and Wales.

The appearance of the 'milk-white mare' in the folk-tale from Alderley Edge has clear ritual and Celtic connotations. It may also be significant that in this same area of east Cheshire there appears to have been some kind of horse cult which survives in the form of the Wild Horse. The horse is a character in the weird Soul-caking plays, which are still performed on the eve of the great Celtic festival of the dead, Hallowe'en.

Before the First World War the ritual play, which has an unbroken tradition in the village of Antrobus, was performed before local gentry in the big houses of the district; now the teams travel around the local public houses. The mummers play involves a fight between the Black Prince and King George, with the former being killed and then revived by a magical potion, symbolizing the boundary between summer and winter which Hallowe'en marked. The team also includes a 'Letter-in' who opens the play, an old woman, Beelzebub, a doctor and the impish Little Dicky Derry Doubt. But the most revered member of the team is the Wild Horse itself, made up of a man in a sheet, carrying the head of the horse, who prances and snaps its jaws. Although horses like this appear elsewhere in British folk tradition, it is only in Cheshire where they emerge on Hallowe'en. Dozens of villages in this part of the country at one time jealously guarded their own horse skull, a symbol of luck and fertility, which was painted black and carefully hidden away after every performance.[19]

18 Garner, 1977, op. cit. Other sources of legend consulted: Kathleen Briggs, *A Dictionary of British Folktales. Part B: Folk Legend* (Routledge & Kegan Paul, 1971); J. H. Ingram, *Companion into Cheshire* (London, 1947)

19 Pickford, op. cit.

The Padstow Obby Oss is the best-known example of a 'horsing' ceremony in Celtic Britain. Two horses now appear annually on May Day morning in the small Cornish fishing port, whose inhabitants celebrate the Beltane festival with powerful enthusiasm.

Horses were of foremost importance to both Celtic tribes and the late Roman cavalry regiments of which an historical Arthur may have been one war leader. The symbol of the horse goddess combines a number of important religious and martial symbols, and among the many cults which flourished in Gaul and Celtic Britain was that of the goddess Epona, whose very name means 'horse' or 'sleek pony'. Epona was the divine protector of the Gaulish cavalry units in the Roman army, and appears in later mythology as the Irish Macha and the Welsh Rhiannon. She was probably worshipped by the British tribes who built and cut her image upon the slopes of the hillfort at Uffington

Castle on the Ridgeway of southern England as early as 1400 BC, when Stonehenge was still under construction.

Throughout ancient Europe the symbol of the horse goddess was part of a pagan solar cult; the sun was perceived as being carried across the sky in a chariot pulled by a team of horses. In the archaic May Day celebrations at Padstow in Cornwall, the Obby Oss dances at dawn, and this may give a clue to the significance of the 112-metre-long (365-foot) Uffington horse, which actually appears to run from east to west, as if galloping out of the dawn.[20] The complex cult of Epona, connected with the sun, fertility and the dark mysteries of life and death, was one of the longest lasting in Britain, and even today her name and divine presence are remembered in one part of the Peak District hills 2,000 years after the 'end' of Celtic Britain.

In the context of the Alderley Edge wizard legend, a farmer rides the sacred horse along a specific route in a sacred place at a special time of the year – sunrise at Samhain, the end of October. Symbolically the horse can be said to be taken, or offered to, the sleeper or god who lies beneath the hill awaiting the rising sun. Taking all these elements together, the oral tradition which has survived in this part of Cheshire seems to have preserved a fragment of race memory which may date back as far as the Bronze Age, when the first Celtic settlers farmed, mined and bred their horses on the sacred landscape we now call Alderley Edge.

LIVING THE LAND

Our tradition may have been of immense antiquity, or it could have been of fairly recent origin. To me it didn't really matter. It felt right, and knowing what I do now about other traditions in these isles, it seems clear to me at least that we had a fragmentary knowledge of something far older, something which enables us to make sense of the world and something which gave us a real sense of belonging to the land and each other. It's almost gone now, and that's a great shame.

To us these things are not all that easy to explain to outsiders. In fact I never really knew just how hard they were to articulate properly until I had to try and write it down for you. Fundamentally, the belief that was handed down to me was this: that the world and everything in it was driven by an awesome power which could be seen everywhere – but only by its effects and results. This power was generally considered to be female, mother nature if you like, although that expression is now so overused that it seems it's become a cliché. We didn't need to make representations of her like statues and the like because she was all around, everywhere, and it was simply a matter of looking and learning how to find her. To put it another way, why have statues and so on when the whole valley you live in can be seen as the living body of the mother on which we lived? But although the primary source was seen as female – and I think this was because all life comes from the female of the species and so it was logical we should believe the main

20 Archaeologists from Oxford University have recently discovered the famous White Horse hill figure is actually 2,000 years older than previously thought. Using a new scientific method which dates the last period at which soil was exposed to sunlight, it was found that the figure was in existence in 600 BC, and possibly as early as 1,400 BC – the late Bronze Age. As the first documentary evidence for the figure is from the twelfth century AD, this demonstrates how unsafe it is to assume the first written mention of an artefact or tradition disqualifies it from an earlier existence. See 'White Horse Trots Back to the Mists of Prehistory' (*Guardian*, 17 February 1995)

creating power was also female – the god, or male power, was also there. This was usually seen as manifesting in a different way, in the weather, the stars or certain high places in the landscape. But the two were just manifestations of the same thing. Split into male and female powers because that's how we see life, as male and female, so it just seems natural that we see the gods that way too.

As I said, aspects of the landscape could be referred to as being part of the god or goddess, male or female. In and around the valley of the Wharfe there were many legends of male and female giants from the distant past who had moved, thrown, carried or dropped piles of stones and peaks of hills. Most of these places were important to us and visited frequently for a number of different practices which I can't go into here. But in the area we lived Beamsley Beacon, Simon's Seat and the three so-called fairy hills above Thorpe were key points, but there were many more and almost any secluded point was important within our tradition.

The legends may be just stories now but I'm sure they relate to the actual creation process, when the hills were raised by the primeval creating force. If we are talking about splitting the landscape into male and female, god and goddess, then obviously

Depiction of a horned Celtic warrior god on a stone from Mouselow Hill, Glossop, Derbyshire, on display in Buxton Museum.

The High Peak District

Opposite: This beautiful upland area of the Pennines in northwest England is the source of much of the less well-known Celtic lore. Towns, villages and landmarks mentioned in the text are also highlighted.

things such as the river, springs and certain hills or fells were seen as places of the goddess and the high moors, rocky scars and peaks such as the Beacon were the places of the male power. The core of the old faith was the constant coming together of these two, whether it be in the creation of human or animal life or in the creation or destruction of the year or on a different timescale altogether the coming and going of worlds. The actual length of time involved was immaterial to us. We knew things were eternal and the power involved in each process, from the flight of a bird to the creation of a mountain or the destruction a storm brings was equal and from the same source. Our actual practices are difficult to put into words, but this was the core of what we believed, and was the best way our people knew how to explain and live with the constant mystery of nature and our existence.

I think I should make it plain as soon as possible that what we believed and practised was not witchcraft or even remotely connected to what I've seen and heard about witchcraft since leaving the north. I've never met a witch and from what I've read about them I'm not sure I want to. There were, to the best of my knowledge, never any witches in the areas we lived in. I know some of the old books on the Dales refer to some local characters as being witches, and some of these people were related to us and still others must have followed the same or a similar tradition but from other family lines or areas. But they were not witches; if anything the label 'wise woman' or 'wise man' was more strictly true.

Let me assure you that we were not in any way anti-Church. I think this view of people who follow the old traditions has been invented as much by the media as by the Church itself. We were quite prepared to accept the Church in our valley and our people have always frequently attended services, and even helped with their festivals. Also, by and large, we went along with the various rites of passage held within the church. There was never any conflict. Most of us were baptized, married and all of us buried within the rites of the Church. That may come as a bit of a shock to outsiders, but as far as we were concerned the Church had been there as long as we had and we had no problems at all with it really.

There was another reason why we have always been close to the Church. Churches act as attractors for all kinds of practices connected with the old traditions, and often when people who don't understand these things find something in their house or land which they can't explain, they take them to the nearest church. So you can often find old and odd carvings in churches and where would they end up if the church wouldn't take them? They'd be sold, lost or thrown away and part of our history would be lost. And it's a fact that the same people who carved the heads in and around the dale also often worked on the local churches and left their mark there. The clergy usually let these objects remain in their buildings, many of them in full knowledge of what they represented but happy to leave them there and have the patronage of those who followed our tradition as well as that of the Church. If truth be known, there have been more than one or two members of the clergy in our area who were as comfortable out on the wild moors at night as they were in the pulpit, if you see what I mean. If there have been any problems with the Church, it has been only recently with the coming of the more evangelical clergy, those people who want everyone to bend to their beliefs and their beliefs only.[21]

21 Pers. comm., 1994

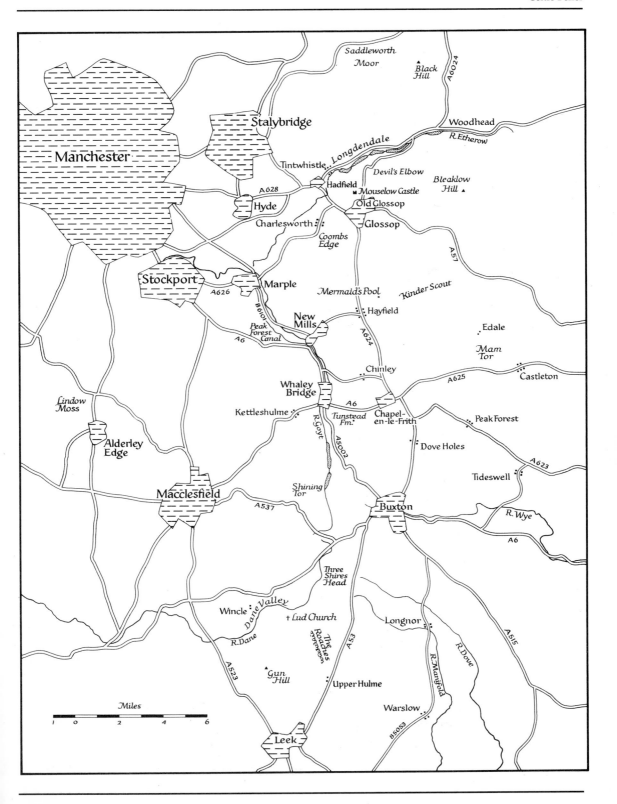

THE LONGDENDALE MYSTERY

'In spite of present-day enlightenment, with its electric trams, its motor cars, and its patent medicines, superstition, or rather a belief in semi-witchcraft, still has a firm grip of many minds in some of the more out-of-the-way villages and hamlets of England. Such parts of this kingdom as the wilder corners of Cornwall, Dartmoor, and the High Peak of Derbyshire, have both given birth to legends and wonders, and, what is more, retained many of them at the present time.'

A writer in the Derbyshire *Reliquary*, 1890s

At the dawn of recorded history, during the Iron Age, the mountains and valleys of the Pennines, stretching from the Scottish lowlands south to the Peak District, were inhabited by a Celtic tribe known as the Brigantes, who took their name from a mother goddess they worshipped, Brigantia. During the Roman occupation the native religion merged with religions brought to the new province by soldiers from far-flung parts of the empire. This resulted in a vibrant mixture of cults, ranging from those surrounding Celtic deities to exotic new cults like that of Mithras, which at one time was competing directly with Christianity for followers.

Place-names are very important pointers to a Celtic presence in the High Peak, part of the southern border of Brigantian territory in this troubled period. In his study of place-names of Derbyshire, Professor Cameron found the largest cluster of British names in the extreme northwest of the modern county, around the border with Cheshire. Around the hamlet of Rowarth, between Hayfield and Glossop, he pinpointed a cluster of seven Celtic place-names, which suggested to him that was 'the area of the county settled latest in Anglo-Saxon times'.[22]

Professor Cameron's conclusions neatly fit an area of land we know is redolent with archaic traditions which many believe date back far into the mysterious Celtic past. This is an area where until recently the old pagan deities were remembered, the important calendar feasts acknowledged, human and stone heads kept and venerated and the spirits of water propitiated.

An important river-name with Celtic roots in this part of the Peak District is the Etherow, significantly one of the three tributaries which feed the Mersey. It begins life in the Peak District hills and runs westwards through Longdendale valley, following a very ancient salt route for packhorses and coaches travelling from Chester to York. Experts believe this river valley may have acted as a tribal border between two Celtic peoples when the Romans arrived in this frontier region, with the Brigantes to the north and west, and the Cornovii to the south.

Two thousand years ago the landscape of the High Peak was very different from the one we see today. The high hills and river valleys were heavily forested then and the little villages which visitors adore today began life only during the Anglo-Saxon period. Frisian auxiliary troops, part of the Roman advance on Brigantian strongholds in the Pennines, arrived in the remote valleys of the Dark Peak in the second half of the first century AD. They built their first fort of turf and timber in a strategic position on a hill upon the

22 Kenneth Cameron, *The Place-names of Derbyshire* (Cambridge University Press, 1959)

42

Stone well-head carved with three archaic faces, from the banks of the River Etherow near Melandra Roman fort at Glossop, Derbyshire. Like many other guardian stones in Celtic tradition, it once marked a dangerous boundary – the junction of the river with a tributary.

southern side of the river, close to the entrance to the valley. This was near a crossroads by a ford which provided a communications route between the Brigantes in Yorkshire and North Wales via the Cheshire plain.

The remains of the fort known to the Romans as Ardotalia, now the modern Melandra, are situated today on the edge of a housing estate on the outskirts of Glossop. Melandra may take its name from a word meaning abounding in oaks, and refers to Longdendale's once extensive forests. Old traditions describe a 'mighty forest, whose trees were so thick the squirrels could leap from branch to branch from Mottram to Woodhead'.

Melandra stood on the junction of three Roman roads. One route linked it with Brough-on-Noe and Templeborough in Sheffield, another went west to Manchester and the third led south to the shrine of the healing springs at Buxton, Aquae Arnemetiae. Inscribed stones from the fort show it was garrisoned by the First Cohort of Frisians, but some of the most important finds were native Celtic and testify to a period of settlement and trade between Romans and native farmers and tradesmen.

After the departure of the Romans there is little historical evidence for life in the valley until the Norman Conquest, when Longdendale was described by the Domesday Survey as 'all waste . . . fit only for hunting'. The valley later became the largest of three wards in the medieval Royal Forest of the Peak, ruled by William Peveril from Castleton. In 1157 the manor was granted to the Abbot of Basingwerke in North Wales and the trees were gradually cleared by monks to make way for sheep-farming. Glossop, the principal market town of the region, itself remained a small settlement through the Middle Ages, until a late transformation with the arrival of the cotton mills during the eighteenth century. By 1820, the town and neighbouring area had become part of the new industrial Midlands, when the turnpike roads opened up the area to outside influence for the first time. But for centuries before, the stage coach had been the chief link with the outside world, when today's main roads were nothing more than packhorse tracks across a treacherous moorland morass. And despite the presence of the Christian Church, the influence of old ways and customs established in the tribal past remained very strong.

Memories and traditions die hard in this part of Peak, where farming communities were hemmed in by the encircling hills for generations. Remote topography and an economy based upon livestock farming make an ideal context for the survival of archaic beliefs, especially in areas like Ireland and Wales, where we know old traditions have been preserved and transmitted by a strong oral tradition. Although there is no Peak District equivalent of the Irish

Dindsendchas ('Tales of Eminent Places') or the Welsh *Mabinogion* to help us interpret its mythological past, the hills and valleys retain their memories and personality as clearly as any written page.

The influence of old ways can be seen most clearly in the text of region's best-known piece of literature to survive the medieval centuries, *Sir Gawain and the Green Knight*. Linguistic experts have traced the author of the fourteenth-century epic to a small corner of the Peak District on the borders of present-day Cheshire and Staffordshire.[23] It seems that the story was actually written by a Cistercian monk from Dieulacres Abbey who was reviving the traditions of the warrior King Arthur and in the process drawing upon the pre-Christian mythology of the region in which he was born. Its central character, the Green Knight, embodies of the power of nature and the old religion, a shape-shifting trickster whose colour identifies him with the foliate heads carved by masons in churches throughout the region at roughly the same time.

The story also features other archaic symbols such as the head cult, magical mists as a gateway to the Otherworld and the remote pagan temple or Green Chapel, which has been identified as the awesome rock chasm known as Lud's Church above the Dane valley. These elements explain how the story fits so neatly into the pre-Christian mindscape conjured up by the *Mabinogion* and the earlier Irish tales and sagas. It suggests the tribes of Brigantia shared a common cultural milieu with those of Ireland and Wales, an attitude to the world which has never entirely died out.

There are many other folk-tales and legends in this region, so many that it seems almost every field, road and hamlet has its own explanatory story, resident spirit or *genius loci*, much as the stories from the Irish *Dindsendchas* suggest. At the turn of the nineteenth century, historian Thomas Middleton collected some of the legends of Longdendale, including a yarn about a ferocious and desperate battle which took place between the Celtic tribes and the advancing Roman army. The story describes this battle as the final engagement in this part of the Pennines, and to ensure victory the tribe's druid priests made the ultimate sacrifice to the gods in the hope that they would support the tribe in victory. A beautiful girl, the daughter of the British chief, went willingly to her death on a rough altar before the tribe went to battle.

Taking advantage of topography, the tribesmen gathered on the rugged gritstone edge southwest of Glossop. Known today as Coombs Edge or the Nab, part of this strategic area was sacred to the horse goddess Epona, and she may have received offerings or oblations before the cavalry charged into battle against the auxiliary troops. The Roman legions employed well-worn tactics, stood firm and drew the tribesmen on to Ludworth Moor, where, exposed to the superior tactics and weapons of the empire, the tribesmen were abandoned by their gods and soundly defeated. According to the local tradition, hundreds died, including their chief, Edas, and their bodies were buried in barrows which are still pointed out on the moor.

This defeat must have left an indelible impression upon the psyche of this area, for the escarpment remains an eerie and brooding presence today. Local people avoid certain lanes and paths, for many have had strange experiences here. Writing of the local beliefs in his *Legends of Longdendale*, published in 1906,

23 Ralph W. Elliot, 'Sir Gawain in Staffordshire: A Detective Essay in Literary Geography' (*The Times*, 21 May 1958)

Middleton reports: 'it is said that at certain seasons of the year, when the moonlight falls upon Coombes Rocks, the ghosts of the ancient heroes marshal on the battlefield, waving in phantom hands their phantom axes, as though ready for the coming of the Roman foe.'[24]

THE OLD WAYS

Ancient beliefs and traditions classified as 'Celtic' have always been associated with Ireland, Wales, Scotland and Cornwall, because they are the lands on the western edge of these islands where ancient legends and lore from the pagan past are believed to have survived for longest. Here relics of a native British or Celtic past have lingered perhaps in a way more obvious than elsewhere – in language, traditions and attitude. But there are also places in England where very archaic beliefs and practices have continued – in parts of the Pennines, the West Country and elsewhere, where it was once believed the Anglo-Saxons had displaced all previous lore and language.

Probably the most difficult feature of the Pennine traditions is their very nature. The practices followed by those who observe the old ways are often furtive and 'undisclosed', sometimes hidden beneath the more widely known and practised customs and ceremonies. In 1977, when the BBC *Chronicle* team were making their seminal documentary in the north of England, Dr Ross and the film crew were told how in one valley wells, springs and water-sources were decorated with simple bunches of flowers at important festivals, Beltane bonfires were lit on farms, stone heads were carved and buried in the valley, and a strong belief persisted in the power of a divine mother goddess and a male horned god.

One of the names still in use for the goddess was Anu, a word of very ancient vintage. In the form of Arnemetiae, the goddess in a sacred grove, this was a name recorded in Roman times at the sacred springs of Buxton, in the same region of the High Peak. The horned god is remembered in numerous carvings, symbols and the oral tradition as the leader of the Wild Hunt. Belief in both deities was and still is strong in this area.

How widespread are these traditions? Ten years of research in the north of England have led us to suspect that they are far more widespread than even we at first imagined at the beginning of our quest. Patient and careful enquiries have found traces of archaic beliefs and traditions surviving in four regions of the southern Pennine foothills. It is clear there are many others in Cumbria, Scotland and the West Country, where similar clues have surfaced.

Discussing the nature of her own Peak District upbringing, a guardian of one tradition told us, 'Longdendale is by no means unique. These traditions survive over most of England, but they are so innocuous that they go unnoticed – they do not "stick up" above the landscape as odd practices to be remarked.

24 Thomas Middleton, *Legends of Longdendale* (Manchester, 1906)

You could find the same thing in most countries, away from the cities, where the population has been fairly static for a couple of hundred years. I know some of it survives in Devon and in Yorkshire.'[25]

This lady – we met her in a previous chapter – inherited the local traditions from her grandparents when she was a child in one part of the Longdendale valley. She also seems to have brought others into the area from a branch of her family which originated in Northumbria. A second informant, a man to whom this guardian is distantly related, is acquainted with a slightly different tradition, although the two once lived only a short distance away from each other in the same valley. This is typical of the situation in this part of the hills, where communities living quite near to each other seem to have inherited slightly different versions of pan-Pennine traditions. He also says that the tradition he was exposed to when he was a child in Glossopdale came from grandparents and other members of the family, including his father, who travelled the county as part of his business, learned the stories and tales firsthand and 'knew Derbyshire like the back of his hand'.

'On top of this, the stuff which to me was authentic and old came from my grandmothers, both of whom fed me with different stories from different areas,' he said. 'The old people of my grannies' generation in the High Peak were the source of all sorts of interesting practices.' Like many residents of this and other adjoining Pennine valleys, he is able to trace his family tree back a considerable distance to the seventeenth century and beyond. His roots were in Glossop, the pre-industrial revolution centre of the valley, where various branches of his family have been established 'time out of mind'. The rich tradition he was exposed to in childhood has stayed with him throughout adult life and was further enriched by experience of other parallel traditions during travels throughout the world, and latterly the Celtic west.

'You go away and become sophisticated and educated and all the rest, but it remains with me and very easily surfaces up again,' he told me. 'I don't disbelieve in this stuff at all. It is there and part of my psyche, and not in any way connected with any of this modern neo-Celticism or New Age stuff, which just seems false. This tradition was old and it was the sort of stuff that makes the hair on the back of your neck stand up – it still does with me.'

He added, 'There was a layer of belief when I was a kid in the Peak that was not Christian. It was old, and people knew it was not Christian. But they didn't regard it as being inimical to Christianity, because everyone I knew was a church- or chapel-goer, but these were like two separate compartments in their lives.

'It was not a theology or philosophy or any kind of organized religious thing. It was more like the fairy-faith in Ireland, all to do with *genii loci* – spirits of the place. It was stories about fairy hills, trees and wells and things like that, all tied up with certain places. There were deities as well, but not forming part of any religious system.'[26]

Old traditions like these are not confined to these two particular valleys; it is simply that people here have been prepared to discuss their tradition in public, although often only with a certain degree of anonymity and after considerable persuasion. Not far distant to the south, on the high rocky

25 Pers. comm., 1993

26 Oral tradition; notes from pers. comm., October 1993

Hannah Pickford was born on the Bluehills on the Roaches in the mid-nineteenth century. She was one of many wise women or healers who were important in preserving the oral tradition in these remote hills. Hannah was the great great-aunt of writer Doug Pickford, who still lives in the area.

moorlands called the Roaches in north Staffordshire, on the southernmost flanks of the Pennine hills, a parallel ancient tradition has survived.

Here local writer Doug Pickford was taken to see a large natural gritstone outcrop in a field near a remote farm around which within living memory the Beltane bonfires were lit, and at one time sheep were 'run' round the rocks. 'I was shown on my visit charcoal deposits which are evidence of fires being lit in the not too distant past,' said Doug. 'There are very few real locals around there now, but the current farmer has been told that this was where they used to have the fires. The name of the place was Ballstone Rock – presumably because of the Beltane fires.'

Doug, who is the editor of a weekly newspaper in Macclesfield, was himself born and brought up in this conservative moorland region and has a rich family tradition of his own. 'My interest was nurtured by my family, who were one of five living on the Roaches at the turn of the century,' he told me. 'They have been there since goodness knows when, but it seems they were squatters originally. It seems the Pickfords arrived when the rule was that if you could build a house within 24 hours, with four walls, a roof and have smoke coming out of the chimney, you could settle there for good.

'My great-grandfather, besides being a "man of the hills", possessed a knowledge of the landscape that had, I am told, been passed down from the seventeenth century. His wife, my great-grandmother Hannah Pickford, was the "wise woman" of the area and there are countless stories related of them both. Hannah died at the age of 85 around the turn of the century and now most of the people who have moved to live up there are outsiders. None of the original families are left.'

Doug explained that his great-grandparents were both aware of pre-Christian traditions in the area where he still lives. 'You imagine what sort of place it must have been like at the turn of century, when it was still isolated.

The Bawdstone on the Roaches, a rock escarpment on the Staffordshire moorland, was the centre of Beltane rites until the turn of the century. People visited the natural boulder to be healed, and it was whitewashed annually on the morning of 1 May.

There was no organized "pagan" religion, there never was, other than this modern revival, which is a recent thing.

'These were just families who had a great respect for the earth – you have to when you live in a place like that. The religion they followed was one of their own making in a way; although it was nothing organized, they always knew exactly what to do and when to do it.'[27]

HEALING STONE

It was through family tradition that Doug Pickford traced the origin of a story which had been handed down by word of mouth from his great-grandparents' generation. This concerned a unique 'healing stone' on the Roaches. This huge glacial erratic is called the Bawdstone and it sits upon three smaller stones, creating a tiny chamber beneath which water occasionally gathers. The chamber is just large enough for a person to squeeze underneath and out the other side, a procedure which played a significant part in local tradition.

In the past, the stone was the focus of an extraordinary procession on the morning of 1 May, the festival of Beltane, which marked the beginning of summer. Dozens of people, some helping sick and infirm relatives, would follow a well-worn path from the market town of Leek and villages round about, travelling by foot many miles to the rock escarpment. Here they would crawl beneath the Bawdstone 'to knock the Devil off their backs'.

This 'gathering' at the Bawdstone apparently continued until the turn of the century, and Doug was able to trace a man now in his eighties who knew of the procession in his youth and had visited the stone himself in secret when he was sick. 'He couldn't say why he went there. It was just the tradition that was where you went when sick,' he said.

Processions to and gatherings at megaliths are an important feature of folklore, and evidence of feasting and dancing has been found by archaeologists at some important prehistoric sites. It seems that rituals may have taken place at special times of the year, and these may have evolved into the later Celtic 'fire' festivals. In 1879 a writer who visited the Bawdstone described how there was a tradition that the boulder was always whitewashed 'with some ceremony' on the morning of 1 May. The whitewashing of the stone, performed by the farmer who owned the land, continued until the 1920s. When he was asked why he did it, all he was able to say was that 'it has always been done', a tradition followed by his father and grandfather before him.[28]

The Bawdstone was of course not the only sacred stone venerated on that May morning, and it seems that the whitewashing or decorating of pagan stones was a feature of the Celtic tradition in this region. In Ireland, a number of prehistoric standing stones have been painted white both at Easter and Beltane for reasons long forgotten. In antiquity, whiteness equated with

27 Doug Pickford, pers. comm. and notes, 1993 and 1994

28 Ibid. Doug Pickford, *Magic, Myth and Memories in and around the Peak District* (Sigma Press, 1993)

holiness, and white chalk or quartz pebbles were often used to decorate the surface of both chambered tombs, Bronze Age barrows and holy wells. Whitewashing was probably a development from this tradition.

At Roe Cross, on a Roman road near Mottram-in-Longdendale, there is another 'white stone' with its own medieval legend which is still whitewashed every summer by the villagers. There are other examples in the Peak and on the North York Moors. At Luddenden Dean in the Calder valley in West Yorkshire, there is the Whiterock, a large natural boulder which glistens from an isolated hillside every May morning. This rock is believed to mark the burial place of a British chieftain of whom nothing is known, but the custom continues in secrecy. No one knows how old the tradition is, or who performs it, but it has become so well established that it features in a collection of poems from the valley by Poet Laureate Ted Hughes, who is a native of nearby Mytholmroyd.[29]

Certain special stones have been venerated from time immemorial by farmers and residents in the Pennine foothills. One informant in the High Peak knows of several stones which are not necessarily ancient but appear to have been left alone by farmers. Some say they are just the remains of gateposts, left for cattle to scratch on. 'Often they have got a hole right through them, and they say that's where the bolt of the gate went through,' explained one local. 'Nevertheless, when I was a kid we believed you could descry the future by peeping through the hole at the right time, and touching it brought luck. Only in recent years I have seen flowers put out by it, and other small offerings left there.'[30]

Stones such as these may have been regarded in some areas as being the dwelling places of gods or guardian spirits of the land – *genii loci* – who may have required offerings or propitiation to ensure their power to fertilize the earth or heal the sick continued. Offerings to standing stones were often in the form of flowers or food, and sometimes sacrifices. At the beginning of the nineteenth century, a writer described how the inhabitants of the village of Urswick, in the Lower Furness region of southern Lakeland, were accustomed to dress a 'rough piece of unhewn limestone as a figure of Priapus' on Midsummer Day. The stone, which was about 90 metres (less than 100 yards) from the parish church, was smeared with sheep salve, tar and butter and covered with coloured rags – 'the head ornamented with flowers'.[31]

How long these ceremonies continued is an intriguing question, for although the Christian Church was officially hostile to all kinds of pagan worship, this often continued in remote areas, even under the very nose and sometimes with the involvement of clergymen. For example, in 1351 the Bishop of Exeter ordered the destruction of a pagan statue and the chapel which housed it at the hilltop priory of Frithelstock ('sacred stone'), in the heart of the oak forests of central Devon. The chapel, built in a grove by the monks of the priory, was drawing a considerable following from surrounding parishes, but the statue, rather than being of the 'most lowly and obedient Blessed Virgin Mary', was 'of proud disobedient Eve or of unchaste Diana', presumably a pagan forest deity.[32] There is in fact plentiful evidence that pagan groves and temples were later adapted for Christian use, and anecdotal evidence of very recent Christianization has been uncovered in the Pennine hills.

29 See Andy Roberts, *Ghosts and Legends of Yorkshire* (Jarrold, 1992)

30 Oral tradition, collected 1994

31 William Bollinson, *Life and Custom in the Lake District* (J. M. Dent, 1974)

32 Theo Brown, 'The Black Dog in Devon' (*Report of the Transactions of the Devonshire Association*, vol. xci, 1959)

THE DOLLY AND THE STATUE

The strange God Dolly found in the cellar of a house at Hollingworth, Cheshire, and used as part of a local tradition.

Offerings to pagan standing stones are one thing, and in some areas perhaps commonplace. More occasionally, historians hear about mysterious and shadowy figurines and statues – perhaps representing the grim pagan gods or goddesses themselves – which are still fashioned, used and sometimes buried in great secrecy.

One strange figurine which may have once been the focus of pagan rituals is a 12.5-centimetre-high (five-inch) stone carving unearthed in the cellar of an old house at Hollingworth, in the heart of Longdendale, during the 1960s. According to local historians, it has been 'known for many years'. The vile-looking figurine – nicknamed 'Little Mannie' – has large, lentoid eyes and prominent horns which curl around the sides of the sheep-like head to give the little carving an eerie, malevolent appearance. The house where the figurine was discovered dates from the seventeenth century, and a story concerning its discovery tells how it was found along with another broken statue depicting a female deity. Both were surrounded by candleholders and chicken bones – clear symbols of witchcraft.

Today, the figurine has joined a group of other puzzling Celtic carvings in the cellar of a museum in the northwest of England. Despite the level-headed nature of its new custodians, Little Mannie has been blamed for a catalogue of unusual mishaps and other 'mischief'. Several staff at the museum have refused to handle or touch the figurine, which has unnerved the most seasoned of archaeologists. Historian Tony Ward, who obtained the figurine for the museum's collection, said, 'The stories of its "influence" amuse me. I carried it in my jacket pocket for a couple of weeks, but I have seen people react to it.'[33]

33 Kevin Ludden 'There's No Flies on Little Mannie' (*Sun*, 2 July 1991); pers. comm., Martin Petch, 1991; pers. comm., Tony Ward, 1993

Opinions about the age of the figurine vary, with one expert suggesting it is of 'considerable antiquity', of possible Celtic origin. Another has compared it with the tiny hermaphrodite 'god dolly' excavated from beneath a Bronze Age trackway in the Somerset fens in 1966. Recent evidence, however, suggests the Glossop figure may be of African origin, as a tribal fetish imported as a traveller's curiosity centuries ago. However, perhaps the most important clue to the subsequent use, if not the origin, of the figurine were the words used as its finder showed it to Tony Ward: 'This is just the sort of thing grandfather used to make.'

Clearly there are other carvings of a similar nature hidden away in the hills, performing a function known only to those who practise the old ways in secrecy. Clues that archaic pagan rituals are still practised in the Pennine hills come to the authors' attention quite regularly, and often quite by accident.

Straddling the borders of Greater Manchester and West Yorkshire, the district known as Saddleworth is a collection of moorland villages clustered on the hillsides watered by the Chew Brook and the River Tame. Like Longdendale, the isolated terrain is an ideal context for the survival of archaic traditions and in Saddleworth the familiar beliefs about the spirits of place who inhabit mountains, streams, trees and other natural phenomena can be found.

Carved stone heads, representing the guardian or protective spirits of the Celtic tribesmen, have turned up occasionally in the architecture of cottages and farm buildings in this conservative Pennine region. They may have been used, like sprigs of magical rowan, horseshoes, witch stones and other 'amulets', to protect the household against evil. But perhaps the most intriguing information about the deep-seated – and *continuing* – nature of the pagan tradition came less than ten years ago.

A group of ramblers from the Oldham area of Greater Manchester regularly visit the wild and beautiful moorland region surrounding the ruins of the Roman fort at Castleshaw, a popular destination for weekend walking expeditions. In the summer of 1987 the group were pioneering a new route on the moors west of the fort, on a ridge of land above the Castleshaw reservoir some three kilometres (two miles) from the foothill village of Delph. That summer the moor had been burnt and was completely clear of heather, and as the walkers climbed the blackened earth one morning they were surprised to see a shadowy form staring back at them from a 1.2-metre-high (four-foot) stone pillar by the side of the rough path.

The sculpture, which looked freshly cut and recent, was of a powerful and archaic-looking face filling the width of the isolated stone gatepost. Carved on one side of the stone only, the face had sunken black eyes with deep eyelids, a triangular nose and thick double lips. Most striking of all – from either side of the head sprang expertly carved ram's horns.

'Only part of the carving was done when we first saw it,' said walker Alan Chattwood. 'Some months later we passed the stone again and found another bit had appeared. Whoever was carving the statue was obviously taking some time over the job and putting a lot of artistic effort into it.'[34]

Photos taken of this elaborate sculpture in its final stages show a powerful form very evocative of the pagan gods, a seemingly hermaphrodite deity with

34 Pers. comm., Alan Chattwood, 1991 and 1995

both ram's horns and female breasts. It was almost a year later before the presence of this stone on the isolated moor came to the attention of fieldworker Martin Petch, who is conducting a survey of Celtic stone heads and associated sculpture in northwest England. He alerted the authors, who made two visits to Castleshaw to locate and photograph the stone.

It was not until the second visit in October 1988 that we located the carving. By that time, we were astonished to find that it had been deliberately attacked and the solid gritstone pillar shattered completely into two separate sections. The face of the mysterious god or goddess had clearly been the target of the attack, and the features were badly defaced.

We never found out who carved this statue and why. It would have taken considerable time and effort to create such an image, slowly, in a number of stages, on hard gritstone rock on a remote moor literally 'in the middle of nowhere'. Did the person who created the image of this deity then deliberately destroy it as part of some mysterious ritual act to nullify its power? Or was the carving a victim of a fundamentalist backlash against a potent symbol of a living pagan tradition?

THE RIDDLE OF THE MOUSELOW STONES

The Romans spent many years attempting to subdue the warlike Brigantes in those troubled centuries of which no native record remains. Historians believe the Celtic tribes in the Peak may have made a stand against the Romans on Mouselow Hill, above Old Glossop. Mouselow is from the Saxon words, 'Mous hlaw', meaning a natural hill used as a burial mound, but the origin of this strange place can be traced back 2,000 years before the arrival of the Pecsaetan or 'Peak dwellers' in this region. There are traces of ramparts, perhaps dating from the late Bronze Age or Iron Age, close to the summit of the hill, and it is possible that the original barrow or pagan graveyard dates from this earlier time.

Mouselow's position at the head of Longdendale makes it an ideal location for a fortress, and there is some evidence that the earlier fortifications were replaced with a short-lived castle following the Norman conquest. In the reign of King Stephen, tradition tells of a terrific battle at nearby Mottram – another 'holy hill' in this valley – which gave rise to the name War Hill. It is likely that when, in 1157, the manor of Glossop was granted by King Henry II to the Abbey of Basingwerke, this put an end to the use of Mouselow for military purposes. It remained a lonely and eerie place, surrounded by the Royal Forest of the Peak, until centuries later, when the manor passed into the hands of the Howard family.[35]

35 Tony Ward, 'The Mouselow Stones' (unpublished essay, 1993); Glynis Reeve, 'The Mouselow Stones' (unpublished essay, 1985); pers. comm., from Buxton Museum, Anne Ross, Tony Ward and Glynis Reeve, 1988–95

The Mouselow Stones, on display in an arch at Buxton Museum. This group of puzzling carvings, found on Mouselow Hill in the early nineteenth century, depicts a number of pagan symbols.

The Howards were and are still England's premier Roman Catholic family, and during the religious persecution which followed the Reformation they were forced to follow their tradition of worship in secret. Despite his Catholic faith, the Duke remained officially a Protestant in order to benefit from the livings of the church and school in his manor. The association of his family with the High Peak may well have reflected their need for a safe and remote base from which to practise their faith away from persecution. But Catholicism was not the only 'secret' religious tradition practised in this region.

At the end of the eighteenth century, Parliament was in the final stages of passing laws to allow Catholics to worship openly. It seems that around the year 1780, when the Act of Religious Toleration was before Parliament, the 12th Duke of Norfolk, Bernard Howard, drew up plans to build a small chapel on top of Mouselow Hill. Exactly what happened here is not known, but an old tradition describes how work on the foundations was halted suddenly when the labourers broke through into 'something,' downed tools and refused to carry on.[36]

Soon afterwards the hilltop, which the Howards named Castle Hill, was planted with trees and its slopes abandoned once again to pasture. Fifteen years after these events, a Manchester historian described seeing quantities of stones on the hilltop, but the next record of activities there comes in 1840, when a retired Wesleyan minister, the Reverend George Marsden, was building a house in the nearby village of Hadfield. Along with other residents, he got permission to remove building stone from the ruins at the top of the hill, and while walking there it was said he 'found some curiously marked stones'.

36 'Attempt to Unravel Mouselow Mystery' (*Glossop Chronicle*, 8 August 1986)

Removing them from the hilltop, the vicar incorporated them into the gable end of his house in the village, following an ancient and still continuing Pennine tradition. According to one historian, the Rev. Marsden was 'following the tradition that they might ward off evil spirits, but, in reality so I am told, as a warning to his parishioners that he would not tolerate un-Christian activities'.[37] The stones remained in the wall of the house until the end of the ninteenth century, when Lord Howard, curious about the origins of the stones, removed them and presented them to the Glossop Antiquarian Society. An account of 1905 describes how they had been examined by experts who had decided they were 'early Anglo-Saxon' in origin, following the fad at that time among Victorian antiquarians.

Although experts were as puzzled a century ago as they are today about the meaning and significance of the strange symbols carved upon this collection of stones, the Victorians were clear that they had ritual – and pagan – origins. The account continues, 'Some of the symbols have been recognized as representing the river of life, the wind blowing from the four quarters of the earth, Thoth, one of their gods and other objects which they worshipped.'[38]

This account is puzzling, because Thoth was an Egyptian not an Anglo-Saxon deity. However, before more work could be done, the Second World War approached and the 'Mouselow Stones' were donated, along with a collection of stones from Melandra Roman fort, to Buxton Museum, where today they can be seen displayed, appropriately, above an archway. Ten in number, they are covered with strange Celtic-influenced symbols, the most obvious of which is a crudely incised face with what appear to be horns sprouting from the brow of the head. This could be the figure described as 'Thoth' in the 1905 account. The figure is similar to others found on the Roman wall, and may represent a pagan Celtic horned god – perhaps Cernunnos.

The caption which accompanies the Mouselow Stones gives few clues to the bizarre story which surrounds their 'rediscovery'. It reads, 'Their precise origins are unknown, but the concensus of opinion is that they are of Celtic (Iron Age) origin, and may have belonged to larger groups of carvings of cult significance.'

The Mouselow Stones have made two return visits to their home in Glossop since the Second World War, when they were first moved to Buxton Museum. Their second trip, in 1985, triggered a series of odd events which led an archaeologist to bring to a temporary halt an exploratory excavation on Mouselow Hill itself. The archaeologist who masterminded the dig, Glynis Reeve, was a local woman herself and had always been intrigued by the unanswered questions which hung over the prehistory and history of the town, particularly the 'lost' period between the departure of the Romans and the Norman conquest, when Longdendale became part of the Royal Forest of the Peak.

In 1984, with the backing of Manchester University and the Peak District National Park authority, Glynis undertook an extensive fieldwork survey of Mouselow and planned a small excavation upon the summit of the hill across part of the defensive earthworks. The excavation, which continued over three summers, concluded there had been four main phases of use, beginning with a burial mound of Bronze Age date, which was cut through by ramparts of Iron

37 Pers. comm., Glynis Reeve, 24 August 1991

38 Hamnet and Jenkinson, *Glossop in a Sketch* (1905); articles in the *Glossop Chronicle*, 1901–13

Age date. These in turn were superseded by a short-lived Norman motte and bailey. There was also evidence of building work dating from the eighteenth century, supporting the local tradition about the abortive attempt to build a chapel on top of the hill.[39]

The archaeologists also found evidence of water on Mouselow, whose summit is crowned by a grove of oak trees, and a large wet area caused by a small pond or spring which might have originally functioned as a sacred spring. More evidence of the sacred nature of the hilltop was the presence of hundreds of small quartz pebbles similar to those which were used to decorate Bronze Age barrows. Quartz is not indigenous to the site, but similar pebbles once decorated a spring below the hill.

The work at Mouselow was overshadowed during the course of the three summers by a series of strange events which have left ill-feeling in the region to this day. It seems that Glynis unearthed something more than she bargained for when her research touched a raw nerve with the followers of the Celtic tradition, who, it seemed, disliked the publicity and attention which the dig was attracting to the area.

Speaking ten years later, Glynis recalled how it was not long after volunteers began work on the hilltop that things began to go wrong: 'We had not been working up there for very long – a few days, I think – when we started to get phone calls – anonymous phone calls – quite late in the evening from people obviously very concerned that we were digging on a site which had some special significance for them.'[40]

The calls asked, 'Why are you digging up there?' and 'What are you trying to find? There isn't anything to find anyway.' Glynis described how the group also received warnings about horned figures and 'the Old Ways'. At this time the volunteers were based in a small field centre in Glossop, and soon a number of people began to come in demanding to know what they were doing, some of them 'quite annoyed that I should be so presumptuous to dig a site which had nothing to do with me and which should be left undisturbed'.

Relations with local people were soon to worsen when Glynis began researching the history of Mouselow in an attempt to find out what was behind the mystery. She came across several old references to the discovery of the strangely carved stones, but could not trace what had happened to them after the Glossop Antiquarian Society disbanded during the Second World War. In an attempt to track them down, she placed an article in local newspapers appealing for information. Soon afterwards the curator of Buxton Museum replied, saying he believed the stones from Glossop were lying in the basement gathering dust. Soon arrangements were made to transfer them to the excavation's field centre in Glossop for an exhibition. 'I thought we would perhaps arouse some local interest and maybe find out some more about them,' said Glynis. 'But I was totally unprepared for the reaction.'

Local people did come in to look at the stones – but they did not stay long. Several looked at them and then walked straight out without saying a word. Shortly before Christmas of that year, a man came in and looked at the stones for a long time. Then he turned to Glynis and, shaking from head to foot, he said, 'I don't know what you have got those in there for. They're quite evil and

39 'Mouselow Castle' (unpublished excavation notes by Glynis Reeve, Derbyshire County Council Archaeological Unit)

40 *The Call of the Celts*, BBC2, October 1986

you should have them under glass. Just looking at them makes me shudder.' The man was unwilling to say much more, only that 'they reminded him of something he had once been involved in and wished he hadn't'. That was all he was prepared to reveal, but some time afterwards there was another visitor to the field centre who had shown an interest in the dig on Mouselow. When Glynis said she was puzzled by all the problems and wished she knew what it was that she wasn't supposed to find up there, the visitor turned and said, 'What you did not find was the entrance to hell.'[41]

Undeterred by the attitude of local people, Glynis reopened the dig once again in the summer of 1985. This time, every member of the team suffered an accident on that site. 'We found it very hard to put to the back of our minds, especially when everybody had drawn blood, and we had to get to the bottom of what it was that was disturbing people so much,' Glynis said afterwards. Her suspicions about Mouselow's secrets were confirmed when Celtic scholar Anne Ross and Professor Rosemary Cramp, of English Heritage, who had been sent pictures of the stones from Mouselow, both said they believed the stones were Celtic in style if not date, and might have once formed part of some kind of religious shrine.

Glynis believed that the team had been digging upon, not, as they had originally thought, a Christian religious site, but possibly a place where people who followed an old tradition still met to worship. When the strange nocturnal phone calls continued, this increased her belief that Mouselow was still being used for some kind of secret worship. Eventually, the volunteers became so nervous that some wondered what would happen if they returned again the following summer, and it was suggested the dig should close early.

In an effort to calm nerves and extend the hand of friendship to nervous locals, Glynis suggested that on the eve of the festival of Beltane, 1 May, they should try to communicate with these people in a way they would understand. She explained, 'a member of my team and I decided we would go up on to the site at night. It was very dark and lonely, and we were frightened, because we kept hearing rustlings in the trees and couldn't tell whether it was the wind or perhaps someone watching us.' When the two got to the top of Mouselow, Glynis stood in the middle of the dig and said, 'You have nothing to fear from us', then slowly walked down to where another member of the team was waiting in a car. He told them that while the pair had been on the hill, there had been a number of lights moving about on the lower slopes.

'I don't know who they were, but after that night the harassment stopped,' said Glynis. 'There were no more phone calls, nobody else came into the field centre and made a fuss, and it was made known to us that we were perfectly welcome to carry on with our excavation so long as our interest remained purely archaeological.'[42]

Despite the lifting of the unusual atmosphere generated by the dig at Mouselow, the 1985 dig finished early because of bad weather. When the team returned the following summer to complete their survey, the atmosphere had improved markedly and soon a BBC TV crew arrived to film Glynis and the Mouselow stones for a one-off documentary programme planned for transmission on Hallowe'en that year.

41 *The Call of the Celts*, BBC Radio 4, October 1986

42 Ibid.

On that programme Glynis said she believed that the team had received so much harassment during the dig because a certain group felt they were trespassing upon a place which was sacred to certain people in the area and, she believed, 'They were afraid we would desecrate it and trespass upon their beliefs and expose them.'

It was through the TV producers that Glynis learned that another woman would be interviewed as part of the programme. She was a local housewife, but was not to be identified on the programme. On hearing her voice, Glynis immediately recognized her as the person who had taken part in the 1977 *Chronicle* documentary on pagan traditions in the Peak District.' I had been told there was a "Guardian of the Old Ways" but I didn't know who she was. I knew nothing about her at all,' Glynis told us. 'It was the producer of the programme who unearthed the earlier documentary and when I heard the voice, I put two and two together. When I first heard about these beliefs, I could not believe it – it was like something out of a children's story. But there are parallels for guardians in Celtic history, where traditions are handed down through families.

'I don't know how far back this tradition goes. The minute you start talking about "Old Ways", people say – ah, witchcraft. But I don't think, from what little I have seen of them, that they are connected with witchcraft.' She added, 'In the end, I was told that as long as I kept to the archaeological side of things, everything was fine. So after that I deliberately avoided researching on the folklore side, I kept to the archaeology and we finished the dig over the next two seasons without a lot of hassle. They were doing us no harm any longer, so that's how we left it – we had our interpretation of the site and we left them and their beliefs to history.'[43]

For her own part, the guardian who appeared on the programme blamed the dig for generating all the 'bad publicity', which she claimed had led 'her people' to become defensive and worried. 'It was just the thought of exposing private things to the light of day that really was at the root of everything,' she said. According to the guardian, the organizer of the dig had been advised not to bring the wrong sort of publicity to the site, because 'it distressed some of the old people'. She claimed this advice was ignored and it was then decided to 'think very hard at her', in an attempt to deter her by making her feel nervous. This, she said, was a perfectly valid way of deterring someone 'making them feel uneasy about what they are doing, so they stop. Unfortunately she misinterpreted that as some sort of threat.'

She said the phone calls and harassment received by the team were nothing to do with her people, because 'that isn't the way we operate . . . You don't harm people, you might sort of block their thoughts so they turn back on them, but that's the most we would ever do. There's no point in believing if you're going to hurt people.'[44]

Whatever the intention, the controversy and ill-feelings actually fuelled the publicity surrounding the events at the Mouselow excavation. In addition, the subsequent transmission of the TV documentary and the publicity which followed have now ensured that any further enquiries about the Old Ways and the Longdendale tradition from 'outsiders' will always be met with a stony silence. One historian in the valley said the effect of the publicity was to make

43 Notes from pers. comm., Glynis Reeve, 1993

44 *The Call of the Celts*, BBC Radio 4, op. cit.

a number of informants clam up and refuse to discuss their tradition, for fear of being labelled as weirdos, eccentrics or worse.

Celtic expert Anne Ross also appeared in the TV documentary on Mouselow screened on Hallowe'en 1986. She was, of course, fully aware of the existence of an archaic Celtic tradition in this area of the High Peak and guessed that Glynis had stumbled across what she called 'a strong local feeling about certain stones which had been sacred, which were believed to have certain powers'.

What of the stones themselves? What was it about them which aroused such intense feelings? No clear answers can be found, because so many stones from the original grouping are now missing. Not all the stones appear to be of the same date, and although some have Celtic affinities, others are clearly medieval and may have been used as gravestones in more recent times. What is clear is that, as with other collections of stones which once functioned as part of a living tradition, exposure to unwelcome attention from outsiders was bound to trigger an adverse reaction from the community to which they belonged.

Archaeologists have been baffled for years about the significance of the unique collection of stones from Mouselow. According to historian Tony Ward, who has studied them for over 20 years, 'Some of the stones have symbols which could be linked to some known Celtic icons, but it is impossible to relate them to a particular cult or to ascertain their original purpose, though the possibility that they were gravestones was considered.' He concludes, 'All that can be said is that the stones are not Roman, but that they have some affinity with the Celtic tradition of the area.'[45]

What may be significant is the fact that the grouping originally included at least three carved stone heads of the Celtic tradition. Dozens of similar heads of varying date have turned up in Longdendale valley, some medieval and others with clear Celtic affinities. Many seem to have been deliberately buried, seemingly to neutralize the power they were believed to contain. As with other examples, it is impossible to date cult heads of this kind, and in the past many which have been ascribed an Iron Age origin have later been reassessed as products of an archaic carving traditon which was thriving in the Pennine foothills as late as the nineteenth century.

Stone heads are often associated with fertility and one stone contains a phallic symbol set in a Roman-influenced design. Another appears to be a side view of a horse's head. Others contain Celtic 'roses' and the letter 'A', which may have formed part of an inscription or dedication to a long-forgotten deity. A number of the stones have symbols which connect them with a woman or women whose graves they perhaps originally marked. At least two of them feature a strange symbol made up of five holes grouped like a domino. This symbol is known in Longdendale as the 'valley pattern' and was used locally to mark the death or burial spot of a woman who died on the moors, a tradition known at the end of the last century.[46]

The valley pattern may be one of the finest examples of the survival in this area of the Peak of a tradition dating from pagan Celtic times. The pattern was clearly regarded as a magical symbol as early as the fourteenth century, when it was mentioned in Chaucer's *Canterbury Tales*. One combination of holes,

45 Ward, op. cit.

46 Tony Ward, pers. comm., 1988 and 1993–4; for 'puer et puella' pattern, see Roninson edition of Chaucer's *Canterbury Tales*, note 2041 on *The Knight's Tale*, p. 677.

Sheela-na-gig hag or goddess carving from Sier Kieran, County Tipperary, Ireland. The function of the drilled holes is a mystery, but they are similar to the 'valley pattern' symbols found across the Irish Sea in north Britain.

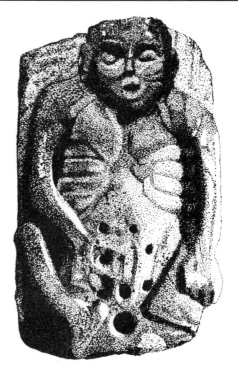

known as 'puella' (Latin for 'girl'), appears in a list of symbols associated with geomancy – earth magic – drawn up at the request of King Richard II. The stone at Woodhead, at the head of the Etherow, mentioned earlier, also contains a variation of this pattern, and the authors know of other examples from elsewhere in the Celtic lands, including one on an Irish Sheela-na-gig female figurine and several drilled in stone heads from Brigantian territory.

What may actually be the most mysterious stone in the Mouselow collection, and also seems to be the earliest in date, is a tapered stone which reveals its secrets only when placed upright and cross-lit. Then, what appears to be a pattern of lozenges turns itself into the figure of a woman wearing a distinctive 'tartan' garment with her hair drawn up into a bun. According to experts who have studied this stone, the nearest comparison to this strange figure is from a context in Bronze Age Denmark, and it is possible this stone may be truly Celtic and carved by the people who buried their dead on the barrow below Mouselow Hill.[47]

Movement of sacred stones, or their handling by people outside the tradition which created them, has always been a taboo in the Celtic lands. In 1985, when the Mouselow stones were being stored in a house in Glossop prior to their return to their museum home, a number of strange electrical disturbances are said to have occurred, including a power failure and the malfunctioning of computers. Clearly, in this part of the Peak District, centuries after the countryside became nominally Christian, those who still live close to the earth and follow the old ways continue their respect for sacred places and certain stones which have special powers, and questions from outsiders will always be unwelcome.

47 Ward, op. cit.

2

CELTIC LANDSCAPE

One impulse from a vernal wood,
May teach you more of man,
Of moral evil and of good,
Than all the sages can.

William Wordsworth, 'The Tables Turned'

THE STONES OF THE CROOKED GLEN

Longdendale and the neighbouring Pennine valleys where ancient pagan traditions have survived from the Celtic twilight are not unique in the British Isles. Other secret valleys exist in Ireland, Wales and Scotland, where one in particular has preserved a living Celtic tradition which reached its twilight only within existing memory.

Deep in the Grampian mountains known as Drumalban, the backbone of Scotland, lies the village of Fortingall, which guards the entrance to the most magical glen in the Highlands. Lying to the north of Loch Tay and the village of Killin, isolated Glen Lyon begins at the wooded Pass of Lyon and is surrounded on either side by towering mountains. At 40 kilometres (25 miles) in length from its head in the mountains east of Bridge of Orchy to the confluence of the rivers Lyon and Tay near Kenmore, it is one of the longest – and most mysterious – in the highlands.

The encircling hills guard the strange stones and forts around which clansmen have woven their legends from time immemorial, for in the Gaelic, Glen Lyon is *cromghlearn nan clach*, meaning 'the crooked glen of the stones'.

Tigh nam Cailliche, a rocky Celtic shrine in Glen Lyon, Scotland.

Each pass into this secret valley is guarded by ruined stone 'castles', which are believed to be a series of stone-built Iron Age ring forts, known in this part of central Perthshire by the name 'dun'. One at Loch Tummel has a rowan tree growing through its centre.

A strong tradition in the valley associates them with Fionn MacCummail, a hero god king (also known as Fingal), who kept the peace in a far-off age not only in the Highlands but also across the Irish Sea. Fionn is really another form of the Celtic father god Lugh, and Glen Lyon was, say the old tales, his home and the ruins were manned by his 9,000 warriors. An old Gaelic tradition, attributed to Oisin, Fionn's son, runs, 'Twelve castles had Fionn, in the Crooked glen of the Stones . . .' Until very recently, tales and traditions surrounding the adventures of Fionn and his war band, the Fiana, were told by the people of this valley, who referred to him as if he were a real or living personality.[1]

A large standing stone in a field at Killin (Cil-Fhinn – 'cell of Fingal') is supposed to mark Fionn's final resting place. However, like King Arthur at Alderley Edge, some believe he really lies deep inside a cave in Skye, surrounded by his faithful warriors. In other tales he is a giant who could stand with his feet on two hills overlooking Loch Tay. In Celtic mythology the gods and goddesses were always of huge size, and this belief survives in folk traditions. Tales of witchcraft, ancient magic and the god Fionn are all part of the rich archaic tradition which has survived in central Perthshire, which in Glen Lyon has taken root so strongly in the psyche that mythology and tradition have been imprinted into landscape features.

Near one of Fionn's forts or duns at Cashlie is a 60-centimetre-high (two-foot) standing stone which resembles the head of a dog; it is known as the Bhacain ('dog stake'), and villagers believed this was the stake to which Fionn's warriors tethered their hunting dogs when they returned from the chase. This stone was regarded in 'superstitious awe' by the residents of valley, according to an historian writing at the end of the last century. It was then that old folk believed in the power of the stone to grant and take away the gift of fertility from local girls – 'When the girls returned from gathering the harvest in the ungodly Lowlands, under the stone they went. It was better than all your modern pills.'[2]

Other stones too had mysterious supernatural powers, and their resident *genius loci*. In the Black Wood of Chesthill stood a tall monolith, Clach Taghairm nan Cat ('the stone of the devil cat'), a gathering place for felines on Hallowe'en, and nearby was the Stone of the Demon, associated with witchcraft.

The ancestors of Celtic scholar Anne Ross originate from this mountainous country, and when she revisited the region during the 1950s, she was in an ideal position to rediscover much firsthand lore of the locality. Dr Ross spoke the Gaelic and, through friends and contacts, found to her surprise how the valley was still very much a ritual landscape, with a living Celtic tradition still continuing. She was shown stones along the glen which locals believed represented personalities from the mythology of the valley, and saw other strangely shaped water-worn stones, drawn from the bed of the River Lyon, which were thought to have healing and evil-averting powers.[3]

In the village of Fortingall, pairs of these strangely shaped stones, which resemble lions or fantastic creatures from mythology, can be found guarding

1 Julia Smith, 'Me and Finn McCoo' (*Northern Earth*, 56, winter 1993–4); Duncan Fraser, *Highland Perthshire* (Montrose, 1958)

2 Fraser, ibid

3 Anne Ross, lecture on Celtic landscapes, Ley Hunter Moot, North Wales, September 1991

gateposts at Glen Lyon house and the parish church itself, where there is also a famous yew tree said to be more than 1,000 years old. Although guidebooks say the stones are merely decorative, local folk tradition suggests they were used in much the same way as the archaic carved heads and talismen found in other Celtic regions, channelling their power to bring luck to the household and guarding entrances and thresholds.

The stones are actually drawn from the bed of the River Lyon, which wears them into fantastic shapes as it flows through this part of the central Highlands. These water-worn stones were also believed to have healing powers, and one grouping is associated with a Celtic saint who in the eighth century AD founded a monastery near Glen Dochart, which runs west from Killin. Like many Celtic saints and their druid predecessors, St Fillan had a reputation as a healer and is said to have used a set of stones, each of which resembled a part of the human body. Two centuries ago, a writer in the *New Statistical Account* described them as 'round stones which had been consecrated by the saint and endowed with the power of curing diseases . . . each had a peculiar merit'.

At some point the healing stones passed into the hands of the owners of a mill founded by the saint beside the Falls of Dochart. The owner became their guardian and for centuries they were kept behind iron bars set inside a niche in the gable wall at St Fillan's Mill. Early in the nineteenth century the guardian was an old woman whose office was hereditary and 'had been held for centuries by her ancestors'. This guardian would rub the stones round the diseased body part three times one way, three times the other and three times the first way again, at the same time muttering a Gaelic incantation.

It was also the job of the guardian to carry out an annual ceremony to honour the stones on Christmas Eve. This custom continues to this day, when the owner of the mill goes down to the riverbank and gathers rushes washed up by the current – but under no circumstances must they be cut. He or she then takes them to the mill, removes the old bed of rushes and replaces them with new for the coming year. Today the tradition is said to represent the changing of rushes in the cradle of the baby Jesus, but it is clear that the stones were originally part of the pagan cult of stones which lingered in this valley.[4]

The eight surviving stones are now temporarily stored at the local tourist centre while work to restore the old mill continues. It is many years since they were used in this Celtic healing ritual, but the Christmas Eve custom continues, for it would not do to neglect the old traditions. Stones like these are imbued in popular tradition with strange powers, and stories about them abound not only in Scotland but in Ireland too. In Ireland stones imbued with magic were used for cursing and divination as well as pagan worship.

Folklore scholar Patrick Logan writes of one anthropomorphic stone which was kept on an isolated farm in the Beara peninsula of western Cork. Like the Glen Lyon stones, it was naturally worn by the action of waves to resemble a human head and body. Local people were reluctant to speak about the 'god stone' or idol, as it was known, but Logan was able to establish that it was dressed perhaps to resemble a woman – at 'certain times of the year'.[5]

Cult stones and wells always had guardians, both male and female. An account written in 1852 describing the island of Inniskea, off the coast of County

4 Julia Smith, 'A Walk around Killin' (*Northern Earth*, 58, summer 1994); Fraser, op. cit.

5 Patrick Logan, *The Holy Wells of Ireland* (Colin Smythe, 1980)

Mayo, tells how the 350 inhabitants even then practised 'a curious form of fetishism' whereby a stone 'carefully wrapped in flannel is brought out at certain periods to be adored, and when a storm arises this god is supplicated to send a wreck on their coast'. The account adds how whenever the aid of this malevolent pagan god is sought, a 'flannel dress' was dedicated to it, and this was sewed on by an old woman who performed a role as its priestess or guardian.[6]

In Scotland it was believed that idol stones like these could grow, give birth to baby stones and even return to their accustomed place if they were moved. Disturbing them could be a dangerous business. Many years ago two special healing stones were removed from a burial ground on the shores of Loch Tay by a farmer who knew nothing of their reputation. He intended to use them as ornaments outside his front door. But it was not long before a member of the McDhairmids, whose burial ground they belonged, arrived in person to make sure the sacred stones went back to the gravestone to which they were attached.

THE OLD WOMAN'S HOUSE

Ancient Celtic traditions cling to the mountains and valleys throughout central Perthshire, but it is in the wild upper Glen Lyon itself where their echo can be heard the strongest. Once again the symbols of *genii loci*, sacred stone, river and guardian, feature in this tradition. The most mysterious part of the glen is little known and hidden away in a fold of the mountains at the very source of the river which produces its magical stones. To the north of the twisting valley towers the fairy mountain of Schiehallion (1,090 metres/3,547 feet) and even higher and closer to the south is Ben Lawers (1,225 metres/3,984 feet).

It is said there are farmhouses in the hollow between the two mountains and when we paid a visit one August morning, the ominous grey clouds hung across the encircling hills as we drove towards the huge hydroelectric dam which 30 years ago swallowed up two small lochs, a hamlet and a connecting road. Today, Loch Lyon, with its modern electric pylons and massive concrete dam, sits uneasily at the head of a glen where the reality of Britain's living pagan tradition has survived.[7]

Although the upper glen is now depopulated, 200 years ago it supported a thriving and substantial population, with large hamlets at Carnban, Bridge of Balgie and Innerwick. It was a tough existence for the crofters, whose livelihood depended entirely upon livestock and what they could scratch from the land. Their lives were ruled by the weather and the movement of their livestock. In May the cattle, replaced by blackface sheep when the glen was depopulated, were taken to the shielings pasturage on the higher ground, and in October they were brought back down to herbage closer to the settlements. These were both important times of the year – boundaries in both mind and landscape – and were marked by special rituals.

6 J. E. Vaux, *Church Folklore: Survivals of Heathen Customs* (London, 1902)

7 David Clarke, 'The Hags' House' (*Ley Hunter*, 120, midwinter 1993–4)

That was the Celtic past. Today the magic of the valley remains, despite the flooding of the loch, the building of ugly pylons and more recently the influx of tourists. Mairi MacDonald of Oban, who writes a series of guidebooks about Highland customs, has told how she once took a group of historians up the glen to see the old shielings. It was May, and she said she felt impelled to take with her the traditional bannock of oatmeal to re-enact the old Beltane ritual, casting offerings to the sun, wind and rain and to the birds and beasts of the hill. 'It was a most magical and moving experience,' she said afterwards.[8]

For young and old in the superstitious Highlands, the annual migrations were the happiest time of the year if the correct time-honoured rituals were followed. Before setting off for the upland shielings along the shore of Loch Lyon, past the Old Woman's Pool, the ancient ceremonies had to be performed on 1 May, as all your ancestors had done before you.

In Glen Lyon the Beltane rites took place before the men set out to reach the fertile lands of the mysterious Glen Cailliche, 615 metres (2,000 feet) up in the marsh, which branches west from the arm of Glen Meran. This isolated glen, four kilometres (two and a half miles) in length, is one of the few places where the magic of pagan Britain has survived from the Celtic past. For here lies a strange little house known as Tigh na Cailliche. 'The Hag's House' or the house of the goddess. Tigh na Cailliche is in reality a crude rocky shrine, a miniature Highland crofter's 'black house', perched in the middle of nowhere above a rushing burn.

This rocky shrine is in all probability connected with the pagan Celtic cult of the Mother Goddess. It may be the only surviving example of its kind in the whole of the British Isles. But this is no lifeless pile of stones, for the shrine is part of a living Celtic tradition which has been continued into recent years by a guardian – a lone shepherd – who has performed a vital ritual at the little shrine, as his father and grandfather had done before him. At the door of the little stone house, from May to October, sit three strange stones, keeping watch over the glen. The tallest, 46 centimetres (18 inches) in height, is known as the Cailleach, Old Woman or Hag. Her partner is the Bodach or Old Man and there is a third, the smaller Nighean, or daughter.

Historian Duncan Fraser wrote that in olden times, when the upper glen was inhabited, there was never any doubt about how it got the name of the Old Woman. 'Others grew old and died, but she seemed blessed with eternal life,' he said. 'Like the unchanging hills, she had been there longer than anyone remembered. People showed something more than just an ordinary respect for her years.'[9]

In those days before the arrival of Beltane, when the advance party prepared the shielings for the summer migrations, nothing could be done until the vital ritual to propitiate the goddess had taken place. The stones were removed from the shrine, which was re-roofed and thatched. The stones were then brought out into the air and carefully washed in the waters of the Allt na Caillich – the burn immediately below her little house. While the ritual took place, special Beltane bannocks were made and eaten. And when October arrived and it was time to leave the shieling for another year, the very last thing they did on Samhain Eve was to remove the thatch from the roof and carefully fill in every nook and

8 Rennie McOwan, 'Ben Ledi and Beltane' (*Scots Magazine*, May 1988)

9 Fraser, op. cit.

cranny with moss to keep the stones warm, 'so that when the icy winds of winter came sweeping down the glen and the snow rose high over the little house, she would be snug and safe inside – with her husband and family'.

Anne Ross first visited the little house in the 1950s along with a colleague, a well-known archaeologist. They had heard about the existence of the shrine while studying at Edinburgh University and, intrigued by the story, became determined to visit it. Setting off from the village of Crianlarich on the morning of 1 May, they walked 25 kilometres (16 miles) across snow-covered mountains and crevices until they entered the deserted glen and saw what they first thought was a seagull nestling in the glen below. The 'seagull' was in fact a white quartz stone, lumps of which are scattered across parts of this glacial landscape. When the pair eventually came down from the mountain and saw the 'house', they realized that the shepherd whom they had been told maintained the tradition had indeed performed the rites on May Eve, because all the stones were outside the little house and were sat looking down the glen.[10]

Thirty years later, when we visited the lonely shrine, we arrived after a lengthy trek across a treacherous bog and rushing burn before an ascent into Glen Cailliche brought us to a triangular stone suspended upon a rock outcrop. This was a specially placed marker, pointing towards the lair of the Cailleach. There were in fact not three but six stones in the family, all gazing down the glen, as they have done for centuries. Local legend says that every hundred years or so, the Cailleach, Old Woman or Hag bears another, and though the baby of the family is still very small, people swear it is growing and will one day be just as big as the others.

Although some of the stones appear carved, the Cailleach and her children are in fact natural water-worn stones, shaped like dumb-bells, a shape that is found only in one special part of the burn below the little house. In certain lights the Cailleach is said to take on human features. The stone in fact has a face on the top of her 'head', along with a weird neck ornament which may represent a torc. The torc or necklace is a cult symbol associated with the goddess from the earliest times.

Dr Ross has recorded a unique oral tradition which has been passed down through generations to explain the ritual connected with Tigh nam Cailliche, which she says runs like a Scots version of the *Mabinogion* or one of the ancient Irish tales. It tells how centuries and centuries ago during terrible snows on Beltane, the first day of summer, a man and his wife who was heavy with child came over the mountains and sought shelter in a bothy by the rushing burn. The man was huge and powerful and his wife was twice as large, a regular feature in Celtic mythology, where the god is big but the goddess is always bigger, and they were homeless in a wild and rugged country in deep snow. The couple came down to the burn, and the people who lived in the glen built them a large stone house and thatched it.[11]

And, so the story goes, the woman brought forth not a son but a daughter, 'and they lived there for ever and ever and blessed the glen and all its flock and stock and progeny, provided the correct ritual was carried out'. Parallels have been drawn between this legend and a passage in the second branch of the Welsh *Mabinogion*, a collection of medieval stories drawn from an earlier pagan

10 Ross, op. cit.

11 Ibid.

Celtic milieu. This describes a scene witnessed by Matholwch, King of Ireland, who saw while hunting in the mountains a monstrous man with yellow-red hair emerging from a lake with a cauldron on his back. The giant is followed by a woman, 'and if he was big, twice as big as he was the woman'. In this tale the woman gives birth to a fully armed warrior who proceeds to lay waste to the island.[12]

In the Glen Lyon legend, which is clearly drawn from a mythological mindscape, similar to that which fuelled the writers of the *Mabinogion*, the three deities have become weather gods and guardians of the pasture. Dr Ross was told by the stones' guardian how 'people in the lower glen believe that if this isn't done their crops and stock will suffer'. The tradition of the valley tells how the three anthropomorphic stones which represent the deities guarantee good pasturage and fine weather, but strange and unpleasant things will happen if they are disturbed from their winter's sleep. One writer says, 'When she was displeased there was nothing but bad weather, bad crops and disease among the cattle, all through the summer months. It was almost uncanny how it happened.'[13]

Upon their first visit to the shrine, Dr Ross and her archaeologist friend immediately wanted to take a photograph of the hag stone or Cailleach. He made the mistake of moving the stone to obtain a better picture, and as he took the photos both visitors were petrified when the heavy stone slid very slowly towards him, rolled forward and, according to Dr Ross, 'we could clearly see a rather baleful, malevolent face on top of it . . . It was a very frightening moment.' Strangely enough, none of the photos taken of the stones during that first visit came out. It was not until Dr Ross returned in the company of the shrine's guardian that a successful photo was obtained.

Other strange stories are told about the Cailleach and her shrine. On one occasion, an archaeologist who visited removed one of the small baby stones from inside the shrine and left the glen with it in his sack. However, as he walked, the stone became heavier and heavier and the man became terrified by weird voices shouting for him to return it. Following a series of frightening events, the stone was eventually returned to the guardian of the shrine, who in turn returned it home – no doubt with an appropriate ritual to propitiate the deities who inhabited the glen.[14]

Up until the First World War, this miniature house was annually thatched on May Eve and the stones brought out to watch over the flocks. But since the flooding of the glen, and the emigration of many of its former inhabitants to work in the Lowlands and North America, the little house has been roofed with stones, which until recently included the lump of white quartz, acting as a marker in the wild hill country. Now the shrine has a rough roof of rock, but it is no longer clear whose duty it is to perform the ritual which was once so very important to the inhabitants of the lower glen.

Whatever the future of the tradition may hold, the stones are still treated with honour and respect, and are seldom visited by outsiders, for it is a long, hard and exhausting trek from the nearest road before one can get anywhere near the magical glen where 'this family forlorn' live. The seasonal movement of the stones in and out of their little house, with the ritual washing in the burn

12 Gwyn Jones and Thomas Jones (translation), *The Mabinogion* (Everyman, 1949)

13 Fraser, op. cit.

14 Notes from pers. comm., Anne Ross, 1994

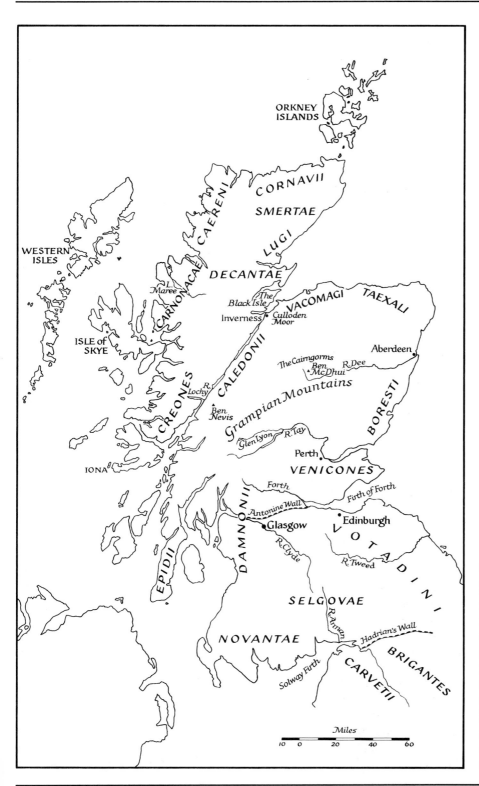

Celtic Scotland

Map showing the territories of the major Celtic tribes of Scotland as found by the Romans. Also illustrated are some of the important rivers, mountains and sites mentioned in the text.

at Beltane, is probably the last lingering remnant of a prehistoric cult which reaches back far into the distant past. There is no doubt that the Cailleach and her children have been here for a long time, so long that four centuries ago, when the first place-name was recorded, the glen bore her name.

Many hills and mountains in the Highlands of Scotland have preserved the name of the goddess or cailliche, a name which means an old woman or nun who wears a hood or veil (the *caille*). Above Ballachulish is Beinn a'Beithir, the hill of the goddess of wind and storm, while on Jura there are the Sgrìob na cailliche or Hag's Scrapes. But nowhere else are there such a concentration of place-names as Glen Calliche, where the house, the river, the mountain and every major landscape feature takes its name from the ancient hag.

These names may provide an important clue to the antiquity of the tradition. The abbot Adomnan of Iona, in his seventh-century *Life of St Columba*, mentions two compound river-names in the Highlands which contain the word '*dea*', meaning goddess in old Irish, as their second element. One of these rivers in Lochdea, which he says in the language of the Celts 'may be called nigra dea, the black goddess'.[15] Lochdea is in fact the modern River Lochy, which flows into Loch Tay, on the southern fringes of the mountain range below Glen Lyon itself, which may point to the antiquity of the Glen Lyon tradition.

'Dea' is found also in the River Dee in Aberdeenshire, a name which may simply mean 'goddess', as perhaps does the Welsh Dee, which reaches the sea near Chester (Deva to the Romans). Dozens of other loch- and river-names in the Highlands are thinly disguised memories of former pagan goddesses – the River Annan in Dumfriesshire takes its name from Ana/Anu, the mother of the gods, and the Clyde is from Clóta, the washer at the ford. The connection was so clear to Dr W. J. Watson, in his *Celtic Place-names of Scotland*, that he concluded, 'the feeling of divinity pervades and colours the whole system of our ancient nomenclature'.[16]

WOMEN OF THE MISTS

'The Cailleach Bheur of the Highlands, the blue-faced lean hag who personifies winter, seems one of the clearest cases of the supernatural creature who was once a primitive goddess, possibly among the ancient Britons before the Celts.'

Kathleen Briggs, *A Dictionary of Fairies*

15 Alan and Marjorie Anderson (eds.), *Adomnan's Life of St Columba* (Thomas Nelson and Sons, 1961)

16 Quotes in F. Maire McNeil, *The Silver Bough* (Glasgow, 4 vols., 1957)

There is much evidence in the early Celtic literature and folk traditions of belief in a primordial mother goddess whose origins can be traced from the mists of Indo-European mythology. She is one of the oldest and most powerful religious icons. She is connected with wild nature, the weather and the reaping of corn, but she also has a dark side as a goddess of death. Belief in the goddess as a representation of divine power is widespread and fundamental in the British tradition, where she was known by many names and depicted in many forms – both as one and as three.

In the Highlands she is known as the Cailleach or hag; she is the Caillaigh in Ireland and the Isle of Man, and is also known by the more ancient name Anu or Aine, which can be found in the Peak and in Leicestershire tradition as Black Annis, a monster who lived in the Dane Hills. She is always connected with the weather and the earth. In the rich Somerset tradition, 'the woman of the mist', like the Highland Cailleach, herds the deer and is seen on the hilltop road at Loxley Ford, near Bicknoller. People say she has been seen 'face to face' as recently as 1950 – 'She sometimes looks like an old, frail crone and sometimes as a great, misty figure. She just becomes part of the mist.'[17]

In the Cromarty Firth, fisherfolk knew her as Gentle Annie, a weather spirit who controlled the squally gales which were feared in one part of the coast. A similar Highland tradition tells how she wore a great grey hood, which was washed every new year at the beginning of winter in a great whirlpool – the Cauldron of the Hag, at Corrievreckan, between the islands of Jura and Scarva. In the eighteenth century Martin Martin described this as 'a dangerous gulf in which the sea begins to ferment with the tide in flood, until it boils like a pot and rushes up in a spout as high as a vessel's mast, making a loud report'. This treacherous sea, where the waves crash, meet and spout, is called the Cailliche, and tradition says that when the old woman puts on her handkerchief of the white waves, it is fatal for any mortal to approach her; but when she lifts cloak or plaid, the hills will be white with snow.[18]

These traditions demonstrate how the goddess was a deity or force which controlled the elements of life and death, as well as the fates of men. When the storms of the vernal equinox were passing away, the people of the glens would say the Cailleach 'had thrown her mallet under the holly' and vegetation would return again. Until the end of the sixteenth century, 25 March, now Lady Day, was Latha na Cailleach or Old Wife's Day, when she gave up her struggle to hold back the sunshine and new season of growth.

The symbol of the divine goddess is the new moon, known in the Gaelic as Banrigh na h-Oidhche or 'Queen of the Night'. The moon was revered for its strange power over the tides, weather, the seasons and the human body. The waxing moon was thought to have a fecund influence upon every task connected with the crops and livestock, while a waning moon was beneficial for tasks like digging peat or cutting timber. Throughout the Celtic world, the goddess was regarded as too sacred to be fully personalized, except in abstract form. She was usually believed to manifest in the landscape or nature itself, particularly in mountains, caves and strangely shaped stones, such as those in the valley traditions of Glen Lyon and Longdendale.

In 1927 folklorist Eleanor Hull wrote, 'In Ireland the goddesses are held to be both more numerous and more powerful than the gods and still regarded as the builders of mountains, the impersonators of winter, and the harbingers of spring.'[19] In Scotland, as in Ireland, there are the same mountain-building traditions concerning the Cailleach or hag, who created dolmens and hills, and became the guardian of rivers, springs and mountains.

17 Ruth Tongue, *Somerset Folklore* (Folklore Society, 1965)

18 Eleanor Hull, *Folklore Journal*, September 1927

19 Ibid.

In the Emerald Isle the goddess is identified with the landscape and its sovereignty. In the province of Munster are the Da Chich Anainne, or the Paps of Anu, two great breast-shaped hills with twin summits in the Gaelic-speaking area of County Kerry. Associated with the Paps is the hero/god Fionn, whom we met in Glen Lyon and is said to have gone into the mountains to sleep with his younger self. In County Meath, the goddess/hag appears as the guardian of three sacred hill summits in the prehistoric Loughcrew passage-grave complex, where the most prominent peak (278 metres/904 feet) is known as Sliab na Caillighe (the Mountain of the Hag). The central hill summit is crowned by Cairn T, an impressive tomb which contains megaliths carved with elaborate sun symbols. It was inside the stone womb of a nearby tomb on Slieve Gullion that Fionn was said to have been swallowed up and turned into an old man.[20]

In Irish tradition, the territorial goddess is described as offering a cup to the man who is destined to be king, with the king representing human society and the goddess representing the divine power which is manifested in nature. And it is in Ireland too that the slow transformation of the power of the female goddess from paganism to Christianity is most clearly marked. In the ninth century AD she is depicted as an elderly Christian nun in a beautiful poem, 'The Lament of the Hag of Beare', which depicts human life as being ruled by the ebb and flow of the sea tide, on the turn of which life will dwindle, while with the in-coming tide it waxes to its full powers and energy.

The manuscript from which the poem is taken, now in Trinity College, Dublin, is preceded by a note which connects the Cailleach or hag with three other pagan priestesses or deities: Brigid, Liadan and Uallach. Three out of these four were transformed in the Christian era into saints or nuns, and the story of the goddess Brigid/Bride, later St Brigit, is one of the finest examples of the way the old religion came to terms and merged with the new. In folk tradition Brigid's stronghold was the territory of Leinster, at Kildare, where her temple stood beside a sacred grove of oaks. Inside her temple, later her cathedral church, was 'a perpetual fire'. The Welsh historian Giraldus Cambrensis described how the nuns there continued to tend this sacred fire until it was extinguished by the Anglo-Norman invasion of the twelfth century.[21]

Brigid's day, 1 February, is the pagan Imbolc, a fire festival associated with fertility, light and livestock. As a Christian saint, St Brigid continued in the role of the pagan earth goddess as the mother of tribes and a divine protector of their territory. In many tales Brigid the goddess and saint appears as the equivalent of Anu, the mother of the gods, and in fact all the miracles associated with the saint were connected with fertility and livestock. This happy mixture of pagan and Christian tradition allowed her cult to thrive and Brigid or Bride's popularity as a female deity was such that the Brigit cult spread from Ireland to northern Britain, where there is a Celtic tradition running parallel to that of Ireland.

In the territory of the Brigantes many early churches, megaliths and holy wells are associated with her. The Romans equated her with Victory and Minerva, and throughout the Pennines she was worshipped as the high goddess for a proud and independent people. The cult of the goddess survived both in the guise of female saints and the special reverence for the Virgin Mary

20 Michael Dames, *Archaic Ireland* (Thames & Hudson, 1992)

21 For sources on the Brigid cult, see Proinsias McCana, *Celtic Mythology* (Hamlyn, 1970); *Gerald of Wales: The History and Topography of Ireland* (Penguin Books, 1982)

and St Brigid, foster mother of Christ, and the female dedications of many early churches, particularly those associated with holy wells and river sanctuaries.

In the Western Islands of Scotland and the Isle of Man, Bride's day on 1 February was formerly of very great importance, a time when housewives would invite the fertility goddess into their homes. Martin Martin, writing in the eighteenth century, described how on 1 February in the Hebrides the mistress and servants of each family took a sheaf of oats, dressed it up like a woman and then:

> put it in a large basket and lay a wooden club beside it, and this they call Briid's bed; and then the mistress and servants cry three times 'Briid is come', 'Briid is welcome' . . . This they do just before going to bed, and when they rise in the morning they look among the ashes, expecting to see the impression of Briid's club there; if they do, they reckon it a presage of a good crop and prosperous year, and the contrary they take as an ill omen.[22]

The goddess had many different personifications, all reflecting the different aspects of womanhood in the traditions – virgin, lover, mother, crone. In the western Highlands of Scotland, the last handful of corn cut at the end of the harvest in September and October was identified not with the fertile Bride, but with the Cailleach or Old Woman. Very similar harvest traditions have been recorded in Ulster and in Wales, where the last sheaf was known by three names: Y Gaseg Fedi (the Harvest Mare), Y Wrach (the Hare) and the Neck. These survived in some areas in a symbolic form long after the arrival of the combine harvester.

One nineteenth-century traveller described how there was great rivalry between crofters in Scotland as to 'who will first have the Cailleach', with some even going out at night after their neighbours had retired, so they might cut her before the others.

> When all have finished the last sheaf is dressed up and made to look as like an old woman as possible. It has on a white cap, a dress, a little shawl over the shoulders fastened with a sprig of heather, an apron turned up to form a pocket, which pocket is stuffed with bread and cheese, and a hook is stuck in the string of the apron at the back, the idea being that in this attitude and costume she is ready to join in the harvest toil.

At the feast which followed, the Cailleach, was dressed and placed at the head of the table, and as the whisky was passed around, each of the company toasted her, saying: 'Here's to the one who has helped us with the harvest.' When the table was cleared, dancing commenced, and the figure was taken out by one of the lads, who danced with her – 'And should the night favour it, the party may go outside and march in a body a considerable distance, singing harvest songs, the old wife accompanying them, carried on the back of one of the men.'[23]

22 Martin Martin, *A Description of the Western Islands of Scotland* (original edition published 1716, reprinted by Mercat Press, Edinburgh, 1970)

23 *Folklore Journal*, vol. 6, 1895

LAND OF THE GODDESS

Sheep farming has been an important way of life in the Pennine valleys of northern England for many generations. In the Celtic past, the beginning of lambing was marked in the farming calendar by the festival of Imbolc on 1 February, the time when the ewes began to lactate. It was also the feast day of the goddess Brigid or Bride, who was the divine guardian of the flocks and hills.

Because of the remote and solitary nature of the shepherd's job, farming families have preserved traditions of great antiquity. One of the best known of these, which survived as a historical quirk in some upland areas like Cumbria and the Yorkshire Dales, is the traditional system of counting sheep which used numbers based on the archaic languages of Britain. Several forms of the old numbering system exist, consisting of a mixture of Celtic and Latin, Anglo-Saxon and Norse words. The two most familiar to the National Sheep Association, are 'yan, tan, tethera, pethera, pimp, sethera, lethera, hovera, covera, dik' and 'onetherum, twotherum, cockthorum, quetherum, setherum, shatherum, wineberry, wigtail, tarrydiddle, den'. These words can be compared with modern Welsh numerals which, phonetically, are 'un, day, tri, pedway, pum, chwe, saith, wyth, naw, deg'.[24]

As in many aspects of Celtic life, the supernatural world and the propitiation of the gods who inhabited it pervaded all aspects of life, flocks included. The Celtic empathy with animals is reflected in the older tales from mythology and later folk tradition. One pagan deity remembered in areas where sheep played an important role was the horned god, or lord of the animals, who may be the same as the deity known in Peakland tradition as the lord of the crossroads. He was often depicted in carvings with stag antlers or ram's horns, and a number of stone heads depicting a half-man, half-animal hybrid are known from the north of England. One, found in a garden wall at Mirfield, on the eastern fringes of the Calderdale valley, displays a ram's head carved on the opposite side of the block.

Similar carvings are known on churches in the same area, and may well reflect both the economic and religious role of sheep in the regional folk tradition. The role of beliefs such as these in the life of the farmer is demonstrated by this account, provided by a Lancashire woman Christine Wade, who was an apprentice shepherd to an old Sussex man in the mid-1950s. She described how she was taught to count sheep from one to 13 in the traditional way. 'At the end of each 13, I had to make a notch on a stick, multiply the notches by 13 and whisper the total in the shepherd's ear or show him the stick,' she said.

'At first I wasn't allowed to know the reason for this strange rigmarole. But eventually he explained that the gods always listened to the sheep count, and if any man was overly proud of his flock they were likely to send a *murrain* [plague] to shorten the numbers. Counting in a strange language in thirteen was sufficient to confuse the gods.' She added, 'My 14-year-old disbelieving titters earned me a cuff around the ear but to this day I still count sheep, and anything else I value, in the old way in 13s.'[25]

24 Letters published in the *Daily Mail* (London), 15 June 1994

25 Ibid.

Celtic sculpture often combined human and animal symbols into one hybrid image. This powerful carved head from Mirfield, West Yorkshire, joins a baleful human face with the horned head of a ram.

Similar traditions are found in the pastoral farming communities which cling to the moorland foothills of the Derbyshire High Peak. In this area lambing often came late in the hills, and snow blizzards could catch the shepherds unawares. One informant remembers from childhood how during the February snows there was always concern and worry about the safety of the sheep who had not yet been brought down from the moors and hills for lambing. It has stuck in his mind how the young shepherds were reassured by the old folk, who would say, 'Oh, don't worry about it. Biddy'll take care of her own.'[26]

Biddy appears to be a dialect version of Brigid/Bride, who in Hebridean tradition was the guardian of the hearth, flocks and herds. According to Ruth Tongue, the name is also found in the tradition of the Brendon Hills of Somerset. She may be the same benign female deity found in High Peak tradition as Th'Owd Woman. A particular area on Bleaklow Moor, above Glossop in the High Peak, is associated with her. She was visualized as a shapeless form or apparition, who sometimes appeared in the guise of a dark horse and foal which the lonely traveller could meet upon the moors.

One informant, referring to Biddy or the Old Woman, told me, 'There was quite a lot of belief in the mother when I was a kid in the High Peak, though not exclusively, and muddled up of course with Catholic piety, so you sort of wandered in and out between saints and deities as in the Irish and Hebridean tradition.' Flocks, herds, hills and weather all played a role in beliefs about the great Celtic earth mother. In the living Celtic tradition of the High Peak, the divine Mother Goddess is known by three names: Anu, the One and She Who Devours Men. The goddess remains active and powerful in the living tradition of this region and natural images of her are still revered.

One striking carving may depict the goddess in her triple form. The faces are on a rectangular, concave block of millstone grit, and appear to be surrounded by water weeds, symbolizing her role as a water goddess. According to local stories, other carvings similar to this one were once kept

26 Oral traditions, collected in 1993 and 94; see also Ian Taylor, 'Bride and the Old Wife' (*Northern Earth*, 53, spring 1993)

buried near a spring on the moor and unearthed for a special ceremony where a lamb was offered to the deity on a certain day every year. The stone is now in a museum, but the belief in the mother continues.[27]

There is considerable archaeological evidence for a cult of the Tres Matres (three mothers) being followed by native Celts and Roman soldiers in the north, of which these folk traditions may be direct survivals. Carvings of *matres*, sometimes singly, sometimes in pairs, but most often in triple form, have been found in every part of England, with the best evidence coming from the Brigantian frontier region of Hadrian's Wall. Altars dedicated to the Tres Matres have been found at a number of forts along the Wall, often depicting babies, baskets of fruit, loaves of bread – symbolizing fertility, childbirth and the harvest.

The cult of the goddess attracted followers among the soldiers garrisoned in Brigantia precisely because so many were drawn from Celtic tribes from other regions of Europe, including Gaul, Spain and Germany. Dedications to 'the Goddess across the Seas' have been found on Roman sites in County Durham, while an inscription 'to the Witches Three' was found in a temple at Benwell on the River Tyne. Others talk of classical goddesses, 'the Syrian Goddess' (identified as Ceres), and Brigantia, tutelary deity of the native Celts.[28]

At Carrawbrough, near the fort of Procolitia, dedications were to a local goddess of a sacred spring, Coventina, and 'to the Goddess, Mother of the Gods' in the language of the classical world. Conventina herself was depicted on a relief as a trio of nymphs, one floating upon a water-lily. The native shrine here sat alongside a legionary temple to Mithras, an exclusively male mystery cult. Despite the nature of Mithraic worship, it seems he was not a jealous god, for a carving depicting a native goddess was found in an anteroom of the temple. This seems to suggest even the all-male followers of this Persian cult felt the need to acknowledge the tutelary goddess of the land. She had been spared in an attack in the fourth century AD by Christian iconoclasts, who had defaced and beheaded the Mithraic statues.

There are a number of stones dedicated by both soldiers and natives to the tutelary goddess identified with the landscape of northern England. One, found at Castlesteads on the western edge of the Roman wall, was dedicated to 'the nymph Brigantia', linking her with water sources, and elsewhere she is depicted as a healing goddess. The name Brigantia, which became Bride or St Brigid, is also found in river-names, including the Braint in Anglesey and the Brent in Middlesex, and experts believe the element 'brig' means 'high' or 'holy'. In a study of her cult, historian Nora Joliffe concluded that Brig or Bride was 'an honourable epithet for both rivers and hills of peculiar sanctity, which were associated in northern Britain with a more definite divine personality'.[29]

Dedications to the goddess on the southern border of Brigantian territory have been found at Greetland in West Yorkshire and Doncaster on the River Don. Some of the few surviving landmarks left by the people of Brigantia in the Peak District are the distinctive defensive earthworks and hut platforms, dating from the late Bronze Age, which crown the summit of the Shivering Mountain of Mam Tor above Castleton. The word 'mam' is yet another reference to a mother goddess, this time joined to a second Celtic word, 'tor', which occurs in Derbyshire as well as Cornwall and Devon.

27 Anne Ross, 'A Pagan Celtic Shrine at Wall, Staffordshire' (*South Staffs Archaeological and Historical Society Transactions*, vol. xxi, 1979–80)

28 John Billingsley, 'The Saddle: An Ancient Landscape?' (*Northern Earth*, 57, spring 1994); Craig Chapman, 'Druids and Stone Circles,' (*Northern Earth*, 61, spring 1995); Anne Ross, *Pagan Celtic Britain* (Routledge & Kegan Paul, 1967)

29 Nora Joliffe, 'Dea Brigantia' (*Archaeological Journal*, 1942)

Speaking on the 1977 TV documentary, the guardian of the Longdendale traditions said that there were 'quite a lot of mothers around here', referring to the Derbyshire Peak. She said they were generally represented in stone, but would not always be recognizable to outsiders, who wouldn't know what they were looking at if they saw one of the images.

It is plain she was referring to landscape or natural images of the mother goddess, like those found in Scotland and Ireland. She says that although very often people will see odd-shaped stones and think they look like a seated woman or statues they have seen in museums, they look no further; if they did, they might see that at one part of the stone there is a 'V' and at another part there are two indentations 'symbolizing the female of the species'.[30]

Another informant from north Derbyshire told us, 'In our tradition the gods could never be depicted in human form. It was just a recognizable symbol of the god or goddess which was used, often as a house guardian or marker. This could just be a stone or a piece of wood with a special mark or symbol which identified it to those who knew.'[31]

Describing the importance of the goddess in the Longdendale valley, the guardian said that respect for the mother was a very old tradition, one of the last aspects of 'pagan' belief to survive into living memory. She has always known her as the mother or the One, and it is clear that the mother is basically a name for the earth – the Earth Mother. She said there was the old trio of the Virgin, the Mother and the Woman Who Devours Men, but because the significance of them came from so long ago, 'sometimes you don't quite get the message as it started out perhaps . . . but that is the belief that there is the mother and there are three faces of the mother'.[32]

The triple form of the mother is also found in Roman Britain and in Christianity, and it seems that when Christianity first came to Britain, the missionaries didn't take the old ways away from the people but instead just fitted certain new ideas into the older beliefs, and the tradition just continued to evolve over the centuries.

Perhaps unique to north Derbyshire, within living memory there was also 'the living mother', a woman who represented the mother and who was a mother to her people, 'and long ago there was the problem that the mother belonged to all, and she was available to all, and she was not allowed to prefer one above the rest'. But nowadays, she said, 'the mother doesn't have to belong to everyone . . . you can prefer one man above all others; it's more a mother in spirit than in body'.[33]

This tradition has a parallel in other Celtic lands, particularly Ireland, where there is some evidence for matriarchal inheritance in certain families. It seems there were even special living women who were identified with the goddess or hag. In the seventeenth century, a diocesan synod in Kilmore, County Galway, banned all women known as *gierador* from receiving sacraments, and it seems that these were the local wise women or hags, the intermediaries between the tribe and the goddess.[34] This suggests that the *gierador* were possessed in some form by the female deity, in this instance a Celtic mother goddess – perhaps the ancient hag Anu or Aine of the Irish traditions, whose name is also remembered in this part of the High Peak.

30 *Chronicle*, op. cit.

31 Oral tradition, collected 1995

32 *Chronicle*, op. cit.

33 Ibid.

34 Jack Roberts, *The Sheela-na-gigs of Britain and Ireland: An Illustrated Guide* (Key Books, County Cork, 1995)

Opposite:
Ludchurch or
Lud's Church is an
awesome rocky
chasm in the Back
Forest above the
Dane valley in
Staffordshire. The
name is from the
Celtic father god
Lud. The 'church'
was the 'Green
Chapel' of the
nature god
depicted in *Sir
Gawain and the
Green Knight.*

In northern England, traditions of this kind can be found described in a unique seventeenth-century account which talks of the 'trance possession' of a Yorkshirewoman, Helen Fairfax, who became entangled in a series of witchcraft allegations. Her father was the general Edward Fairfax, who produced a volume on his campaign against local witches which was first published in 1621. The Fairfax family lived in the Washburn valley region of the Dales, which, like neighbouring Pennine valleys, has an archaic Celtic tradition. In describing the fits experienced by Helen, Grainge, the editor of Fairfax's volume, said, 'She had perfect symptoms of the disease called 'The Mother', and he goes on to note how the herbalist Culpeper prescribed motherwort as a cure for this 'disease'.[35]

Possession by the divine mother, prophecy and visions of the past and future were one aspect of the archaic and completely pagan tradition which has survived in two Pennine valleys. Another relates to a stone focus possessed by the mother. In Longdendale, the guardian recalls how, alongside the living mother, according to her tradition, there was also the 'stone mother' – a focus which was particular to that person. 'When she died, or when she got removed, that was buried and it wasn't used again,' she states.

Every human mother, she said, at one time had her own personal stone mother, often a small triangular stone or talisman with nothing but a triangular mark 'at a strategic place' to indicate it was female. A second informant describes the stones as symbols of the clan or family: 'Some of the older groups use a glyph, and from an early age the stone imprints upon you. It's a way you identify if you belong to a particular family, like a primitive form of identification badge.'[36]

Special stones like these are of course not unique to Peakland tradition, for in Scotland, Cumbria, Ulster, the Isle of Man and elsewhere many families kept small charm stones as treasured heirlooms. The most famous is the Lee Penny, immortalized by Sir Walter Scott in *The Talisman*. This was a triangular or heart-shaped stone given as ransom by the wife of a Saracen chief to Sir Simon Lockhart during the Crusades. The stone developed strong healing powers, and these could be focused by drawing it sunwise round a vessel of water, then dipping it in three times. It was also said to promote fertility in cattle and give protection against the evil eye.[37]

Amulets of special stone and rock crystals were often regarded as having protective properties against a range of supernatural horrors, and as we have seen, author Alan Garner made much use of this motif in his first novel, *The Weirdstone of Brisingamen*. In Norse mythology Brisingamen is a magical necklace or torc made for Freya, 'the most lovely of the goddesses', by the Brisings, or dwarfs. Stones like these were often used in the Staffordshire Moorlands region of western Peakland as protection against witches and the evil eye, if holed and worn around the neck. Elsewhere in the Yorkshire Dales and Cumbria another variant is the Dobbie Stone.

In the Western moorlands, protective stones were most effective if they came from the rock escarpment known as the Roaches, or from the spectacular rock chasm nearby called Lud's Church. The valley of Dane, below Lud's Church, is a remote and beautiful place where once again the divine goddess of Celts is remembered both in tradition and in landscape. Eerie Lud's Church, or

35 Phillips, op. cit.

36 *Chronicle*, op. cit.

37 For charm stones and lucks, see J. G. Lockhart, *Curses, Lucks and Talismans* (Geoffrey Bles, 1938); see also Phillips, op. cit.

the Green Chapel where Sir Gawain faced the Green Knight, is hidden away in heavily forested Back Wood, an area full of associations with the old ways.

Below the pagan chapel, the Black Brook meets the River Dane, whose name is derived from the goddess Danu/Anu. The Dane rises from the earth on desolate moorland at Featherbed Moss and travels southwest towards the beautiful and numinous Three Shires Heads, where a packhorse bridge straddles the boundary of the counties of Cheshire, Derbyshire and Staffordshire. Writing of Three Shires Heads in 1864, a local vicar spoke of the reddish-yellow ochre which flowed into the River Dane from local streams. It was, he said, regarded as having magical properties and could protect against witchcraft and the evil eye if quaffed nine mornings in a row.[38]

The iron-rich springs feeding the Dane come from the hills around Gradbach, a name said to be derived from the words 'sandy stream'. But in local dialect Gradbach is known as 'Great Bitch', and that vernacular name is found on gravestones of residents in a local cemetery. The 'Great Bitch' is said to refer to Gradbach Hill itself, where a prominent rock formation may represent the goddess. If you know what to look for and if you find the right place and the right time, you may see her image appear on a sacred rock above the river at Gradbach Hill. As you sit, look into the lovely valley below and see a stream running red, rich in ironstone – a symbol of her menstruation and the everlasting fertility of the earth.

THE CURSE OF THE SHEELAS

Earlier we saw how the pagan goddess had a dual nature in folk tradition. The early Irish tales and legends emphasize the female deity's power over life, death and the seasons as virgin, mother and crone. In oral tradition too, the divine mother is both benign and malevolent, maternal and martial. She heals and presides over childbirth, but at the same time can be dark, menacing and fatal for those who fail to respect the raw power of nature which she represents.

The Celtic king was often described as having a symbolic marriage to the land – in effect, a mating with the territorial goddess, to whose womb, the burial mound, he would return in death. In Ireland this was formalized in the Feast of Tara, where the Irish high king united with the goddess of sovereignty in a Hallowe'en ritual. In these tales, the goddess would often transform from hideous hag to beautiful girl once the union had taken place. This sexual aspect of the goddess is apparent from her association with the land and also perhaps from medieval images of a grotesque female figure displaying her genitals.

In the Ulster cycle, the goddess of sovereignty takes the form of three war goddesses, Macha, Badb and Morrigan, and the hero Cuchulain encounters a number of divine hags who are described as blind in one eye and represent a primeval sexual force. These fearful descriptions bring to mind the many

38 Doug Pickford, *Myths and Legends of East Cheshire and the Moorlands* (Sigma Press, 1992)

powerful carvings found throughout the British Isles of hideous hag-like beings who may represent the Celtic hag or Cailleach. Their features often display a repulsive leer, with the naked body in a crouched or squatting position, the grossly exaggerated genitals pulled apart by the hands.

These carvings were given the generic name 'Sheela-na-gig' by antiquarians during the nineteenth century. The term was drawn from vernacular Irish meaning 'old hag of the paps', but it has become the source of much controversy because breasts are not a feature found on the carvings. In the oral tradition of the areas where these carvings are found, 'Sheela' seems to be drawn from the word *sile*, meaning a hag or fairy woman, or *suil*, a term for the evil eye.

A recent survey found 140 Sheela-na-gigs in Britain and Ireland, 80 of which appear to be in their original locations above doorways and entrances to old churches, abbeys and castles. The largest collection is in the National Museum of Ireland, which has 15 from the variety of locations.[39] Many more are missing, but clearly figures like these were once displayed on religious buildings not just in Ireland, but in northern and western Britain.

Scholars have classified Sheelas as just one of a range of sexually 'exhibitionist' figures of Norman or medieval date, but 100 years after their 'discovery', scholars continue to be fiercely divided about their true pedigree and function. Although attempts have been made to trace the origins of Sheelas to the Continent in the early Middle Ages, as part of a Christian attempt to warn pilgrims against the temptations of the flesh, there are clear prototypes for the image in pagan Iron Age sculpture.

Anne Ross favours a Celtic origin for the Sheela-na-gig, suggesting that 'in their earliest iconographic form they portray the territorial or war goddess in her hag-like aspect, with all the strongly sexual characteristics which accompany this guise in the tales'.[40] And as scholar Etienne Rynne concludes, 'The Irish merely adapted their [traditional images] to the newly introduced motif and then forced ahead with renewed enthusiasm . . . producing more and better Sheelas than anyone else.'[41]

Whatever their original intention may have been, in the folk tradition of many rural areas Sheelas are still used for promoting fertility, healing the sick and turning away the evil eye – a function similar to that performed by the archaic stone heads in northern England. In local tradition, Irish Sheelas are known by a number of names, including the Devil Stone, the Idol, the Evil Eye Stone, and as the protective hag of the local castle or river. Because they were usually positioned high on the walls of castles or bridges, often overlooking the boundaries of tribal territories, it is possible that some of these fearsome images were meant to represent the local territorial goddess, put there to ward off evil or attack.

Many of the figures have strange attributes which associate them with pagan deities and ancient fertility rites. Some hold discs or objects which may be solar or lunar symbols associated with the different personifications of the mother. A number of carvings kept at little-known rural shrines have evidence of continual rubbing of the genital area, which was seen as the centre of the feminine power itself. Others have holes drilled in a pattern similar to that

39 See Anthony Weir and James Jerman, *Images of Lust: Sexual Carvings on Medieval Churches* (Batsford, 1986); J. Andersen, *The Witch on the Wall: Medieval Erotic Sculpture in the British Isles* (London, 1977); Stella Cherry, *A Guide to Sheela-na-gigs* (National Museum of Ireland, 1992)

40 Anne Ross, 'The Divine Hag of the Pagan Celts', in *The Witch Figure*, V. Newall (ed.) (Routledge & Kegan Paul, 1973)

41 Etienne Rynne, 'A Pagan Celtic Background for Sheela-na-gigs', in (ed.), *Figures from the Past* (Glendale Press, 1987)

known in the Longdendale valley of the Derbyshire Peak District, which may have been a magical symbol associated with the goddess.

The Sheelas' connection with a goddess is confirmed by the association of some carvings in western Cork with the sacred name Catherine/Cathleen. This name is synonymous with the hag or Cailleach, whose home on the Beara peninsula was itself near an ancient church dedicated to St Katherine. Many of the carvings are found in monasteries, churches and pagan temples associated with women, like those at Clonmacnoise, Iona and Tara. One important Sheela, high on the wall of Ballinacarriga Castle in western Cork, appears to be dedicated to Catherine Cullinane, the wife of a local chieftain, who is associated with goddess symbols. The surname Cullinane can be traced back to the early Celtic tribes of western Cork, who seem to have had a matriarchal system of inheritance like that suggested for the Picts in Scotland.[42]

Plainly, furtive beliefs about the continuing powers of the pagan goddess with certain stones and wells continue in rural areas of Britain and Ireland to the present day. The deep-rooted nature of these powers upon the human mind exists below the surface in twentieth-century society, and archaic beliefs can easily resurface when the circumstances are right.

Strange phenomena, 'curses' and other sorts of bad luck have been experienced by people who have moved or disturbed artefacts associated with pagan shrines or used as part of furtive traditions. Carved stone heads, heirloom skulls and idols have all been associated with strange happenings in folklore and in living memory. Recently, it has been claimed that camera equipment refuses to function when attempts are made to take photos of Sheelas and other Celtic idols, a problem met by visitors to the Glen Lyon goddess shrine, and to a strange hill figure known as the Black Horse in the western Pennines.

It is clear that in many places, these artefacts or images continue to exert a powerful influence upon the human mind – some would say an evil influence, which may explain why a number of Sheelas and related Celtic sculpture have been destroyed in the centuries since their creation. In Ireland, the clergy issued specific orders in the seventeenth century for priests to hide away, smash or bury Sheela-na-gigs and other idols; this was happening as recently as 1844, when a parish priest in County Meath buried a stone known as the Idol, which continued to exert power over his flock.[43]

Sidney Jackson, an antiquarian and fieldworker based at a West Yorkshire museum, recorded a number of strange experiences involving Sheela figurines he had examined during the 1960s. In particular, he describes a visit to an image built into the entrance wall of the parish church at Croft-on-Tees, on the North Sea coast near Newcastle. The carving is described by the church guide as Romano-British in origin, and represents 'a local deity of the sea'. Before it came to the church, it was formerly built into the masonry of a bridge, probably in a guardian position.[44]

Jackson wrote after a visit to the church, 'I wanted to photograph it, but from the start things went wrong. First, the flash wouldn't work, then the shutter amazingly wouldn't work, until, having wasted eight exposures, with the last on my film, I came away without a picture.' Some time later Jackson learned that a fieldworker from Denmark, Jorgen Anderson, had had the same

42 Roberts, op. cit.

43 Ibid.

44 Sidney Jackson, 'The Curse of the Croft Sheela' (*Bradford Telegraph and Argus*, 16 July 1974)

experience when he tried to obtain a picture of the Sheela at Croft. Similar problems were encountered by another colleague of Jackson, Jean O'Melia, who also failed to obtain pictures of Sheelas at Bridlington Priory and in a ruined church in Ireland. It is easy to scoff at stories like these and attribute them to coincidence or wishful thinking on behalf of incredulous fieldworkers, but even as we were writing this book, a colleague in West Yorkshire sent one of the authors a number of colour slides showing the Croft Sheela, along with another from the same region. Those pictures all disappeared without trace in the post!

FREYA

The fertility connotations of Sheela-na-gig figurines continue to this day in living traditions on both sides of the Irish Sea. This statement is supported by strong folk traditions which surround a number of these emotive carvings. One 46-centimetre-high (18-inch) example is set on a wall at Holdgate Church in Corvedale, one of a group of churches with their own 'female guardians' in the Welsh Border region. Formerly young men in the parish would take their brides 'and introduce her to the Sheela to bless his marriage with plenty of children'.[45]

The fecund power of the goddess and her role as guardian or protector of the ground on which she was sovereign continue at a village in southern Cumbria to the present day. The part of coastal Cumbria where this tradition has survived was settled, along with the Isle of Man, by Norse people who migrated from settlements in Celtic Ireland during the early medieval period. Paganism continued here well into the era when England was said to have become officially a Christian country. As late as the tenth century Olaf Ball, a thane of King Ragnald, who then held all the land from the Eden in Cumbria to the River Wear, continued to 'swear by the mighty gods, Thor and Othin'.[46]

The latent paganism of the Norse settlers can be judged by the images on the famous Gosforth Cross, a wheel-headed stone which has stood in a churchyard on the western coast of Cumbria for almost 1,000 years. The stone base represents the Tree of Life, Yggdrasil; and three sides of the face depict scenes from Ragnarok, the Norse doomsday, and images of the pagan gods. Even the Crucifixion image is executed in the form of a crude, pagan Norse style.

Although nominally converted to Christianity, the Norse farmers and tradesmen brought their goddess cult to this part of northern England, which was then occupied by Celtic tribes with a parallel tradition. Scholars have noted a concentration of early medieval churches on the coastal plain of Cumbria dedicated to the goddess St Brigid, many of them associated with healing wells. It is quite possible that religious fusion took place during the migration period, with the Norse goddess merging naturally with that of the indigenous Celts.[47]

Hidden in the hills about three kilometres (two miles) south of Ulverston, is the twelfth-century church of St Michael and All Angels at Pennington. The

45 John Hargreaves, 'Dallying with the Sheela in the Sanctuary' (*Weekend Guardian*, 28–29 October 1989)

46 William Chaney, *The Cult of Kingship in Anglo-Saxon England* (Manchester University Press, 1970)

47 Mike Haigh, 'The Cumberland Bride-Church Cluster,' (*Northern Earth*, 57, spring 1994)

building perches at the centre of a raised circular churchyard, a common indication that it stands on a numinous or early sacred site. Several years ago Andy Roberts, who was holidaying in the area, visited the church at the end of a long cycle ride in order to inspect a curious carving of a female figure which he had heard resided in the porch. The church, as is often the case today, was locked, but an elderly villager soon emerged from the porch and began to relock it behind him.

Asked about the carving, the man at first said it had been removed to Kendal Museum, but then suddenly changed his mind and admitted it was actually stored in the cellar beneath the church itself. 'Current parson's superstitious,' he said. 'He thinks it is an evil influence. Old parson used to have it in the porch. It was taken out of the church wall and must be 1,000 years old.' Eventually, the old man led him down into the cellar and there opened a dusty ammunition case to reveal a full-length female figure carved on to a block of sandstone about 75 centimetres (two and a half feet) long by 30 centimetres (one foot) wide. The vulva took the form of a deep hole which looked as though it had been rubbed, either by the human hand or perhaps by farm implements. As he examined the carving, the old man said, 'The new parson thinks Freya might have put a curse on people and that's why she's going.'

Intrigued by the use of the name Freya, Andy asked if the man was referring to the carving. 'Aye, lad,' was the reply. Andy then asked if he had always called it that, and again the reply was 'Aye, all the time.'[48]

Why, he didn't know, or he wasn't saying. Enquiries revealed that the first record of the carving, in a local newspaper dated 1929, described how it had been discovered or found three years earlier built, as the old caretaker had said, into the east wall of the church. The article reported that the vicar of the day had specifically asked workmen to look out for strange carvings during the alterations, but when the figure was found the men decided to smash it, believing 'the parson would not like to see it'.

Luckily the vicar of that time retrieved it at the eleventh hour, and later it was noted how the stone was 'deliberately and secretly built into the church beside the altar – thus propitiating both new and old gods'. One account from the 1930s specifically described the carving as a depiction of 'the goddess of fertility Frea or Freya', and it seems this identification – whatever its origin – remained in the oral tradition for more than 70 years. When scholar Richard Bailey, of Newcastle University, examined the carving in the church porch in 1979, he said that one of the residents 'identified the figure to me as Freya'.[49]

Folklore scholar Hilda Ellis-Davidson writes that in the Scandinavian tradition Freya was the tutelary goddess, sister and bride to the god Freyr, who together were known as 'Lord' and 'Lady'. Freya was their territorial goddess, a Norse equivalent to the Celtic Brigid/Bride. 'She was connected with the water and the sea . . . she was regarded as a giving goddess, bringing bounty to the fields, animals and mankind,' she wrote.[50] Furthermore, it would seem that the Pennington Freya was not the only one of its kind in existence. Earlier this century, other accounts refer to similar goddess stones found in early churches at Egremont and Cross Canonby – both now missing. Have they been destroyed or are they being used secretly as part of some local tradition?

Opposite: Sheela-na-gig, Pennington, Cumbria. Feared by clergyman, revered by villagers, this pagan relic now lies in Kendal Museum.

48 Andy Roberts, 'An Encounter with Freya' (*Northern Earth*, 56, winter 1993–4)

49 Richard Bailey, 'Apotropaic Figures in Milan and Northwest England' (*Folklore*, vol. 94, 1983); *Cumberland News*, 14 September 1929; F. Welsh, *Companion Guide to the Lake District* (Collins, 1989); pers. comm., Lynn Fade, Kendal Museum, 1994

50 Hilda Ellis-Davidson, *The Lost Beliefs of Northern Europe* (Routledge, 1993)

When we contacted the current vicar at Pennington, the incumbent since 1991, he confirmed that his predecessor would not have the carving in the church. Soon the true nature of the 'curse' which a previous vicar believed Freya had put on locals became clearer. 'I was told it was Freya, a goddess of fertility, and it's something many people round here knew about. I know it was originally found in the church wall but I don't know where the name came from originally and it is possible it was known about before that time,' he said.

'My predecessor was worried about the pagan connotations of the stone and I think I would share his concern. He wanted to get rid of the carving, but because it was in the inventory of the church he couldn't give it away or smash it. Apparently, during his time at the church, there was some kind of village festival and Freya was brought out and put on display, along with other historical artefacts. It was said that as a result the vicar's wife became pregnant soon afterwards, along with several other village women who had taken part in the festival. That was a coincidence that local people thought was significant.'

In the end the vicar left, and under his successor it took a special vote at the Parish Church Council and the approval of the diocese of Kendal before the carving could be removed on extended loan to a museum. 'It was not a unanimous vote but we won it. Some people did not want it to go because it was church property; others wanted to retain it inside the church "because it is ours," he said.[51]

Not all parish vicars share the reticence of their Cumbrian colleagues. The Rev. Michael Stedmon, whose church plays host to a well-known Sheela at Church Stretton, Shropshire, told a writer in 1989, 'To be honest, I would prefer it not to be there but I would strongly resist any attempt to remove it. It is part of the genius of the church.'[52] Similar feelings were echoed by the people of Kiltinan in County Tipperary, whose Sheela was stolen from the parish church by persons unknown in 1990. As the local museum curator put it, 'Sheelas hint at feelings and emotions not normally evoked by academic study.'

THE WELL OF THE
TRIPLE GODDESS

The influence of the Celtic twilight can be seen most clearly upon human belief, even among archaeologists, in the following story. Early in 1990, a team of amateur archaeologists began to investigate remains that suggest the existence of an early Anglo-Saxon nunnery beneath a Norman abbey on a hilltop on the Isle of Sheppey, Kent.

The leader of the team, historian Brian Slade, is an advocate of an unorthodox method to find the site for excavation which is frowned upon by archaeogists in public but often used by them in secret. Mr Slade used two bent

51 Pers. comm., 1995

52 Hargreaves, op. cit.

pieces of metal and a hazel twig to pinpoint what he believed to be the site of the Monasterium Sexburga complex, founded by St Sexburga, queen of Kent, in the late seventh century AD.

Excavations on the site chosen by Mr Slade soon revealed dozens of bronze dress pins, coins, pieces of glass and contemporary pottery which seemed to confirm the identity of the site. Suspecting the history of St Sexbuga's holy place stretched back before the Anglo-Saxon period, the team decided to explore the bottom of a 12-metre (40-foot) shaft known as the Minster Abbey Gatehouse Well. In the summer of 1991 a six-man team began work in the mud and darkness, with workers being slowly lowered by rope into the cold mineral well for one-hour shifts. The excavation of the well revealed its ancient stone lining, but the most exciting discovery came from below the water table when a flat cut-out metal shape depicting in silhouette a triple-headed deity was found.[53]

The central head looks out directly in front, while those flanking either side look left and right. All three share a large swollen body, symbolizing a pregant goddess, a very strange symbol to find in a Christian monastery complex. In addition, the excavation found broken fragments of beeswax which fitted together to form the same shape as the metal figure. This image appeared to have been Christianized by the addition of an equal-armed cross before it was deposited, perhaps as a votive offering to the goddess of the well.

The first person to touch the cut-out figure was archaeologist Ian White. At the time of the excavation, his wife, Sharon, had suffered four miscarriages of much-wanted children. But almost exactly nine months later, she gave birth to a healthy baby girl, Emily. She was followed by another baby, Hannah, and the couple told a local newspaper how they began to believe the power of the fertility goddess may have played some mysterious part in their private joy.

'I would certainly like to believe the image of the fertility goddess helped us. Sharon had been to see specialists about her miscarriages, but was told they didn't know what the problem was,' he said. 'If this image was believed in all that time ago, there must be something in it. But whatever the significance of the goddess, I've now got two daughters and to me that really is a miracle.'[54]

The finds in Minster village and the gatehouse well – now renamed as the Well of the Triple Goddess – have since prompted English Heritage to schedule certain land in the vicinity as 'a site of major archaeological importance'. And shortly before Christmas 1994, residents noticed how on several occasions beautifully wrapped bunches of flowers would appear on the stone slab which had been used to cap the mysterious well following the excavations.

Brian Slade said he was surprised when he discovered the Whites knew nothing about the flowers and guessed that another local couple, desperate to have a baby, were placing the flowers on the well in the hope that the goddess would help them too. He said, 'If modern high-tech medicine fails them, perhaps married couples experiencing difficulties having a baby should see if handling this fertility goddess can help. For a fact, superstitious women who fear becoming pregnant are already refusing to touch it!'[55]

53 Brian Slade, 'The Minster Wells, Parts 1 and 2' *Holy Wells Journal*, new series 4 & 5, 1995)

54 Ibid.; *Sheppey Gazette*, 6 October 1993

55 Ibid.

THE RIVER

Verbeia, 'She of the Cattle', was the goddess of the River Wharfe in North Yorkshire. She is carved on a stone from the river, now in Ilkley parish church, West Yorkshire.

I can well remember one spring day when I was about nine years old. My grandmother took me on the bus to Ilkley to the church there, and right in the darkness at the back of the building pointed out a carving which she said was the goddess of the river. To me it was just a stone with wavy lines being held by a figure in some kind of dress. I've visited it many times since she passed over and have come to see it as one of the few representations of the mother which manages to capture her with any degree of success. And it's in a church, which goes to show what I wrote earlier about churches and the tradition.

My family have always been with the river. In this part of the Dales you can hardly get away from it, when every slope and fellside is alive with streams and pools which feed into the river. No matter what part of the year we were in, the river remained constant. In winter it helped sweep away the detritus of the year which had gone and in the spring and summer it brought the dale to life again. I was always taught to respect water – that it was the source of everything. It helped create and also, by washing away, to destroy, and was never the same.

People talk glibly today about specific gods and goddesses connected to rivers and water, but we never really had such distinctions or limitations. The river and its sources were expressions of the one power and that was that. The power of creation is, as I've said before, beyond being male or female, although it can show itself as those distinctions. We treated the river and its power with the utmost respect and, like other points on the land, there was a time when its power should be 'acknowledged'. For the river May Day was the right time. And it always had to be May Day, and like most of our practices it was simple yet demanded energy and commitment. Just the effort of gathering on one specific day was enough, with people often returning from quite some distance.

On the eve those of us who lived in the dale and who had time to spare would spend time in the fields and fells gathering tributes to the May and the river. Anything we found beautiful and appropriate would fit the bill – organic or inorganic, it didn't matter, although we tried to keep a balance between the two. Sometimes stones or bones, but always flowers, and considerable time could be spent making posies from those available at that time of the year.

Late on the eve we would gather together at a farmhouse within a few miles of the source of the river and have, I suppose, a bit of a wake or party. No strange rites or anything like that! Just a gathering and a good time. A bonfire could be lit in the yard, and we knew that the people who couldn't be with us for one reason or another would also be marking the occasion with a fire, even if it was just a candle placed in their window bottom. It didn't matter how it was done, so long as it was done.

At first when I was young, all this was just treated as a bit of a game. But as I grew up the understanding came, just clicked into place, and I would miss this event only if I was working away and couldn't manage to get back in time. Part of the tradition involved a walk to the source of the river, about seven miles away at Cam. The bonfire was always left to burn itself out. When we arrived, the time before dawn would be spent in quiet contemplation. No one spoke at all and it could be very eerie, just the sound of the water and the wind. At this time and place there was a point in the night when we were all hit by a certain sense of an in-coming rush of life and then we knew the year had turned once more and the warmth of summer was on its way back. And we were all part of that cycle in some mysterious way. As dawn came, we would busy ourselves around the head of the water, arranging the flowers and offerings we had brought with us. When this was completed, we would eat and drink, again usually in silence, although one of the older people might say a prayer of some sort, a blessing of thanks for the river's continuing benevolence and to the coming summer season. Then we returned to our homes to carry the May festivities on in our own family way.

The Wharfe had quite a reputation for demanding and taking life in the past, and this still carried on, although people see it in a different light now. One location our tradition held in great respect was the Wharfe near Bolton Abbey, and in particular the part near where it plunges beneath the rocks at the Strid. This is a spectacular and beautiful place and here the gap from one side to the other is only a matter of feet wide. It is here the river takes its sacrifices. I suppose at one time it might have been an organized thing and the victims were the old or the sick who chose to give themselves, but that was in a more primitive time and really there was never any need for it.

The challenge of trying to jump across what seems an easy gap is too much for many people and sacrifices come this way. I suppose the act of leaping across a powerful river in full spate is some people's idea of conquering the power of nature in some small way. Most of those who have been foolish enough to try manage it, but over the years many have failed and are sucked out of sight into the swirling pit that lies beneath the waters. As my grandmother said, the Wharfe could represent both the creative and destructive powers of the mother. Although all water sources were considered special by our tradition, a bit of competition must have existed at one time, for the Wharfe was compared with the nearby River Aire in one old couplet: 'Wharfe is clear and the Aire lithe. Where the Aire drowns one, Wharfe drowns five.' One old book I have on the dale describes how parties of people would visit the Strid with the intention of jumping across, and it says of one guide, 'Two or three times he had brought parties to the Strid *and gone back with one short, and he seemed to feel the futility of it.' My grandmother also used to tell me how a white horse was to be seen rising from the Strid, always just before or after a sacrifice had been taken.*[56]

DARK WATERS

It was late on a winter's evening and a lone traveller was hurrying along the banks of the Derwent towards Cromford village, where his ailing mother awaited him. He knew nothing of the river's evil tradition. Suddenly an old woman dressed in green emerged from the hillside and greeted him: 'And where are you bound for so late? The sun has gone down and it will be dark soon. This is no road to travel at night.' Undaunted, the traveller remained silent, for he knew that to reply to a witch was to place yourself in her evil power. Sensing he was in danger, the old woman offered him a posy of St John's wort, saying, 'I wish you well. You once freed a bird from a fowler's net and I knew that bird. Take the posy and show it to Crooker.'

Before he could ask who Crooker was, the figure vanished and the traveller continued on his way. But before long he saw another old woman dressed in green standing on the lane, this time holding a posy of primroses – magic plants. She warned him not to travel the road and, when the advice went unheeded, said, 'You freed a rabbit from a snare. I knew that rabbit. Take these and show them to Crooker.' Once again, before he could phrase his question, the woman vanished. At the corner of the lane he met a third green woman who held a third posy – this time of daisies. She told him to take the posy, saying he once saved a vixen from a trap. She offered this advice, 'Keep as far from Darrent river as you can and Cromford Road that runs beside it. You must be on Cromford Bridge before the moon rises.' With that she faded into the hillside and the traveller found himself standing alone and in the darkness, clutching the three magic posies and with the rushing of the river echoing in his ears.

Before he could reach the bridge, the moon was high in the sky, the river swirled and crashed below and beneath the full moon huge ash trees cast weird shadows on the foam and spray. As he hurried towards sanctuary, their branches stretched out eerie fingers towards the fearful traveller.

As he broke into a run, keeping as he thought well away from the river, he heard the water roar as if saying, 'Hungry!' Suddenly the moon appeared from beneath a cloud and he realized he had turned a corner on the bank and was within inches of the river and death. The huge shadow of a menacing ash tree stood directly in his path. Gasping the word 'Crooker', the traveller hurled the daisies over his shoulder and ran. There was splashing noise and Darrent moaned 'Give!' Immediately the ambling form of Crooker cast its shadows across the road in front of him. Again, he hurled the posy of primroses over his left shoulder. Crooker stopped in his tracks. There was another splash. Darrent

56 Pers. comm., 1994

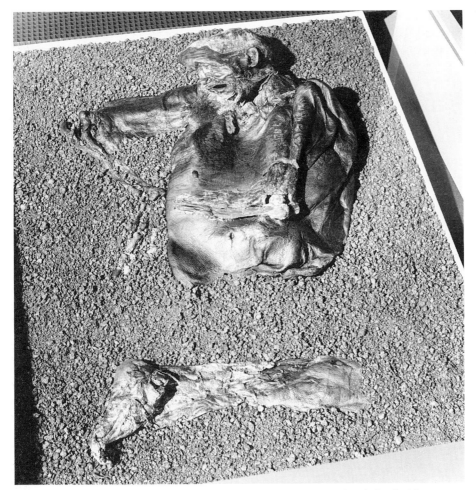

Lindow Man – the 'body in the bog' – now preserved in a display at the British Museum in London.

again cried 'Give!' The traveller was almost within reach of the bridge now, with fear driving him on. Crooker tried a third time. With his last bit of strength, he cast the posy of St John's wort at the evil spirit. It screamed and the river groaned as he flung himself at the foot of the sanctuary shrine and safety.

In the village, the people heard the river's cry and looked at each other with ashen faces. 'Darrent and Crooker,' they whispered. 'We must go first thing in the morning and get the priest. There'll be another body for the churchyard. Remember the old beggar woman we found with a broken neck? Drowned in Darrent at night she was – he roared then!' But come morning, when the throng reached the bridge, all they found was a tired traveller saying his prayers at the medieval shrine. Soon he got up and wandered off towards the village alongside the riverbank, past the great ash tree beside which the Darrent ran shallow and contented.[57]

This folk-tale was told in villages around the beautiful Peakland villages of Cromford and Matlock around the turn of the century. The River Derwent – in local tongue Darrent – flows through this central part of the Peak District, watering some of the most spectacular scenery in the country in daylight. But

57 Story adapted from versions in Ruth Tongue, *Forgotten Folk-tales of the English Counties* (Routledge & Kegan Paul, 1970) and Richard Litchfield, *Strange Tales of the Peak* (Derbyshire Heritage Series, 1992); oral traditions, collected 1993 and 1994

by night, the landscape is transformed and the rushing river has a murderous reputation. When the Romans arrived in this part of Brigantia, they crossed the river at a ford which stands upon the site of an unusual bridge chapel at Cromford, built in the fifteenth century. The hamlet sprang up around the sanctuary of the chapel, where a light was once placed at night to guide lonely travellers across the treacherous ford.

Local people have long known the river was presided over by an evil spirit called Crooker and the road from Cromford to Lea was always a sinister route, particularly around a spot near the ford sheltered by a large ash tree which threw a strange shadow. There have been many dozens of drownings and near escapes from death in the dark waters. Earlier this century, a correspondent of *Folklore Journal* described how she was struck by the way a washerwoman talked of the river 'as if it were a living personage, or deity', to the extent that she could imagine the next step 'would be to take it offerings'.

At that time, in the year 1904, there was excitement around the banks of the river following the drowning of an unwise traveller. But instead of fear, the old woman had a kind of triumph in her voice, uttering, 'He didna know Darrent . . . He said it was nought but a brook. But Darrent got 'im. They never saw his head. He threw his arms up, but Darrent wouldna let him go. Aye, it's a sad pity, seven children! But he shouldna ha' made so light of Darrent. He knows now! Nought but a brook! He knows now!'[58]

The authors heard a firsthand tradition of this kind from a former resident of Longdendale concerning the Etherow, which flows westwards through the valley from the high moorland watershed. The Etherow was seemingly venerated like other rivers in the area, and the family of our informant has a tradition of a child who fell into the river and, like Ophelia, floated downstream singing before he was drowned.

Our informant heard this story from a number of separate sources, one of whom was his own grandmother, who put his family name on this child, saying it had happened 'in our Queen's day'. But it was an incident he has been unable to find any verification of in his family history. And the mystery was increased when he heard the same story from other people in the valley who used a different name for the child. 'Now there can't have been a string of children falling in the Etherow, floating down and singing in Queen Victoria's time, so it seems we have a tradition which has been pinned to a time which is conveniently out of memory – 'back then' in the Queen's day,' he said.[59]

There are a number of versions of this story in the oral tradition of Longdendale, and significantly they all appear to be focused upon a spot below the Roman fort known as Wooley Bridge, where there is a dangerous junction between the Etherow and the Glossop Brook. This area was the haunt of a water nymph whose memory was fading in the 1950s. Her presence was even then remembered in the stone carving of three faces, hidden among water weeds, which guarded the junction of the two rivers.

Places where two rivers meet are traditionally regarded as magical places, like springs and caves, as magical boundaries where contact with the Otherworld was possible. Earth Mysteries expert John Billingsley has written of one such location in Hebden Bridge, West Yorkshire, where an archaic stone

58 M. Agatha Turner, 'Deification of the River' (*Folklore Journal*, vol. 15, 1904); Tongue, op. cit.

59 Pers. comm., 1994; oral tradition

head is built into the wall of an aqueduct above the very spot where the Rochdale Canal crosses the River Calder. The oral tradition here describes how this head was carved to remember a teacher from a nearby school who tragically lost his life as he tried to rescue a child who was drowning in the Black Pool, a deadly whirlpool below the bridge. A snag in this story is the fact that the aqueduct – and its head – was built in 1795, well before there was any school nearby.

'Not only is the head on this bridge; it is also a place where something unnatural occurs. Water is crossing water without mingling, and to cap it all the head is not placed in a visible location,' says John. 'It's very hard to see from the school, and you can't see it from the canal towpath unless you dangle from the parapet over this whirlpool. It has no good vantage point except the river and is obviously not for decoration, therefore the intended audience is the river itself.'[60]

Deification of rivers was not limited to the north of England, for the River Spey in the Highlands of Scotland is spoken of as 'she' and its bloodthirsty waters are believed to require at least one victim every year. On the edge of Dartmoor, the River Dart has a similar murderous reputation, and tradition says it too takes a human life once every year. The Rev. Sabine Baring-Gould said the Dart was heard to cry: 'The sound is a particularly weird one; it is heard only when the wind is blowing down its deep valley.'[61] Of the river, it is said:

> The Dart, the Dart – the cruel Dart
> Every year demands a heart . . .

In Lancashire, the River Ribble was haunted by a less hungry but equally malevolent female spirit known as Peg O'Nell. Peg required a human life once every seven years, unless a bird or other small animal was sacrificed in its place. Belief in the power of Peg O'Nell was still strong in 1908, when a local newspaper, writing of a drowning in the river, stated, 'It is curious that the last fatality in the Ribble took place exactly seven years ago, and the one before that was 14 years ago.'[62]

Sometimes it was possible to persuade the spirit of the river to give up its prey, if the correct ritual was carried out. A story from Nairnshire in north Scotland describes how a man named Farquharson, who was a travelling salesman, slipped and was drowned in a notorious ford on the River Dee within sight of his distraught wife. Immediately, a search was made for the body, but in vain, as were searches further downstream the following morning. That evening, the dead man's wife took his plaid and went to the pool below the Linn of Dee, where he has drowned 'atween the sun and sky'. She folded the plaid in a particular way, then knelt by the pool and prayed to the spirit of the pool to give up the body of her husband. Then she cast the plaid into the water, shouting, 'Take that, and give me back my dead.' The following morning the body, wrapped in the plaid, was found lying on the bank beside the pool. Local tradition had it that the widow shortly afterwards bore a son, who became the progenitor of the clan Farquharson.[63]

In the days before the industrial revolution and pollution, rivers were seen as part of the living body of the earth. They had power over life and death and

60 John Billingsley, lecture on archaic heads at Northern Earth Moot, Bradford, 1994; see also John Billingsley, 'Archaic Heads: Guardians of the Boundaries' (*Mercian Mysteries*, 24, August 1995)

61 Sabine Baring-Gould, *A Book of Dartmoor* (Wildwood House, 1982)

62 John Billingsley, 'The Lady of the Dark Waters' (*Northern Earth*, 54, summer 1993)

63 W. Gregor, 'Guardian Spirits of Wells and Lochs' (*Folklore Journal*, vol. 3, 1892)

Lindow Man. The face of the Iron Age 'body in the bog', found in a raised peat bog near Mobberley, Cheshire, in 1985, has been carefully reconstructed by experts in Manchester and in London.

had to be respected. Upsetting the delicate balance between man and nature was a taboo avoided by everyone except the foolish. In some areas it was even tantamount to blasphemy for someone to interfere when a victim was drowning in the clutches of a river sprite, for once the deed was done, it was thought no further lives would be required until the next cycle in the life of the river. Last century, when a young boy was drowned in the river at Ross-on-Wye in Herefordshire, his brothers were warned about venturing on to its banks in future. But an old man, overhearing the warning, chipped in with, 'Let 'em go, let 'em go. No one else'll be drowned this year. The river has had its dree.'[64]

Variations on this kind of legend can be found in many regions of the British Isles. Some may point to a time within living memory when the waters themselves were believed to be the haunt of spirits which demanded a quota of living victims – both animal and human. In Aberdeenshire, a story was once told about tributes made by freeholders who grazed their flocks on pastureland adjoining a stretch of water known as Lochan-wan ('the lambs loch'). Writing in 1892, a local man described how every man who sent sheep to this common 'had to offer in sacrifice to the spirit of the loch the first lamb of his flock dropped on the common. The omission of this sacrifice brought disaster, for unless the sacrifice was made, half of his flock would be drowned before the end of the grazing season.'[65]

When animal sacrifice was insufficient, it seems that human beings may have been offered to the dark underworld spirits in times of crisis or disaster. In the last ten years, the discovery of ancient bodies buried in peat at Lindow Moss in Cheshire has provided archaeologists with their finest piece of evidence for the practice of human sacrifice in the late Iron Age. At least one of the bodies, whose skin appears to have been painted with mineral pigments, died a ritual death at the hands of the pagan priesthood, possibly at the time when Roman legions were advancing along the Brigantian frontier. Although a number of well-preserved bog bodies have been discovered in Denmark and Ireland, this is the first English example where preservation conditions were good enough to allow experts to analyse the contents of the victim's last meal and draw clues

64 Lewis Spence, *The Minor Traditions of British Mythology* (Benjamin Bloom, 1972)

65 Gregor, op. cit.

about the nature of his life and death. From the evidence, it seems that Lindow Man consumed a last ritual meal of bannock bread cooked on a heather fire before he was subjected to a ritual triple death. His stomach contained traces of mistletoe pollen, a plant which Caesar said was used in druid rituals. The young man apparently went willingly to his death in the pool which became Lindow Moss, where he was pole-axed, garrotted and thrust face downwards into the water, naked other than for one small armband of fox fur.[66]

Although we will never know the names of the grim Celtic gods or goddesses to whom Lindow Man was dedicated, their memory has never entirely left the Lindow area. There are many local tales about other bodies found in the peat bog, and objects offered or dedicated to the spirit which lives there. Until recently, objects unearthed in bogs and sacred mounds were left alone or reburied in secrecy elsewhere because they had been 'offered'. A number of crude stone and wooden idols have been recovered from peat bogs in Ireland and Scotland, and they have often been associated with strange and uncanny happenings. In her book *Prospect of Erne*, Mary Rogers writes of one 'stone figure' which was hastily reburied in a bog in County Cavan after 'several accidents' occurred on the farm where it had been kept.[67]

There are many stories like this from northern England too, and we were told by one Peak District resident of a copper sword and other ritual artefacts which were unearthed when a relative was clearing land near a burial place which had a 'reputation'. They were not kept, but thrown back into a river because they had been 'offered' to the old ones. There is in fact substantial archaeological evidence from Scotland, Ireland and the Continent for the ritual burial of hordes of metalwork, particularly cauldrons, in bogs and dark lakes, which may have been held in superstitious awe and terror by the Celtic tribes. The most famous is of course the ritual cauldron adorned with fabulous pagan imagery which had been carefully dismantled before it was offered to the deities of a bog near Gundestrup in Denmark.

Traditions about pagan deities – usually female in gender – inhabiting pools and lakes are common in British folk tradition and have given rise to dozens of legends concerning mermaids, 'white lady' ghosts and, perhaps most familiar of all, the Lady of the Lake, to whom Arthur's sword Excalibur was finally returned. Stories of mermaids or 'maids in the mere' are commonly connected with isolated pools on the western moors of the Peak District, a belief which is common to many of the regions which have retained a strong oral tradition. In Scotland rivers and pools were often the habitation of the water horse or *each uisge*, which would lure travellers on to its back and then rush blindly into the water, drowning its prey. In England too, the goddess often appeared in the form of a white horse, like the ghostly steed which rises from the foam of the Strid in North Yorkshire on the morning of May Day, preceding a fatal accident in the rushing River Wharfe. Many of these stories may have been manufactured to keep youngsters away from dangerous stretches of water, but they all draw upon an archaic pool of tradition.

High up on the rugged Dark Peak moors at the foot of the dramatic Kinder Downfall lies the Mermaid's Pool, a black acidic mire which one visitor has described as having 'an atmosphere of melancholy, a sense of desolation which

66 Ross and Robins, op. cit.; Ian Stead, J. B. Bourke and D. Brothwell (eds.), *Lindow Man: The Body in the Bog* (British Museum, 1986); see also Denise Kenyon, *Lindow Man: His life and Times* (Manchester Museum, 1987)

67 Mary Rogers, *Prospect of Erne* (Blackstaff Press, 1967)

Eerie Mermaid's Pool is found high up on the slopes of Kinder Scout, a rocky moorland plateau in the Derbyshire High Peak. Local tradition tells how anyone who sees this 'maid in the mere' will either receive the gift of immortality or be dragged beneath the water to their death.

suggests some malign influence has cast its spell over the place'.[68] Local tradition tells how a beautiful nymph lives in a cave on the side of Kinder Scout and comes out daily to bathe in the dark pool. Any man who walks through Old Oak Wood to the pool and is lucky enough to see her while bathing will become immortal, or so the story goes. One local man who lived to the ripe old age of 104 is supposed to have been lucky enough to see the mermaid late in the nineteenth century, although the tale sounds suspiciously like a tradition fixed just outside living memory, as we saw with the child in the River Etherow. Belief in female spirits of these pools remains strong, and there are suggestions that they were regarded as places where the Otherworld could be accessed and the future divined.

On the moorlands between Leek and Buxton in the western Peak District there are two pools associated with mermaids. The mermaid of Blake Mere is of a less benevolent nature and appears at midnight to drag unsuspecting travellers beneath the murky waters, which are said to be bottomless. Earlier this century, the estate that owned the moor on which the pool was situated decided to drain it in order to improve the land for the enjoyment of grouse-shooting parties. A local story tells how labourers from nearby farms were contracted to help dig a drain, part of which can still be seen near the pool. But one morning the men stopped their work and refused to carry on, because they believed so strongly the pool was bottomless and the spirit of the pool would flood the town of Leek if her slumber was disturbed.[69]

68 See Clarence Daniel, *Ghosts of Derbyshire* (Dalesman, 1973) and *Derbyshire Traditions* (Dalesman, 1975)

69 Pers. comm., Doug Pickford, 1995

One of the many
hidden valleys
guarding the
secrets of
Longdendale in
the High Peak
of Derbyshire.
(*David Clarke*)

Below This mysterious, elongated carving from the Mouse-low collection may depict one of the shadowy Celtic gods from the local tradition.
(*David Clarke*)

Right A recent example of a magical-head guardian in West Yorkshire. This has been carved and placed above the entrance to the Sun Inn, Haworth, to lay a ghost which haunted the Inn.
(*Andy Roberts*)

Above The clootie well, Ross and Cromarty, Scotland. This rag well on the Black Isle is one of Britain's largest votive shrines. Over 50,000 rags have been tied to nearby trees and bushes by pilgrims wishing to be healed.
(*Andy Roberts*)

Left Mouselow Hill, Glossop, Derbyshire. An archaeological dig here during the 1980s revealed the existence of a strong, continuing Celtic tradition.
(*David Clarke*)

The Wishing Well, Alderley Edge. One of two springs which emerge from the sandstone rocks in a valley below. Visitors have left pins and coins as offerings at the nearby Holy Well since pagan times. (*David Clarke*)

Stormy Point or the Devil's Grave provides one of the finest viewpoints from Alderley Edge. It is named in the Cheshire folk-tale 'The Wizard of Alderley', which concerns a magical cave, a sleeping army and a white horse.
(*David Clarke*)

Alderley Edge, Cheshire. A magical and numinous landscape which provided the inspiration for a number of Alan Garner's novels.
(*David Clarke*)

Above The Cailleach, Bodach and Nighean. These water-worn stones in the Tigh nam Cailliche shrine are said to represent a trio of protective deities. (*David Clarke*)

Right Carved stone head on viaduct, Hebden Bridge, West Yorkshire. Legend links this with the drowning of a teacher in a whirlpool below the eighteenth-century bridge. (*Andy Roberts*)

The Hag's House, Glen Lyon. Situated in a remote part of central Perthshire, experts believe this rocky house may be one of the last remaining ancient shrines with a living tradition in Britain.
(*David Clarke*)

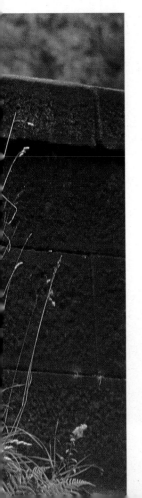

Right The sombre head of a Celtic god – perhaps the deity known to the Celts as Maponus – found at the Roman fort Corstopitum (Chesters) on Hadrian's Wall, Northumberland. The carving has a circular focus on the top which may have functioned as an altar for offerings to the deity inhabiting the head.
(*Chesters Museum*)

Glen Lyon, Perthshire. One of the longest glens in the Highlands, where many archaic Celtic beliefs and practices have survived. (*David Clarke*)

Right Loch Lyon, Glen Lyon. This brooding glen, a physical representation of the goddess, hides a continuing Celtic tradition. (*David Clarke*)

Far right The Green Man, Fountains Abbey, North Yorkshire. A striking image of the nature god in the heart of the medieval church. (*David Clarke*)

Many old houses
in the western
parts of the British
Isles preserve
guardian skulls
like this example
from Flagg Hall,
Derbyshire.
(*David Clarke*)

Three Shires Heads, the source of the River Dane, on the boundary of three modern counties. In Celtic tradition, boundaries both physical and non-physical were of special significance. The sources of rivers were numinous places where the veil between the worlds was thin. (*David Clarke*)

Above The Paps of Anu, County Kerry. One of the best examples of a goddess tradition visualized in the landscape itself. (*David Clarke*)

Left A good example of a Christianized pagan tradition is the annual well-dressing ceremony in Derbyshire Peak District villages. (*David Clarke*)

Left Human skulls and other potent evil-averting artefacts guarded the physical and psychic entrances to Celtic settlements like this reconstructed Iron Age village in the Welsh Folk Museum. (*David Clarke*)

Left Whole Pennine communities still participate in the August rush-bearing ceremony, which has obvious pagan connotations. (*David Clarke*)

Above Burning of Bartle, West Witton, North Yorkshire. An ancient sacrificial ceremony at the end of the harvest in a remote farming community. (*David Clarke*)

Stone head found near the source of an underground spring at Castleton, Derbyshire. The face appears to have one purposeful winking eye, which may suggest it represents one of the baleful one-eyed Celtic deities. (*Sheffield Museum*)

Tree of Life Stone, Snowden Carr, West Yorkshire. A mysterious Bronze Age carving depicting cup and ring markings in the form of a tree, of which an historian has said, 'It is one of the few known to local inhabitants, and marks the site of many May Day religious services.' The outlines of the carving have been marked with yellow chalk. (*Andy Roberts*)

Right Medieval stone head set upon a wall in the High Peak, one of many kept as prize possessions by their owners in this region. (*David Clarke*)

Below The Druid's Head. Focus of supernatural activity after it was found in the roots of a sycamore tree in Bingley, West Yorkshire. (*David Clarke*)

Right The screaming skull of Bettiscombe manor house, Dorset. The skull is believed to have belonged to a prehistoric woman, and may once have been kept in a spring on the hillside above the house.
(Jarrold Publishing)

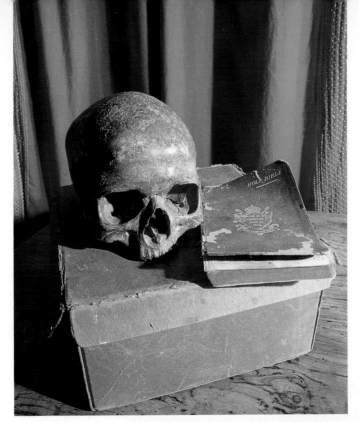

Below Evidence of continuing pagan beliefs and practices can be found in many areas of northern England. Writer Doug Pickford found this sheep's skull decorated with flowers on heathland at Gibb Torr Rocks near Quarnford in western Peakland in August 1992. Two weeks later it was gone.
(Doug Pickford)

Left The Dane valley is one of the most beautiful parts of the western moorlands of the Peak District National Park. This region is redolent with archaic traditions, and provided the scenery for the writer of the fourteenth-century masterpiece *Sir Gawain and the Green Knight*.
(David Clarke)

People have always respected special trees in Celtic Britain. The annual Midsummer custom of Bawming the Thorn Tree at Apperley in Cheshire may be one relic of the ancient veneration of tree spirits. (*Doug Pickford*)

The Strid, West Yorkshire. Near Bolton Abbey, the rushing waters of the River Wharfe are crushed between massive gritstone rocks for nearly 400 metres (440 yards). This is the place where in local tradition the goddess of the Wharfe can appear in the form of a white horse on May Day morning. She often presages imminent death in the river. (*Andy Roberts*)

Should you pass that way, be sure to call at the old drover's inn named in honour of the Maid of the Mere, which stand upon the bleak Morridge Moors. Here you will see an inscribed verse which warns the unwary:

> She calls on you to greet her,
> combing her dripping crown,
> And if you go to greet her,
> she ups and drags you down.'

SECRET SHRINES

During the Bronze Age and the Iron Age almost every stretch of water in Britain was associated with a variety of pagan deities. Lakes and important rivers often received offerings of weapons, valuable metalwork and living sacrifices, and the smaller streams, pools and wells were special too. Water played a significant role in the spiritual world of the Celtic tribes. They saw the springs and wells, particularly at places where water issued to the surface, as a manifestation of the Earth Goddess or divine mother, who usually took a triple form.

Traditions connected with the worship of a goddess of water have very long and deep roots in the Peak District, and the name of one water goddess, Arnemetia, was noted by the Romans and is still remembered by a surviving tradition today. In this region, all the important watercourses have Celtic roots. The Derwent, or Darrent in the vernacular, has already been mentioned. In addition the Dove, Dane, Goyt and Trent all have Celtic roots. The Dane, which waters the enchanted valley below Lud's Church, probably takes its name from Danu/Anu, the Mother Goddess and ancestress of the Irish earth gods, the Tuatha de Danann.

In the Hope valley, a bend in River Noe ('flow') was chosen by the Romans as the site for Navio, their fort at Brough near Castleton, within sight of the Celtic fort on Mam Tor. When the fort was excavated in 1903, inscribed stones were discovered inside an underground strong room. One of these was an altar dedicated 'to the goddess Arnomecta'. Arnomecta was a native Celtic goddess acknowledged by the Romans, for she is the same deity who gave her name to the spa at Buxton, 16 kilometres (ten miles) to the southwest. The Roman *Ravenna Cosmography* identifies Buxton as 'Aquae Arnemetiae', meaning 'the waters of Arnemetia'. The healing springs here were developed into an important religious complex in Romano-British times, for it was one of only two places in the province given the epithet 'Aquae'. The second was Aquae Sulis (Bath), where the famous hot springs of the native Celtic shrine were developed into an elaborate Roman temple and healing complex dedicated to a native sun goddess who was paired with the Roman Minerva.

Arnemetia contains the Celtic word 'nemet', which refers to a sacred grove and appears in place-names widely distributed across Britain and the Continent.

It is found particularly in association with areas where pagan tree worship survived, like the newly discovered prehistoric henge of Nemetstatio at the heart of the oak forests in central Devon.

The Derbyshire name translates as 'she who dwells over/against the sacred grove', the 'she' most probably a reference once more to Anu/Danu. The shrine to this goddess, who was identified with the fertility of the land, originated in the Celtic period and was developed by the Romans when they arrived in the Peak District during the late first century AD. It was centred around two mineral-rich springs, one hot at a constant 82 degrees Fahrenheit and the other cold, both of which emerge from the earth at the bottom of the valley. When the empire was Christianized, Anu became St Anne, but it is likely that pilgrims continued to pay homage to a statue of the pagan goddess in the spa complex. A crude statue depicting 'St Anne', which was in all probability an image of the goddess, was reputedly found in the waters of the spa during one of the medieval restorations. It was destroyed in the sixteenth century during the reign of Henry VIII when the king's agent, Sir William Bassett, sealed the shrine house and took away 'cruthces, shirts and sifts, which was offered'.[70]

When the pool – which is the source of the natural spring water in Buxton – was excavated by Derbyshire County Council in 1975 a collection of 232 Roman coins and two bronze bracelets was pulled out. The coins covered a period of several hundred years of Roman occupation, and are evidence of remarkable continuity of tradition. Even today, in the same area, visitors continue to cast coins into wishing wells 'for luck'.

The spa at Buxton is not the only evidence for the worship of the goddess of water in the Peak District hills. High up on the moors above Buxton is a huge natural limestone cavern named after an outlaw called Poole, who is supposed to have lived in the cave around 1440, during the reign of Henry VI. Long before that time, the cave was frequented by Celts and Roman auxiliary soldiers who visited an underground shrine to make offerings, perhaps for luck and health, to native gods or goddesses of the underworld. Archaeologists believe the cave shrine was in use during the second century AD, at the same time that Roman architects were building the elaborate pagan temple at Bath. Excavations at a spot 20 metres (65 feet) from the cave entrance, in what has become known as the Roman chamber, have uncovered dozens of coins, pottery and jewellery alongside animal and human bones, including skulls. The fine Roman jewellery, manufactured in the mouth of the cave by craftsmen working in a rough workshop, included brooches in the form of dolphins and sea-horses, discs resembling chariot wheels and pins. Most of the bronze objects were found to have been deliberately buckled or bent, ensuring they could not be used again in this world. This ritual dedication of votive offerings is a well-known Celtic practice dating back to the Bronze Age.[71]

Offerings to the spirits of water continue in the Peak District today, both in the well-known custom of well-dressing and in more furtive practices to give thanks to the goddess of springs. Well-dressing – the decoration of springs with flower petals, of seeds and other natural objects pressed on to clay boards to form an eye-catching picture – is a tradition virtually unique to Derbyshire, although a few wells are dressed and decorated in neigbouring counties. The

70 R. C. Hole, *The Legendary Lore of Holy Wells of England* (London, 1893); George Lawrence Gomme, *Popular Superstitions and Traditions* (London, 1887); John Anderson, *Roman Derbyshire* (Derbyshire Heritage Series, 1985); A. W. Dickinson, *Buxton of the Peak* (Gilpin Press, 1991)

71 David Allsop, *A Visitor's Guide to Poole's Cavern* (Buxton Country Park, undated); see also Dickinson, op. cit.

'well-dressing' season opens every year in May, reaches a peak at midsummer and lasts until mid-September, with a Christian blessing of the wells taking place on the feast day of the saint to whom the parish church is dedicated. It is a very long-established tradition which undoubtedly originated in pre-Christian times as a rite to give thanks for the gift of water during the dry summer months.

In practical terms water was an all-important factor for the early farmers and settlers, and as a result of its life-giving properties the tribes would have felt the need to make oblations to the goddess whom they believed provided it. In the limestone hills of the southern Peak, rainfall is easily absorbed through the porous rock and therefore unfailing springs of clear water were vital for the survival of village communities. Although it is unclear how far the tradition dates back in its present form, one theory suggests that it arose after 1348 as a thanksgiving for deliverance from the Black Death and another suggests that it dates back to a drought early in the seventeenth century. Most probably, well-decorating has been revived on a number of occasions during the last 500 years, most importantly during the twentieth century itself. Expert Crichton Porteous notes how in the 1930s only around 14 villages annually dressed wells. In the summer of 1993 the number had risen to more than 48, and every year new villages are creating new dressings for very different reasons – both to revive a community spirit or pride and also to draw in passing tourists.[72]

The instinct to give thanks to the spirit of the water is a very strong one and lies deep within the human psyche. From an early date it seems that the veneration of wells was taken over by the Christian Church, and the custom in Derbyshire today has strong religious links. The church plays a major role in the dressing of five traditional wells on Ascencion Day, 40 days after Easter, at Tissington, which lies at 246 metres (800 feet) on the limestone hills. Here the Christianization of the custom seems to be fully complete, with the church and choir leading a procession to each of the wells, all of which depict biblical scenes, for blessing.

In 1758 Nicholas Hardinge, the Clerk of the House of Commons, saw decorated wells as he travelled through the village of Tissington, where he described 'springs adorned with garlands in honour of these fountains, which are annually commemorated on Holy Thursday'. Forty years later a writer in *Gentleman's Magazine* said it had been the custom in Tissington 'from time immemorial' to decorate the wells 'with boughs of trees, garlands of tulips and other flowers, placed in various fancied devices' on Holy Thursday, 'and after prayers for the day at the church, for the parson and the singers to pray and sing psalms at the wells'.[73]

Another local tradition suggests the custom was actually revived in the nineteenth century when an old woman, Mary Twigg, hung a garland of wild flowers by the Hall Well, along with a verse saying she had been refused garden flowers and had to make do with wild ones, 'and how she had been determined to honour the old custom, which she remembered from childhood'. Perhaps Mary, who was also known as Poll, was one of the guardians of local tradition.[74]

Ever since her time, more than 200 people, many of them living on remote farms and small-holdings, gather together every May in this Peakland village and divide themselves into five teams to create the well-dressings. For

72 Roy Christian, *Well-Dressings in Derbyshire* (Derbyshire Countryside Publications, 1983)

73 Gomme, op. cit., Christian op. cit.

74 Crichton Porteous, *The Beauty and Mystery of Well-Dressing* (Derby, 1949); Peter Naylor, *Celtic Derbyshire* (Derbyshire Heritage Series, 1983)

Heads and skulls are often associated with wells and springs in Celtic mythology. This recently carved stone head acts as a springhead in a farmyard near Bury in Lancashire.

generations farming families like the Shimwells in Youlgreave and Wormhill have participated in the custom, and passed the tradition down to their children and grandchildren. Local people often have to go far afield this early in the summer to find materials to make the beautiful pictures. Following the rule that 'only natural' things can be used, bluebells, wallflowers and wild hyacinths are gathered alongside cultivated flowers like hydrangeas and geraniums. Outlines and detail are provided by the use of alder cones, fluorspar and even coffee beans. Three out of every four pictures used in the Derbyshire dressings have a religious theme, and each village has wells blessed by clergy, who go in procession from well to well.

To many who participate in the twentieth-century form of water worship, the motivation to give thanks to the spirit of the water appears to go back much further into the past. Elsewhere in the small villages and hamlets in western Peakland, veneration of springs and water sources is often done furtively and away from the view of outsiders. In Longdendale, a guardian explained how until recently there was a tradition where 'you might, as we used to do, decorate the springheads where they come out of the hillsides; you put the right wildflowers on them at the right times just to acknowledge the spirit of the waters'.[75]

In Glossop and surrounding villages, wells and springs have been decorated at special times of the year within living memory with flowers, moorland heather and greenery utilized as materials. But an old lady in one village told me very pointedly that there was no Church participation in this custom as in the limestone areas of Peakland; these wells were not dedicated to saints and the ceremonies were completely pagan.

An informant in the same area remembers a spring in fields behind his parents' house which 'had a special reputation'. People would go there in

75 'The Call of the Celts', BBC2, op. cit.

secrecy, he said, to ask the spirit of the well for help, and leave behind offerings, including bent pins just like those left by tribesmen and soldiers in Poole's Cavern nearly 2,000 years ago. On one visit to the area, we were shown a small brass goblet which had been recovered from the spring, now covered by a new housing development, during the 1950s. It may once have been used to dispense spring water, and has since become a family artefact.

The power of holy wells and springs for healing, divination and other practices was particularly strong on the eve of May Day or Beltane, Midsummer Day and on the first Sunday in August (Lammas). Water, trees and stones were a very important part of Beltane rituals, when wells often became the centre of large gatherings of people, each participating in rituals involving divination, the offering of coins or pins to the spirit of the well, and the tying of pieces of clothing to trees overhanging the waters. Individuals who wanted particular favours from the spirit of the water also visited them in secret, telling no one. Until fairly recently it was the custom to decorate trees near springs or wells with coloured rags in Ireland, the Isle of Man and the north of England. One traveller in the Lake District described seeing an oak tree overhanging a spring at Satterthwaite and another at Hawkshead Hill, both decorated with crockery and coloured rags on Maundy Thursday, 1894.[76]

Many of these special places have since disappeared through neglect or direct destruction, but others have survived and become closely guarded secrets for what remains of the living tradition. Some of these decorated shrines, often in isolated natural grottoes, are beautiful places, very evocative of the forest shrines described by the Romans in Celtic Europe. There are a number of famous rag or 'clootie' wells in Scotland which were the centre of rituals on the first Sunday in May for generations. One of them, a Munlochy in the Black Isle, has as many as 50,000 rags hanging from trees around the spring, which is now described by some as an eyesore rather than a beautiful living tradition.

A writer in *The Times* described a visit he made to a similar clootie well on Culloden Moor, near Aberdeen, early in May 1957. The well here, formerly dedicated to the Virgin Mary, lies to the north of the famous battlefield and its crystal-clear water is still a centre of pilgrimage for believers. He wrote:

We came by bus, car, and on foot from all the airts and soon the path leading down hill to the well was covered with a kaleidoscopic mass of humanity. The ritual of those distant days has survived the centuries: first a coin must be thrown into the well, a tribute to the spirit dwelling there; then a sip taken of the water, a charm against evil; and then, after the wish, a 'clootie' or small rag must be tied to the branch of an over-hanging tree. As the path dipped down into a glade of trees with the encircling stone of the well in their midst, we saw clooties all around, far too many for one tree alone, they were tied indiscriminately to the branches of firs, and spruce and beech. Rags there were of all colours, blue and pink and white. Some of the fresh ones were tied in prim little bows, others that had withstood the winds of winter, hung limp and discoloured. So they must hang until another winter has rotted them away; to remove them would bring bad luck, if not a transfer of the very afflictions of which the first owners had been trying to rid themselves![77]

76 Jim Taylor Page, *Cumbrian Holy Wells* (Northwest Catholic History Society, Wigan, 1990)

77 'The Clootie Well: A Highland Tradition from before Culloden' (*The Times*, 25 May 1957)

A similar living tradition surrounding a rag well can be found on the magical West Penwith peninsula in Cornwall. Here stories tell of miracle cures at the waters of the 'Celtic wishing well' at Madron near Penzance. Today this very beautiful and numinous spot continues to possess a feeling of sanctity, and has a special atmosphere. The magical spring itself, said to be beneficial for 'shingles, tetters and wildfires', lies a short distance from a ruined well chapel built by a Celtic monk, St Madron, of whom nothing is known. Trees and branches around the well are still decorated with hundreds of votive objects – coloured rags, clothing, hair and other offerings from modern pilgrims who have come to be rid of their ailments.

It was here in 1640 that a cripple called John Trellile was healed after he 'dreamed that if he bathed in St Madron's well, or in the stream running from, he should recover his former strength and health'. He visited the well on the three Thursdays, washing himself in the waters and sleeping with his back on an artificial hillock known as St Madron's bed. By the third occasion he could reach the well on crutches and soon after was completely healed, so much so he joined the Royalist army as a soldier, and was killed in battle in 1644.[78]

In local tradition pilgrims visited the well on the first three Thursdays in May, when village maidens would drop crossed straws fixed with pins into the waters as a means of foretelling when they would be married. For healing purposes, children were dipped into the water three times as part of an elaborate ritual, and then were made to walk around the well nine times before sleeping on the marshy ground. These rituals were guided in the nineteenth century by a woman guardian, whose function resembled that of a priestess of the spring. Guardians of holy wells and springs are known throughout the Celtic lands, and some of these guardians last relinquished their roles only in relatively recent times.

Anne Ross writes of one such guardian at an isolated township in the wilds of Wester Ross on the far northwest coast of Scotland. This was a man who performed an elaborate ritual to cure epilepsy, using a human skull. The skull, that of male suicide, is associated with a well known as Tobar a'Chinn (the Well of the Head), on a remote hillside. 'The writer was in fact taken to see the well and the head and the ritual was explained in great detail by the guardian himself,' wrote Dr Ross. 'The well lies in a hollow in the hill and it would be virtually impossible to chance upon it.'[79]

Secret shrines like this have survived within living memory in some of the traditions of northern England we have studied. The writers know a number of 'decorated' rag wells in Derbyshire and Yorkshire, and writer Guy Ragland Phillips listed several which retained a living tradition until the middle of this century.[80] The majority of these springs were never Christianized, and often retain names or dedications suggestive of pagan worship, like Thruskell at Burnsall in Yorkshire, which is Thor's Well.

One of the most powerful and evocative of these water shrines is the ancient St Helen's Well at Eshton, hidden beside a peaceful lane in the Dales between Skipton and Bolton Abbey. The sparkling clear water is surrounded by a low stone basin 6 metres (20 feet) in diameter, enclosed within a peaceful grove of trees. The visitor who runs his fingers beneath the masonry beside the

78 M. and L. Quiller-Couch, *Ancient and Holy Wells of Cornwall* (London, 1894)

79 Anne Ross, *The Folklore of the Scottish Highlands* (Batsford, 1976)

80 Phillips, op. cit.

The Rag Well, West Yorkshire. A photo of this secret shrine taken in 1908 before it fell into disuse.

pool will feel the features of three large stone heads all attached to a retaining kerbstone, submerged beneath the waters in true Celtic tradition.

Thomas Whitaker, who visited the well in 1812, said, [The water] 'is very soft and clear and is much esteemed as a remedy for weak eyes and the adjoining bushes are still hung with votive offerings of ribbands . . . by people who either expect, or conceive themselves to have received, a cure through the merits of St Helen.' Today, the visitor can still see ribbons and coloured rags at the well, whose power in local tradition continues. Like Madron Well, there was formerly a chapel here recorded in the fifteenth century which was probably built by the monks of nearby Bolton Abbey. The sanctity of the well – which had its own *genius loci* or spirit – was enhanced by the fact that the spring feeding the pool lay adjacent to two other smaller springs, 'also esteemed sacred', according to Whitaker, and all three of these united at one point and ran eastward into a narrow gill.[81]

81 Thomas Whitaker, *The History and Antiquities of the Deanery of Craven in the County of York* (Leeds, 1807)

The power of St Helen's Well continues, for the writers have been told of 'an extremely strong superstition' by a local resident concerning Midsummer Night, 24 June. 'No local person would pass, or go near on that particular night, and any friend staying in the neighbourhood would be warned that on no account must they pass or go close on this evening,' he said. 'I could never get to the bottom of why, only that if the rule was broken there would be trouble or bad luck. I was camping at a local farm at the time and the farmer told me in no uncertain terms that if I went down there I must get off his land. That was in the 1930s and it was a very strong tradition then.'[82]

The dedication of wells to St Helen was common in northern England, where the Christian saint appears to have taken over the role of a pagan Celtic goddess associated with healing springs. Many wells dedicated to her are associated with ruined chapels, which may have functioned as rustic shrines, each with their own guardian. Edmund Bogg writes of a similar sacred spring and chapel dedicated to St Helen beside the River Wharfe at Thorp Arch. Until recent years this was decorated with votive rags known in Yorkshire tradition as 'memaws', and a photo taken in 1908 shows a little girl tying a strip of clothing on a tree above the spring which stood beside a Roman ford across the river. Here too were the remains of an ancient chapel, probably entirely of pagan dedication, like the others we have mentioned. Writing of the still potent power of the shrine at the turn of the century, Bogg said:

> 'Tis a perfectly natural spot where this well is situated, a paradise of verdure, lovely in all its attributes, a fit habitation of gods, and all but the most indifferent cannot fail to feel the impress of this natural temple. Maidens and others in trouble still make pilgrimages to this holy shrine and so carry onward a custom whose origin goes back to prehistoric times . . .'[83]

THE RAG OAK

The presence of a divine power in the natural world has played an all-embracing role in the beliefs of prehistoric man in northern Europe since the Stone Age. The tree and the spring were enduring symbols of life and the northern peoples had the sacred ash of Yggdrasil, in whose roots the destiny of the world and its people were bound up. The world tree was forever green, and at its foot flowed the sacred spring, whose water gave wisdom and defined the future. The druid priests of the pagan Celts are said to have been given their name from a Greek word meaning 'knowing the oak', and classical authors tell of their secret rituals in sacred groves. Lucan, writing of a druid grove in southern Gaul, tells of 'dark springs running there, and grim-faced figures of gods . . . hewn by axe from untrimmed tree-trunks'.[84]

When Christianity arrived in the dense forests of northern Europe the pagan tree cult was singled out for attack by the early missionaries. St Boniface,

82 Oral tradition, collected 1992

83 Edmund Bogg, *Lower Wharfedale* (Leeds, 1990)

84 Lucan, *Pharsalia* III (quoted in display, Lindow Man exhibition, Manchester University Museum, 1991)

who came himself from an area of southwest England centred upon a sacred oak forest, struck down the sacred oak of the Germans at Geismar. Later, Charlemange presided over the destruction of a giant oak tree, the Irminsul, which formed the central shrine of the pagan Saxons as his Christian empire expanded eastwards. But centuries afterwards, kings were still legislating in vain against pagan practices which continued in the countryside. In England, the Scandinavian king Cnut followed his predecessors by banning 'the worship of idols . . . the sun or the moon, fire or water, springs or stones or any kind of forest trees'. But 1,000 years after these prohibitions, the old ways are still followed, not only in England but in Cnut's own homeland.

In the autumn of 1968 a cold rain was blowing across the roads of south Sjaelland in Denmark. The famous archaeologist Glyn Daniel was visiting a collection of megalithic tombs on the Rosenfeldt estate, along with a group of colleagues who worked for the no-nonsense archaeological journal, *Antiquity*. As the sky darkened, the group's hostess, Hofdam Kontessa Waby Armfelt, pulled the car on to a muddy lane which led into a dark Danish wood.

Eventually the lane came to an end and the group continued on foot into the avenue of trees whose branches slowly joined together overhead, giving them 'a sense of being surrounded and out of this world'. Shortly they turned up an unremarkable side-track, and within moments found themselves led into a clearing in the trees. In the middle of the circle of dripping fir trees was a lone oak which towered above the rest. There was a hole through the middle of it. Surrounding the hole and branches were offerings – coloured rags, torn clothing, bits of handkerchiefs and stockings.

Flabbergasted, Daniel wrote afterwards:

> We were in the presence of a mystery. We were actually in the presence of heathendom, of pre-Christian religion and magic. We realized as one cannot realize when looking at a dolmen or a rune-stone that we were suddenly, only a few miles from a main road, in pagan Scandinavia and, that the present was the past.[85]

In 1966, a Copenhagen newspaper had published an interview with a 90-year-old woman who attributed her recovery from a crippling childhood illness to a visit to this holy rag tree.

> When I was a little girl . . . I could neither walk nor stay upright and I was given up by the doctors. But fortunately my mother, who was a courageous woman, did not give up hope. She went to a wizard, who read an incantation over me, and then advised her to take me to the 'rag oak'. We were living in a poor house not far from the tree. My mother took me to the oak, and drew me through the hole in it, and we left behind some of my clothes on the branches. I remained in bed for some while after our visit to the wood. Then I began to crawl and, in one sudden moment, I found I could walk. I am still a crooked person, but ever since that moment I can jump about like a cat. I have no doubt it was because of my visit to the holy rag oak.[86]

This 'holy rag oak' still exists. It is a living prehistoric shrine, but like others which exist to this day in the British Isles, its exact location is a closely guarded

85 *Antiquity*, December 1968

86 Ibid.

secret. This Danish example can be found only with expert guidance of one of five Danish archaeologists who know where it is. Very few trees alive today are so old that they could have existed in prehistoric times, so clearly there are few if any with an unbroken tradition of healing or worship of more than 1,000 years. But in the case of special healing trees, it appears that particular beliefs or practices handed down from pagan times have become attached to younger trees, especially those which have holes in their trunks through which children or sick limbs could be pushed.

Like other secret shrines in remote country districts, special trees and stones have been resorted to by people in search of cures for a variety of illnesses from time immemorial, and still are. There are a number of magical trees and stones used in this way, not only in Denmark but in Scotland, Ireland and England. In 1994 the authors were taken to see a tree on a leafy lane near the site of Dieulacres Abbey in the western moorlands region of the Peak District which has a reputation of being a 'healing tree'. The tree, an ash, was just one in a line of others on this particular lane, but when we reached it it was obvious that there was something special about it. The trunk of the tree was split naturally into a 'V' and in the notch we found a freshly offered bunch of bluebells. Coins, flints and other small offerings have been left there too in the past and our guide admitted, 'It is very hard to find and I don't know why this particular tree has been singled out, but I know a number of people who have been healed by it, one of whom is a well-known public figure.'[87]

There are dozens of similar trees in the north of England, though their locations are kept secret for obvious reasons. In some cases bark taken from the trunks of the tree was used for healing purposes, mixed into a potion or even hung like an amulet around the neck of the pilgrim. One informant notes how in north Devon, where many archaic and pagan practices continue surreptitiously, there is a tradition surrounding 'toothache trees'. One of these existed until recently at a crossroads near his home, its roots entwined with the base of a medieval cross. Hammered into the trunk, right up to the top, were nails and coins put there by visitors following a tradition that this act would relieve pain from not only toothache, but labour pains too. Recently this particular tree was taken down because it had died, either through old age or the effects of the metal in its bark. But soon afterwards a number of small saplings were planted in the same area, all with coloured rags tied upon them.[88]

A 'wishing tree' was once the centre of pagan practices on the remote island of Eilean Maree in Wester Ross, on the northwest coast of Scotland. The tree was associated with a well used for divination and cures, and its branches were studded with nails, coins and screws and hung with scraps of clothing. One of the pilgrims who hammered a penny into the trunk and made a wish was Queen Victoria, who visited the island during a tour of Wester Ross in 1877, but in the end the veneration it received brought about the end of this tradition, for so many coins and nails were driven into its bark that the tree died.[89]

In Longdendale valley, a guardian of tradition remembers how there were once a number of 'wishing trees' in the area which were considered as being very special. One small and gnarled oak tree once guarded the entrance to an old wood near the river and it was always the custom to greet the tree and say

87 Pickford, *Magic, Myth and Memories* op. cit.

88 Pers. comm., 1993

89 Gertrude Godden, 'The Sanctuary of Mourie' (*Folklore Journal*, 1891)

'hello' to the guardian spirit when one went past. 'All his branches used to have ribbons on them – well, bits of rag really, very often,' she recalled. 'Mostly they were white, but occasionally there might be a red one . . . and later on we realized these weren't just decorations and they weren't some oddity; it was people who had gone to the tree to ask the mother for something – some favour, some help – and had tied a token on to the tree.'[90] She also told how people in her valley were always brought up to respect trees, because there 'might be people or spirits in them or some presence that they were part of'. She said the rowan was regarded as particularly magical, and to this day in one Peak District village sprigs of rowan are placed above the doorways of houses and barns to keep away the evil eye. Also important were the ash, which was said to harbour spirits which could be good or evil, like that of Crooker at the bridge over Darrent; the oak, which was a guardian tree associated with Robin Hood; and the hawthorn.

The sacred hawthorn was also known as whitethorn, the May tree and May bush. It symbolized the change from spring to summer and was an essential part of the May Day celebrations, and was frequently used to make maypoles. The white colour of the hawthorn blossoms was regarded as particularly special, and the tree was seen as powerful against a wide range of evil. In the Scottish Highlands and West County, some people would not have whitethorn blossom in house, as the flowers were seen as 'a symbol of things outside human life . . . an affinity with things beyond the obvious world', but hung outside a cowshed it assured a plentiful milk supply, and when laid in the rafters by someone not in the family it guarded a house against storms, spirits and witches.[91]

Under the Old Calendar, which changed in 1732, the May tree was coming into flower on 1 May, but unfortunately it is rarely seen today, because true May Day now falls on 12 May. Other important plants involved in May Day rites seem to have been the oak, the ivy and buttercup, and all these were involved in keeping evil from animals, and protecting milk and butter. In prehistory, especially sacred trees appear to have been singled out to receive sacrifices. Others were given special names, and to damage one would bring misfortune upon the house and family. This taboo is particularly common today in Ireland, where solitary thorn trees are the homes of the fairy-folk and are *always*, left alone, often to the extent that roads have had to be diverted to avoid interfering with them.

Dermot Mac Manus, in his study of contemporary fairy belief in Ireland,[92] includes a chapter on traditions about fairy trees and gives a number of recent examples of people who have been punished by the fairy-folk for harming sacred thorn trees. As recently as 1968 press reports told of uproar in one small Irish village when roadbuilders were threatening a fairy tree. A number of contractors refused the job of chopping down the tree, and one said, 'I heard of a chap with the electricity board, and he cut down a fairy tree, and the next day he fell off an electricity pole and was killed.'[93] In one case in the Slieve Bloom mountains, a holy thorn dedicated to St Ciaran has been preserved in a small island in the middle of the road, such was the taboo surrounding its power.

Throughout the Peak District too there are numbers of ancient and often long dead trees which have been left to decay in farmers' fields, seemingly

90 *Everyman*, op. cit.

91 MacDonald, op. cit.

92 Dermot MacManus, *The Middle Kingdom: The Faerie World of Ireland* (Colin Smythe, 1959)

93 Quoted in John Keel, *Operation Trojan Horse* (Abacus, 1970)

because of a tradition of fear of what could happen if they were to be cut down. The symbiotic relationship between the tree and mankind, expressed in the form of the prosperity and fecundity of the earth, features in a number of folk-tales. Ruth Tongue, a respected collector of folklore in her native Somerset, has gathered many traditions which suggest individual trees have a personality of their own, and others harbour spirits or fairies. She writes about how as a child she was shown a very old apple tree in an orchard 'and told in a whisper that it was the Apple Tree Man . . . the guardian spirit of the orchard who was said to reside in the oldest apple tree'.[94] In this tradition also the oak was especially esteemed as a guardian tree and there was a strong taboo against cutting them, or planting one kind of tree with certain powers near another.

One important story from this genre comes from the Bakewell area of the Derbyshire Peak District and tells of three tall trees which once stood on top of a fairy hill at the centre of a rich farm. On moonlit nights singing could be heard from the hill and it was said that 'three Green Ladies danced there', but no one dared go near at these times except the old farmer on whose land they danced. He knew the old ways and never neglected to visit the hill once a year on Midsummer Eve, when he would climb up to the summit and lay a posy of late primroses upon the roots of each of the three trees. Because of this respect, the fairy-folk made sure their farmer became rich and prosperous, and he would often say to his three sons, 'My father always said our luck lies up there; when I'm dead and gone, don't forget to do as I did, and my father before me, and all our forebears through the years.'

After the old farmer's death, the land was divided between the three brothers, but the two eldest took no notice of the old ways. They neglected to pay respect to the trees, and eventually the eldest brought men with axes to chop them down for wood for his new barn. But as the axe struck the first tree, it 'screamed like a woman', causing the workmen to flee. Undeterred, the eldest brother continued to strike it and, as it succumbed, a fierce wind blew the tree directly upon him, crushing him to death. His land was taken by the second brother, but the large farm did not prosper and in time he too decided to take an axe to the trees and build a fence around the fairy hill. Taking precautions to avoid the tree dropping his way, he cut down the tree, which lifted a great branch as it fell and struck him a fatal blow to the head.

Thereafter, the youngest brother inherited the farm. He continued the old traditions of his ancestors and took a single posy of late primroses to the lonely Green Lady who remained standing upon the hill, and his land prospered from that day onwards. And even in recent years, there are people who won't climb One Tree Hill, especially on Midsummer Eve, and one or two very old folk remember being told when they were small that the hill must never be fenced because it belonged to a Green Lady.

And the tale as it was told ended, 'The hill and the tree stand there alone – it is a sad and dangerous place to this day.'[95]

94 Tongue, *Somerset Folklore*, op. cit.

95 Adapted from Tongue, *Forgotten Folktales*, op. cit.; oral tradition, collected 1990

3

CELTIC SUPERNATURAL

'When good king Arthur ruled in ancient days
This land was a land brim full of fairy-folk
Or so was the opinion once, I read,
Hundreds of years ago in days of yore.
But no one sees fairies any more . . .'

Chaucer, *The Wife of Bath's Tale*

THE FESTIVALS

There were four main times of the year when we came together to actively celebrate our tradition. These were the eves and dawns of the first days of February, May, August and November. I was told and came to believe that these were the key times of the year for a number of different reasons. They also had significance for those among us who had farms or livestock and the farming year in our area generally revolved round those dates, near enough. February was the beginning of our year and lay in the depths of winter. Those of us who farmed knew this to be the coldest time of the year, the time when most creatures died and the hardest time to do any kind of work with land or animals. But it was also a time of beginning when, even though the weather could be harshest, the days were slowly lengthening, buds were on many trees and the promise of spring and light was upon us. Creation in the heart of destruction was one way we looked at it, part of the regenerative cycle which we tried to experience anew each and every year. As always, these times were marked simply and basically by our families. A gathering at a house, with food, drink and merriment. This would be followed by any people so inclined going to one of the special spots and sitting the night through. At least one small fire would be kindled at dusk and kept burning until dawn, with its ashes scattered to the four compass points. At one time there would have been several such gatherings, but during my youth and early manhood these were down to two or three that we knew about, and by the time I moved away there was just one.

The eve before May Day saw one of the biggest gatherings of the year, and this was mainly centred on springs or water, as I have described elsewhere. However, this was also a time when all those connected in any way to the old ways would somehow mark their houses and farms with a symbol of the season; garlands of flowers and branches were placed on doors and farm buildings, and each family would, if possible, light a May fire in some form. At one time I was told festivities would continue through the night and those who returned from the river or a spring would meet up with others at the fairs or travel to see the maypoles. May Day was also when we would sometimes go up on to the high moors above Ilkley and visit special places. One carved stone, on the edge of our valley, was an ancient meeting place for our people and had special significance for several family traditions. As a child I spent hours there and later as an adult it was one of the places I would go to sit, tracing my fingers around the patterns. On May morning flowers and offerings would be placed in the hollows and water from the river would be cast over it by those of us who lived in the area.

Harvest time was marked at the beginning of August, Lammas as it was known. This was high summer to us, but full with the knowledge of the coming of winter. And we celebrated accordingly with family feasts and also in and around that time with everyone else at the August fairs. I know I've said this before, but you have to realize that while all this was special to us, it was all part of daily life – we didn't see ourselves as in any way different from anyone else in the dale. But these times had to be marked in some way. To have neglected them would have broken the cycle. It was a time of full strength for everyone. The weather was good, food plentiful and it was a time for satisfaction and reflection. All the August fairs in this area celebrated the harvests of the earth and the strength we humans gained from it, and some took this a bit further with feats of strength and endurance, with villages like Burnsall having foot races to the summits of the fells, a very old tradition indeed. One of my favourite writers on the Dales summed this expression of virility and energy when she wrote: 'As the fell runners climbed, the old seemed to rise and swamp the modern element, and the onlookers were no longer of any time, but part of a long line who had watched just such a procession here.' That sentence exactly summed up the feeling I had at all the special points of the year.[1]

BOUNDARIES IN TIME AND MIND

'Boundaries between territories, like boundaries between years and between seasons, are lines along which the supernatural intrudes through the surface of existence . . . And territories, like seasons, must have their boundaries ritually redefined every year.'

Alwyn and Brinsley Rees, *Celtic Heritage*

In regions where Celtic traditions have survived, some of the most archaic features are found in the customs that evolved around the important times of the year, marking the change from winter to summer, from summer to winter and the harvest. Across the world, all religious traditions have had seasonal festivals which marked boundaries in the agricultural calendar, rituals which gave a sense of time and place to the human community. In the areas of Britain we have studied, it seems that the old 'quarter days' were the important times, and they were marked with ceremonies.

Broadly speaking, the Celtic year was split into a warm and a cold period, and the festivals on 1 November and 1 May marked the beginning and end of the farming cycles for communities in the uplands, where livestock were central to the economy. Beltane marked the date when the animals were driven on to the lush upland pastures, and Samhain marked their return to the valleys and the slaughter of the surplus for the coming winter. Both dates were of supreme importance to the British tribes, and were therefore marked with many rituals and ceremonies, as we saw most markedly at Glen Lyon in the Scottish Highlands.

It appears that the Celtic tribes reckoned by nights rather than by days, and attached special importance to the eve of the festivals. In the Irish tradition the year was originally divided into four 'quarter days', the most important of which was Samhain, which marked the end of the year and the onset of winter. This was followed by Imbolc on 1 February, which marked the lactation of ewes; Beltane, which brought the beginning of summer on 1 May; and Lughnasa on 1 August, marking the beginning of the harvest. It does seem, though, that the names of the festivals varied between localities, just as the deities did. These dates were later incorporated into the Christian calendar, with the Church often giving the rituals renewed life within a new framework – a policy laid down by Pope Gregory and St Augustine before him.

1 Pers. comm., 1994

In the archaic tradition of the high Derbyshire valleys, Beltane and Hallowe'en were always important festival dates, marked at one time with family celebrations and great bonfires, but in the words of one informant, 'festivals perhaps isn't the right word nowadays . . . We acknowledge things but we don't necessarily do anything about them.' In Longdendale the fire festival of Imbolc in February marked the beginning of lambing and was sacred to the goddess Bride; in the Christian tradition of the valley it was Candlemas, a feast of purification marked by the lighting of candles.

The harvest festival of Lammas in August was also once marked with great celebrations, as was Michaelmas in September, which marked the end of the harvest, when rents were collected. In addition there was also one 'old and important day' towards the end of December or beginning of January which was known as 'the Lord of Light' and 7 January, which coincided with Twelfth Night or Old Christmas Day. This was known as 'the Lord of the Year' or 'the Lord of the Green Leaves', and marked the heart of midwinter. As one informant put it, 'January was when the god, the old one, Woden or whatever name you want to call him, took his hounds and rode through the sky. It was

The white stone, Luddenden Dean, West Yorkshire. Freshly painted by persons unknown every May Day morning as part of a continuing – and secret – Celtic tradition.

the hardest time of year, when most of the old and weak died, and it was believed the god was active and about chasing his human flock.'[2]

In England and Wales Beltane was undoubtedly the first most important festival following the beginning of the new year. The spelling of Beltane varies, but 'Bel' means a brilliant light, and some authorities believe it refers directly to a Celtic god of light, Belenos. In fact a god known as Belatucadros is named on 40-odd altars in the region of Hadrian's Wall, and carvings depicting a radiant sun deity have been found there. In the pagan past, 1 May was associated with the start of open pasturing, the beginning of summer and the welcoming of the sun's heat to promote the growth of crops. At one time on May Eve great bonfires were kindled as sympathetic magic to welcome back the sun, and carols and songs were sung on high places; even more ancient was the 'Bringing in of the Summer', when the young people of the village would spend the night in woods and then bring back green branches in the morning to celebrate the return of vegetation.

The festival we all know as May Day has very deep roots in the prehistoric past and the words bring to mind deep-seated images of traditions and ceremonies which celebrate the return of the long, warm days of summer, flowers, garlands, the maypole, trees and fertility. In the Christian tradition 1 May became the feast of St Philip and St James, but these saints have no connection with the old ceremonies. As folklorist Christina Hole writes, 'May Day is a festival of purely pagan origin, a simple and spontaneous expression of joy at the beginning of true summer.'[3] In the early seventh century AD in a letter to missionaries in England, Pope Gregory referred to *existing* pagan temples in England and described how they were 'decked with garlands and flowers', which seems to point to continuity in the later decoration of churches with greenery so evident in medieval and early modern churchwarden's accounts of May Day rites.

In all regions of the British Isles there is evidence that pagan springtime ceremonies continued throughout the medieval period, often under the very nose and sometimes with the connivance of the Church authorities. At Cawthorne in South Yorkshire, the inhabitants were censured by the church authorities in 1596 for taking 'towers and garlands and other formes of thinges covered with flowers' into the parish church on 1 May. At Hunsingore near York, in the following year, two men were paraded and whipped through the streets after they were found guilty of 'in a most contemptuous manner bring into the church a Toie, called the flower of the well, in the time of the divine service, whereby the vicar was disturbed'.[4]

It was precisely these primitive origins of the May Day rites that led the Puritans, during the seventeenth century, to recognize many of them as pagan fertility rites. This caused much social hatred and bitterness, when churchmen tried every way they could to denounce maypoles and other spring rites in sermons, and attempted to suppress them by act of Parliament. In one instance, hundreds of people were killed in riots in central London when the authorities tried to remove an offending maypole.

May Day is the favourite festival in the work of medieval Welsh poets, and what may be the first literary reference to a maypole in Britain is found in a

2 *Chronicle*, op. cit.; oral traditions, collected 1994–5

3 Christina Hole, *English Custom and Usage* (Batsford, 1943)

4 Guy Ragland Phillips, *The Unpolluted God* (Northern Lights, 1987)

fourteenth-century poem from Dyfed. Maypoles remain central to most village celebrations in England, and the tall posts with their flowers and ribbons, are unambiguous symbols of the living tree and fertility rites. The earliest maypoles were not permanent, like the well-known ones at Wellow, Nottinghamshire, and Barwick-in-Elmet in West Yorkshire, but young trees brought from the greenwoods. In Cornwall, a tall elm was fetched home on 30 April, painted and decorated, then set up in the middle of the village, and in some parts of Wales a birch tree was similarly used. In Herefordshire maypoles were birch trees decorated with red and white streamers and set up outside the stable on May Day as a sure protection against witches for the rest of the coming year.

BELTANE RITES

May Eve and May Day bonfire ceremonies are rare or non-existent today but were at one time central to the celebration of the festival. In Scotland, the Clan McGregor Society still holds a celebration Beltane bonfire at Kingshouse at Balquidder, weather permitting. Authentic fires were still kindled on farms in one corner of the Peak District in recent years and a visitor in 1977 described them as 'a splendid sight'. Cormac, an eighth-century Irish writer who drew upon earlier material said that in every district at Beltane the fires were extinguished and druids lit two bonfires in honour of the god Bel. They chanted 'numerous spells' over them and then cattle were driven between them, being thereafter divinely protected from disease.

The driving of cattle between two large bonfires was a strong tradition not just in Ireland but also on mainland Britain. The 'new fire' or 'need fire' was still kindled in Highland Scotland and northern England on 1 May, as recently as the turn of this century. Great care had to be taken with every detail of the procedure associated with the making of the need fire, and during the process branches of rowan were carried as magical protection from witchcraft and other evils. All households in the village had to extinguish their fires before the fire could be kindled. It was lighted by friction in the open, with two pieces of wood, often oak, being rubbed together until heat and sparks generated flame.

Usually the fire was made on a high place, and cattle from neighbouring pastures were driven round it or through it. Sometimes oatcakes (bannocks) and a sort of custard was eaten, and everyone would leap and dance around the flames. Blazing logs and red-hot embers would be carried to other farms in the area for new fires to be started as required. In some areas it was customary to burn a live calf in the fire to ensure fertility or in times of scarcity when cattle disease threatened the herds. William Pearson of Crosthwaite near Kendal, a man of standing in the community and a friend of the Wordsworths, recorded a conversation with a farmer who had been present when a living calf was sacrificed in a Beltane fire.[5]

5 R. Clough, 'The Fires of Beltane' (*Cumbria Magazine*, vol. 27, October 1977)

A hybrid carving depicting a fertility god or goddess, carved upon the capital at Melbourne parish church in southern Derbyshire. A vine issues from the mouth of the figure, which appears to be a cross between a Green Man and a Sheela-na-gig.

In many regions of Ireland, northern England and Scotland there are memories of other very ancient ceremonies which involved a Beltane bannock, specially prepared in the traditional way, then broken up and distributed among those taking part in the rites. One of the pieces of the cake would always be blackened, and the person who chose that would become the devoted one, a symbolic 'sacrifice' to the powers. He or she would then have to jump three times through the flames of the bonfire, lit in a specially prepared ritual enclosure, before they were allowed to re-enter the community. It has been suggested that a similar ritual may have taken place somewhere in what is now Cheshire shortly before Lindow Man went to his death in the black pool at Lindow 2,000 years ago, for, as we have seen, experts have been able to discover exactly what it was this sacrificial victim ate before death: namely, a portion of coarsely ground barley bread or bannock, baked on an open fire.

Certainly, in the valleys of the High Peak and central Perthshire a tradition incorporating some features of this ritual existed within living memory. A century ago, a writer in *Notes and Queries* described how every year on 1 May local people used to assemble at a stone circle near Crieff, in Perthshire. There they would light a fire in the centre and each person would place a piece of oakcake in a shepherd's bonnet. After sitting down blindfold, each drew a piece from the bonnet, and whoever chose the piece which had been blackened was referred to be 'devoted' and had to jump through the fire or pay a forfeit. The ceremony also involved a procession around a holy well near the stones, and so deep-rooted was this 'heathenish superstition' that one outraged visitor wrote, 'Many who reckon themselves good Protestants will not neglect these rites even when Beltane falls on Sabbath.'[6]

Human sacrifice was stamped out by the Romans, but pagan practices using symbolic offerings at special festivals survived in the more remote areas of Britain until very recently. In the 1950s an old woman in her seventies took Anne Ross to see a square of deturfed land in the same isolated glen where she said until the First World War people continued to make the ritual square and bake the traditional Beltane bannock. Always at some stage, a black mark like

6 Vaux, op. cit.

a thumbmark appeared on one part of the bannock, which was then broken up and put in a bag. Referring to the person who chose the blackened portion, she said, 'Although we don't talk about it, originally of course that person was sacrificed.'[7]

The act of making the sacred bannock was in itself part of the ritual, with seeds from all the crops grown by the community during the year used in the mixture. The sign of the cross was made over the bannock at all the stages of preparation – when it was cooked, turned or cut. In many areas, bannocks and oakcakes were used for divination, being rolled from tops of hills on May Day morning. If one was broken, those to whom it belonged would come to some disaster or death before the next Beltane; others were carried home and placed under the pillow, to find out if dreams would reveal a future marriage. Parts of the bannock were also symbolically offered by herdsmen to the animals of the district in the hope that their calves or young goats would be safe in the year ahead. In 1770 the traveller Thomas Pennant, writing of the Perthshire Beltane square at Callander, said:

> everyone takes a cake of oatmeal upon which are raised nine square knobs, each dedicated to some particular being, the supposed preserver of their flocks and herds, or some particular animal . . . Each person turns his face to the fire, breaks off a knob and flings it over his shoulder, saying: This I give to thee, preserve thou my sheep and so on. After that they use the same ceremony to anxious animals: This I give to thee, O Fox, spare thou my lambs, this to thee, O Hooded Crow, this to thee, O Eagle!'[8]

THE RUSH CART

August in the Peak District was the focus of the farming year, marking the start of the harvest, and was a time of celebration and thanksgiving for the good things provided by the fruitful earth. Fairs and livestock markets brought the farmers into town and all those who had left the Dales came home to see their families. This was also the time of the village wakes, of which William Wood wrote, 'In the Peak there is no festivity equal to the Wakes or Feast. Every village on this occasion assumes a different aspect; the inhabitants put on their best attire; all employment ceases; the cottages are adorned in rural splendour.'[9]

The wakes coincided with the annual changing of the rushes which then provided the only source of comfort for those who gathered on the cold stone flags of the parish church, where there were no pews for commoners in those days. The sledges used to pull the rushes through the parish to the church were over the centuries developed into elaborate carts, topped with a phallic-shaped pile of specially cut rushes. The appearance of the rush cart – an overtly pagan and rustic object – coincided with a time of merriment, heavy drinking and barbaric sports, which often included bear-baiting and cock-fighting.

7 Anne Ross, 'Lindow Man and the Celtic Tradition' in Stead et al., op. cit.

8 Ibid.; Walter Gregor, 'Notes on Beltane Cakes' (*Folklore Journal*, 1895)

9 William Wood, *Tales and Traditions of the High Peak* (Bakewell, 1903)

In Glossop, the rush cart made its last journey to the parish church shortly before the outbreak of the First World War, an event which marked the end of many previously strong community customs. One hundred years before, local writer Ebenezer Rhodes visited the church and described the annual ritual, which centred on a wagon 'decorated with a pyramid of rushes, ornamented with wreaths of flowers, and surmounted with a garland, bestrewed with the choicest flowers that the meadows of Glossop Dale can produce'.[10]

When prepared, the rust cart was paraded through the village by a team of decorated horses. Men and whips cleared a path through the crowds, and the cart was preceded by groups of Morris dancers and a brass band which stopped only at the gates of the parish church – 'Then the rushes and flowers are taken into the church, and strewed amongst the pews and along the floors, and the garlands are hung up near the entrance into the chancel in remembrance of the day.'

There was often fierce competition between rival villages as to who could produce the best carts, and an early painting shows three separate rush carts arriving at the gates of Saddleworth parish church at Uppermill, a valley further north in the Pennine hills. At Mottram-in-Longdendale an account of 1865 describes how the vicar of the parish headed the subscription for the rush cart with a guinea (£1.05 in today's money). The wagon was surmounted by 'a huge mass of oval-framed rushes' and its front was decorated with a piece of 'furniture print of gay pattern' which displayed silver goblets, watches and spoons, lent by the local gentry. Hundreds of people gathered to see the rush carts pass towards the hilltop church, while high above sat a local character, Joshua Turner, with a tin can on the end of a long piece of string which he used to pull up his share of the beer dispensed at the inns *en route*. Eventually, the cart stopped at an old stone cross at the church gates and the garlands were suspended from the church roof.[11]

Less than 20 years after this account was written a new vicar moved to take up the living at Mottram. He was an Oxford-educated outsider and soon became one of the most unpopular vicars in the history of the parish, his chief claim to fame being his unbending stand against the local tradition and his decision to ban the rush cart from the church, because, he said, it was 'a heathen object'. One hundred years later, this event is still remembered in the area by the great-grandchildren of those who took part in the ceremony, and one of them described how the people could still have the rushes but couldn't take the rush cart into the grounds of the church. 'It didn't stop people decorating it up, putting a white cloth over it so it looked like the mother, and putting all their silver on the front of the cart as a sort of offering to her, to say thank you, for everything,' she said.[12]

To those who followed the Old Ways, the arrival of the teachings of Christianity provided just another addition to an ancient religion which was tied to the earth, the crops and the changing seasons. There was in general no animosity between the two systems, which coexisted happily alongside one another, and as traditions passed from generation to generation over hundreds of years, some elements were dropped and other attractive features from newer religions were added.

10 Clarence Daniel, *Derbyshire Customs* (Dalesman, 1976); Paul Bush, *Neath Ancient Moss: A Short History of Glossop Parish Church* (1987); for rushcarts, see Peter Brears, *North Country Folk Art* (Edinburgh, 1989)

11 Mottram Parish Map, 1994; R. B. Robinson, *Longdendale: Historical and Descriptive Sketches of Mottram and Glossop* (Manchester, 1863)

12 *Chronicle* op. cit.; oral tradition, collected 1993

SERMON FOR THE DEAD

Fifty years ago the giant Ladybower Reservoir swallowed up two villages and 13 farms beneath 504 acres of water in a beautiful, remote valley in the Derbyshire High Peak. Today, travellers heading for Manchester on the scenic A57 Snake Pass road across the Pennines see the awesome man-made dam but rarely catch a glimpse of the tiny Derwent and its church, which disappeared for ever beneath its waters.

The church began life as a chapel founded by monks in the vast Derwent Woodlands, once part of the Royal Forest of the Peak. It was an area largely cut off from outside influence until the Duke of Devonshire built the first packhorse route linking Sheffield with Glossop early in the nineteenth century. And around this time another stranger arrived in the small parish of Derwent Woodlands. He was a curate from the Trent valley of southern Derbyshire, and looked forward to taking over as parson of the parish high up in the beautiful moorlands of the Peak.

An oral tradition in this valley tells how this new parson hoped the clean air of north Derbyshire would help clear his weak chest of a chronic cough, and on arrival he was welcomed by the down-to-earth residents of farms and hamlets across the scattered parish. But although the farmers and shepherds approved of their new parson's energy and enthusiasm, their relationship with him soon began to turn sour. For although his congregation was outwardly Christian, so the story goes, the new parson soon began to learn of what he called their 'superstition and strange practices', which were alien to anything he had ever come across in the south of the county. He was worried by what he heard, and the quarrels came to a head when, shortly before the end of the villagers' year, two churchwardens approached him with a peculiar request.

Hesitantly shuffling their boots on the stone floor inside the small church, they said they had come to see him on behalf of the whole parish. As he was new, they said, they needed to aquaint him with an ancient tradition which had been observed by every vicar of the parish within the memory of man in this part of the Peak. They wanted him to deliver the Sermon for the Dead, which must be given in the empty church at midnight on the last Sunday of the dying year. It was then, they said, that the spirits of those who are due to pass away during the coming year leave their bodies and slip quietly towards the churchyard to hear the special sermon. But the parson was having none of it; such a request was asking him to take part in a pagan rite which had no part in the Christian tradition. 'This is witchcraft and I'll have none of it while I am the vicar here,' he is said to have told them.

The newcomer's refusal to perform the sermon and his general unbending attitude towards the Old Ways resulted in the development of a strained atmosphere in the village during the days which led up to the new year. But when the night came, something drew the parson to the empty church at midnight; perhaps it was his faith that told him he should go there, prove there was nothing in the old superstition and restore the villagers' faith in the true God once and for all.

But when he stood in the pulpit and gazed up into the darkness, he was struck dumb in horror when he saw staring back at him from the wooden gallery, spirits of parishioners he knew and, there among the crowd, his own wraith-like reflection. Stumbling to open the heavy Bible in front of him, he stammered a few words of blessing as his earlier beliefs and certainties melted away into the cold night air. Meanwhile, the spirits gathered around to listen, then slunk away into the shadows of the old building. It is said that after this experience, the parson's contempt for the traditions of his parish melted away like the spirits he saw that night. Alongside that acceptance, he knew that that year would be the last he spent in this world, for he had seen his own fate at the Sermon for the Dead.[13]

THE NEW YEAR

In pagan Britain, 1 November was a Celtic festival of the dead. It was a time of year associated with death and decay of vegetation, hence its old Irish name of Samhain ('summer's end'). The association between Samhain and death was reflected in the natural world: the earth died, the trees were bare and livestock was brought down from the hills, with the surplus slaughtered for the long winter ahead. The eve of Samhain was the end of the year in the Celtic calendar and the surviving folk-tales and mythology tell us it was a special and dangerous time, when the veil between this world and the Otherworld was temporarily drawn away.

In Irish literature it is Samhain which begins the year and was the most important 'feast', when tribal assemblies like the Feast of Tara were held and laws were made. In Wales, Hallowe'en was one of the three 'spirit nights', when the witches, fairies and other supernatural creatures were abroad, and dead ancestors were able to return to the hearthside. Considerable evidence from folk tradition and legend suggests that these beliefs are of great antiquity, for they were held widely not just in Britain but in most of Continental Europe. The sacred nature of the festival continued into Christian times, when missionaries found the beliefs surrounding Samhain too strong to suppress.

The Christian Church may have been so worried about the Hallowe'en rites that in 835 AD they transferred the Feast of All Saints from 13 May to 1 November. A century later 2 November was designated as All Souls' Day, extending the festival further as part of the same process. Samhain was particularly important to rural communities in Ireland, Scotland and northern England, and in some places within living memory it remained the custom to extinguish domestic fires on Hallowe'en and kindle them again the following morning.[14]

Across the north of England, villagers danced around communal bonfires, with young men leaping through flames and carrying burning brands from the

13 Oral tradition, collected 1995; versions published in Richard Litchfield, *Strange Tales of the Peak* (Derbyshire Heritage Series, 1992); David Bell, *Derbyshire Ghosts and Legends* (Countryside Books, 1993); newspaper cuttings in Derbyshire County Council library files, Matlock, Derbyshire

14 Christina Hole, 'Winter Bonfires' (*Folklore*, vol. 71, December 1960)

This medieval church finial from Buxton, Derbyshire, is decorated with four grim Celtic-style faces, illustrating the continuing tradition of head-carving in north Britain.

blaze through the fields. This continued in parts of Derbyshire, Lancashire and Cumbria until the end of the last century, where it was known as Tindles or Tandles Day. In Derbyshire, a farmer would light a small fire in one of his fields and carry a bunch of burning straw on a pitchfork to the highest part of his land, a boundary between this world and the next. Then he would toss it over the surrounding fields. As he did so, the entire household would kneel on the grass round the bonfire and remember all those who had passed over, their ancestors. When the new teaching of Christianity was adapted into their belief system, the family continued to worship in the old way, but prayed for the souls of the dead.

As today, there was a perception long ago at this time of the year that the souls of your ancestors or the Old Ones, as they were known in Derbyshire, were about and could return to the fireside, where the family was gathered. This respect for the dead was continued in the custom of leaving food offerings for the family spirits. In some areas, special cakes were baked and offered to the departed, a tradition which led to the custom of Soul-caking in areas of the Peak District, as at Stannington near Sheffield and Antrobus in Cheshire. This was continued by old people in Matlock and other parts of the Derbyshire Dales until recently, with Thor or Thar cakes baked from a mixture of oatmeal, flour salt and treacle. In some isolated hamlets, these cakes were taken to the churchyard and left as offerings.[15]

Hallowe'en and all Souls' was an in-between time – neither summer nor winter, light nor dark – when the border with the Otherworld was open, and the supernatural had the greatest power to influence the lives of men. At this time of the year spirits could walk around in disguise, and this was the origin behind the tradition of wearing masks or disguises ('guizing') at Hallowe'en parties.

15 Crichton Porteous, *The Ancient Customs of Derbyshire* (Derbyshire Countryside Publications, 1976)

Guizing, playing mischievous games and divination were all part of the elaborate Hallowe'en rites in Scotland, which continue today. In Scotland and elsewhere, rituals involving apples and nuts – both magical seasonal foods – were important parts of the tradition. They all feature in the famous poem by Robert Burns which captures the essence of Hallowe'en:

> The auld guidwife's weel-hoordet nits
> Are round and round divided,
> And mony lads' and lasses' fates
> Are there that night decided.[16]

HALLOWE'EN FIRES

'Some years before the Great War on a crisp autumn night in a far-away part of the Highlands, an old domine revealed to me that Scotland's history was older than the date columns in our schoolbooks. Sitting outside the schoolhouse door, we were looking over the valley to where the dark mountains were silhouetted against the rising moon. For miles and miles the landscape was dotted at wide intervals with bonfires that blazed against the dark hillside. The date was 31 October, and these bonfires were the direct descendants of the fires lit by the ancient druids . . .'

Glasgow Daily Herald, 1920s

In twentieth-century Britain, thousands of people continue to build huge bonfires every year in the days which lead up to the evening of 5 November, following a tradition established nearly four centuries before. The failure of the Roman Catholic conspirators to light the fuse and blow up the Houses of Parliament in 1605 may not evoke the same religious hatred today as it did in the past, but the holiday established by a grateful government continues in popularity.

Bonfires have a deep affinity with people of all ages, and thousands are lit every year on hilltops across the British Isles. A 1981 survey in Sheffield, South Yorkshire, found that more than 60,000 people attended one of the six organized bonfires which were then lit in municipal parks.[17] This meant one in eight of the population took part in the tradition, a figure which does not include those who attended smaller family celebrations. Despite their continuing popularity, today Bonfire Night celebrations are losing some of their former magic, with the move towards large organized events where much of their original meaning for the family and community is missing.

Many centuries before Guy Fawkes and his fellow conspirators were caught and executed for treason, bonfires blazed across the length and breadth

16 From Robert Burn's poem 'Hallowe'en', quoted in McNeil, op. cit.

17 Quoted in Janet and Colin Bord, *Ancient Mysteries of Britain* (Grafton, 1986)

of the British Isles to celebrate an older and more mysterious festival. Bonfires in the traditional sense continued on the eve of 1 November on hilltops in remote areas within living memory, before they were transferred to the familiar date five days later. In the middle of the nineteenth century, Sheriff Barclay, who was travelling between Dunkeld and Aberfeldy in the Scottish Highlands on this date, counted 30 bonfires blazing on hilltops, 'each having a ring of people dancing around it'. In Buchan, some 60 to 80 used to be visible from one vantage point in the mountains.

Writer James Napier told how in 1860 he watched boys and children lighting similar bonfires on either side of Loch Tay in central Perthshire, a region where we know ancient beliefs have survived to the present day. Old people in the area told him how 50 or 60 years before, the fires were made by menfolk who 'all joined hands and danced round the fire and made a great noise'.[18] The tradition had declined when drunkenness and rough horseplay led local churchmen to discourage the rites. In Wales and Ireland similar fires were lit, with villagers dancing round blowing horns, often in disguise.

In all regions, effigies were burnt on fires and the figure or bogeyman of Guy Fawkes was just one in a long series of scapegoats: in the past, there have been witches or hags, the Pope and, more recently, the Kaiser and Hitler. In fact, an old Samhain tradition called 'Burning the Witch' was practised in the grounds of Balmoral Castle as recently as the reign of Queen Victoria. One account of the tradition, says, 'All the while the residents at the castle stand enjoying this curious rite, and no one there entered more heartily into it than the head of the Empire herself.' A large bonfire was lit in front of the castle and a procession of men in Highland garb appeared in the grounds, pushing a trolley containing the effigy of a hideous old woman or witch, whom they called Shandy Dann. As the fire was neared, the group broke into a run, coming to rest only yards from the flames, where with great solemnity the hideous figure was cast in, while the Highlanders cheered and laughed.[19]

This old Scottish custom brings to mind the archaic Burning of Bartle ceremony, which takes place in a tiny North Yorkshire village on the parish feast of St Bartholemew's day, at the end of August. Here a strange Hallowe'en-type effigy called Owd Bartle is made in secret and then paraded through the streets as a special chant is repeated by the villagers. The whole event is completed in under one hour, when Owd Bartle is doused in paraffin and burnt to a great cheer, giving visitors the impression they are witnessing some kind of sacrificial rite. In local tradition Bartle was a sheep thief chased and executed in the distant past, but there are many indications that the ceremony originated in the destruction of a pagan effigy at the end of the pastoral year in these mountains, from when the rite may originally bave been moved at some point in the past.

The supernatural, bonfires, effigies and echoes of ancient sacrifice are all found in one of the strangest and most archaic descriptions of a Hallowe'en tradition we have collected from the High Peak tradition of Derbyshire. Here, as elsewhere, the tradition of lighting family bonfires in the first week of November was a long-established custom until recently. In 1935 a Derbyshire county councillor is recorded as saying, 'I do not know of any place where there has been a Guy Fawkes bonfire longer than in Chapel-en-le-Frith

18 McNeil, op. cit.

19 Ibid.

market-place.' Every October in the small market town all men from 18 to 70 set about the task of collecting ever larger quantities of wood for the huge bonfire, which was built around the ancient cross. One year the heat from the fire became so intense that the cross was seriously damaged and plate-glass windows in nearby shops were split, 'but no one interfered, and the bonfire continued to be lit in the market-place'.[20]

Further north, around the town of Glossop, similar family-bonfire traditions continued until very recent years. As late as the 1950s a visitor to the region could have taken up a vantage point on the moors immediately south of the town and seen dozens of fires burning right across the dales and hills.

A former resident of the valley clearly remembers the bonfires of his childhood. He writes, 'The date for family bonfires in this region was always the traditional one of 1 November or the first few nights of the month, although public fires were also lighted on Guy Fawkes night. We would always watch out for the fires of individual farms and localities around the valley on the nights leading up to 5 November – and know where they were – and comment on whether they were early or late.'

The effigy burnt on the fires was known as Guy Fawkes, Owd Guy of T'Lad. He was made several days beforehand by children and then trundled around town in a special trolley or bogie. 'He was always kept off the fire and in the background until the fire had first flared up and then died down a bit,' he said. 'Then he was carried to and around the fire, clockwise, with a lot of shouting and cheering – either carried shoulder-height or even trundled on the bogie on which he had been wheeled about the streets. On one occasion, at least, I remember him being garlanded in greenery.'

In much the same fashion as the Balmoral effigy, the guy was paraded around the fire and a song was sung:

> Guy Fawkes guy!
> Poke him in the eye!
> Hang him from the lamppost,
> Never let him die!

'The song was usually accompanied by stabbing gestures, or even poking the figure with sticks, and by strangling gestures, as appropriate. Again, I certainly recall, at least on one occasion, Guy having a bit of rope around his neck. I always thought it odd, in as much as I thought about it at all, that we should sing 'Never let him die', when we were doing all that to him and burning him to boot; but there was no sense of Guy being a baddy, and there was certainly no Pope-burning here! Guy was OK, a good lad, a honoured guest at the feast, so to speak.'

The manner in which the guy was treated before his dispatch into the flames has echoes of the Celtic 'triple death' through hanging, stabbing and burning, similar to that suffered by Lindow Man, who was drowned rather than burnt. On this subject, our informant writes, 'It's interesting for us now to reflect on Guy's triple death, but it's possible that the apparent "Celticness" of that practice is coincidence, not survival, because I really don't know how old or traditional all this was. It may well be that practices varied very much from

20 Porteous, *The Ancient Customs*, op. cit.

one little locality or community within the valley to another, and so on throughout the Peak.'

After the burning of the guy, and when the fire had died down, the adults would gather round while the old folk broke up a large piece of oakcake or parkin, a sticky delicacy made from oatmeal and treacle, which were all placed in a tin box. Then there was lot-drawing – one piece would always be blackened, or burnt, and the person who chose this piece would have to leap over the embers, followed by the rest of the young people, 'with a lot of goading, taunting of the hang-backs and bravado'.

Concluding his account, our writers reaches the core of this archaic Hallowe'en tradition: 'I have no idea how widespread our practices were, though they seemed normal and regular enough to me at the time – everyone knew them and joined in. I don't recall any official civic organized bonfires at that time, that came later in the 1960s and it was then that the individuality and, to a large extent, the practice of very local bonfires seemed to die out.

'All those nights, but especially the night on which you had your fire, were nights when the Other, the Supernatural, was felt to come very close. This was really quite palpable – not just among us gullible kids, but even among adults – especially the older ones. There were places you weren't supposed to walk or pass near, just and only then. There was a sense of relief when Guy went on the fire – somehow it was felt that would appease what was out there. It felt a chancy, eerie time – fireworks, the noise and cheeriness, the Guy-burning and fire-jumping were all keeping that Other out in the dark, at arm's length. I don't think that any of that is present in the modern civic bonfire. This bit is the least tangible, least satisfactory thing, but to me it's the most powerful abiding memory. I can remember shivering when Guy went on the fire – there was this feeling, even in a small child, that something important was happening that had *nothing* to do with Parliament and 1605 and *everything* to do with the fields, woods and moors that encompassed us.'[21]

PLACE GUARDIANS

There were many, many local practices which made up the body of our tradition. We would also make offerings at various places in the dale which were special to us either individually, as families or as a whole. These spots could be entrances to valleys, springs and wells, stones or trees. Anywhere really that we felt was 'right' or anywhere where we thought our people had lived and made the same offerings long ago. None of this to the best of my knowledge has ever been written down – it was just passed on from one person to another as the need arose. Some farms and houses held special stones, bones or piece of wood which were house guardians if you like; carved faces were the main ones, and these were treated as having the spirit of the land within them and were acknowledged in some way regularly. This might take the form of just a simple nod or

21 Pers. comm., 1995; oral traditions, collected 1993–4

word on passing, or more elaborate gestures such as offerings of food or drink. Some were painted at certain times.

I was always taught there was a correct way to do things in every aspect of living. Doing things 'right' put us in tune with the powers of creation; it gave us purpose and a sense of belonging. As a part of this, where we lived was very important to us. The land we worked and the buildings we lived in had to be . . . protected, I suppose, or maybe it was just that we had to assert ourselves for being there. Anyway, where we lived had to be protected in some way. Why, I'm not sure now, but we had a few ways of doing this with plants and what might be called small binding spells, although none was as effective or as permanent as the carvings we did. By carvings I mean those of th'owd man. Many of the farms and steadings on which my family lived and worked had these faces on them somewhere and my father and uncle were carving them up until the last war. Why they were called th'owd man I don't know and never asked. But I can guess.

There was no special technique for creating these heads, but they were always done by someone who belonged to us and who knew what they were for. If one of us moved into a place which didn't have one, then it was often the first creative thing we did there,

Field god, Walsden, West Yorkshire. One of many carved stones found in fieldwalls throughout the Pennines, thought to represent local protective spirits or *genii loci*.

or we got someone in to do it for us. Either way it would be done as quickly as possible. Any piece of stone would do as long as it was local. And on it, or should I say from it, a face or sometimes a whole head was fashioned. These were almost always just crude representations of a human face – just two eyes, a nose and a mouth. But generally they were quite well done by people who had knowledge of our tradition. The head was always placed in some significant spot in or on the building; above the door or window, in the gable, chimney or some such place. If the house had a gate it could be set above that or maybe on one of the outhouses, shippens or mistals. As I've said, it didn't really matter other than that it was carved and placed with intent and that its vision wasn't obstructed. At one time you could just tell who belonged to us because they had one of these heads on their property. As I got older, it wasn't so easy; people moved or died and those who came to take over their house or farm often had no idea what these things were for. Some were left alone, others were built into fireplaces or rockeries and quite a few ended up in museums. It's interesting that no one could work out just what they were for and some archaeologists thought they were as old as the Iron Age. Some, just a few, might well have been. But most of the ones I knew about had been carved within the memory of my parents and grandparents. It was part of the tradition that when one of us left a living place, we would never have sold or given them away, and my grandfather often told us what bad luck would come to those who removed heads without knowing of their power.[22]

THE CURSE OF CERNUNNOS

'This story sounds so unbelievable that you might be excused for thinking I have made it up, but it is all absolutely true and happened just as I described it.' These were the words of a Cheshire man we will call Robin, whose experience with the Celtic twilight is probably the most chilling we have ever put on record.

It all began innocently enough. In the mid-1960s Robin was living with his wife in a lock cottage at the village of Marple, on the western edge of the hills. The cottage itself was built at the end of the 1790s, during the construction of the Peak Forest Canal, and according to an old man he once met while walking along the towpath, it had been built upon the site of one of the 'seven ancient wells' of the parish. Besides this single piece of uncorroborated evidence, there was nothing remarkable about the old cottage. But one day in 1965, as Robin hacked away at weeds in the overgrown garden behind the building, he struck an unusual stone with his spade. Carefully, he removed the heavy object from the surface topsoil, which he was clearing to grow vegetables. 'I looked at it and thought it was funny, because it looked like it had been carved into something, and when I cleaned it up a bit, this great grinning mouth began to appear,' he explained.

When fully cleaned, the stone was found to be a representation of a human head carved in sandstone or gritsone, about 30 centimetres (one foot) in height.

22 Pers. comm., 1994

It was grossly rendered and quite deliberately contorted – very similar in appearance to a nightmarish gargoyle. Slightly smaller than life-size, the head was very precisely carved at the front, but flat and uncarved at the rear and side. The semi-spherical eyes with their deep pupils bulged massively, the nose was long and twisted, the mouth was open, with prominent teeth. There were inscribed lines on the face, like tattoo marks which enhanced the malevolent appearance of the carving.

On the top of the head was hair or what could be described as a crown of foliage, and there was some evidence that horns had been attached to the head at one stage because there was evidence of antler pedicles like those of a deer. Almost as soon as this strange stone was discovered, Robin's wife took an instant and violent dislike to it and refused to allow it inside the house; it became a garden ornament.

It was not long after this odd discovery that the couple first heard 'footsteps' inside the cottage. 'They were heavy, deliberate footsteps across the bedroom floor and left us terrified,' recalled Robin. 'There was absolutely no possibility of confusing the sound with the normal sounds of shrinking or expanding wood, and there were no water pipes in the house anywhere near the bedroom. It was the unmistakable sound of someone walking across a bare, boarded floor.'

When the couple moved away to another home in Cheshire, the head was given as a present to Robin's father, who lived in North Wales. He was a very keen amateur archaeologist and had read about the tribe known as the Brigantes and the Celtic cult of the head. 'He was delighted to be given the head, but my mother's reaction was one of violent opposition to having it in their house, despite her being the most mild-mannered of people imaginable,' he explained. 'They soon began to suffer a long succession of problems and bad luck, and according to my mother, they all dated from the arrival of that head.

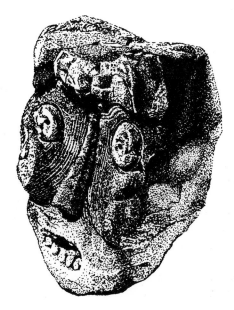

Medieval stone head which may represent Cernunnos, the horned god of the Cornovii, found at Marple, Cheshire.

All kinds of things happened: the house was flooded out not once but twice and my father suffered an undiagnosed heart attack around the time he got the head. My mother was absolutely convinced all their bad luck was connected to the arrival of that object – she said, it's all down to that head, it's evil. She refused to have it in the house and once again it became a garden ornament. This all culminated in the premature death of my father some years late and, the passionate pleading of my mother to "please get rid of that terrible head".'

Robin took the head to his new home in Stockport, where it stood in the corner for some time. 'My wife's attitude to it had not changed and when a female friend of hers visited to see for herself, she experienced such a profound sense of shock and loathing upon seeing the head that I decided I had better find a new home for it,' he said. 'I tended to dismiss all these things, but my wife made it clear that it had to go. I took it to my office, where it was on display for several years, during which time several members of staff either suffered sudden premature death or narrow escapes from death. The number of such deaths and near-death experiences was out of all proportion for the size of the office concerned.'

Finally the firm relocated, the office shut down and Robin was left with the evil, grinning head with no home. 'By now even I was becoming a little nervous about the head. It really did seem to drag a wake of disaster in its trail,' he confessed. It was now the mid-1980s and as he was wondering once more what to do with the strange head, the ideal solution seemed to present itself when some friends of his in Scotland started to look around for a new house. He explained, 'These friends were and still are rather unusual. They belong to a coven of witches spread in the border region of north Cumbria and eastern Dumfriesshire. Recently they had spent a number of months deciding where they wanted to live. They wanted a remote site and a house preferably out of sight of any other. I didn't know very much about the branch of witchcraft they were involved in, but I know they were part of a group who were using some kind of "earth magic" directed against the nuclear power stations in that area. They spent ages using 'pendulum power, ley lines, psychic trances and "automatic writing;" before they were finally convinced that a particular house in a very remote valley was the one for them.'

As a moving in present for his friends, Robin presented them with the strange carved head. 'I said to them, I have got an object that might be of interest to you. How do you fancy this head which I have. It sounds from reading about it that it might be Celtic, but we don't really know for sure. They were delighted with it at first, they thought it was wonderful. They started using it in their rituals and declared it was "very powerful indeed".'

That was 1985. Before long members of the coven began to experience an extraordinary run of 'bad luck' – financial disaster, miscarriages, partial collapse of a house, business failure and family breakdowns. Naturally, the stone head was blamed and soon it was banished into the garden. But the culminating disaster occurred in 1989, when a bomb in a Pan Am aircraft exploded over southern Dunfriesshire, scattering huge pieces of wreckage over a wide area of land.

'This was the most frightening experience of their lives, because they were living in an isolated area to the east of Lockerbie at the time,' Robin explained.

'They knew something horrendous had happened because they heard this explosion and a distance away they could see this vast mushroom cloud lit up, because it was dark and December. They thought it was a nuclear bomb and were so frightened they closed all the doors and windows of the house. They tried to phone for help, but all the telephone lines in the area were jammed and it was a number of hours before they could reach anyone. Eventually they got through to a friend in Edinburgh, who told them about the plane disaster. They were left in a state of shock and stayed in the house until the following morning. At first light, when they left the house, they found it was completely surrounded by fall-out from the crash. Pieces of personal property and wreckage were scattered across the drive in front of the driveway. The shock was so great that they never really got over what happened that night. And as it happened, when a map is drawn of the wreckage distribution from that crash, they were smack in the middle of the biggest concentration of it all.'

The group was still traumatized several days later when Robin drove north once again to visit them. They pleaded with him to take the head away, attributing all their problems to its aura of menace and 'undoubted evil'. But before they would let him put it in the boot of the car for the journey back to Cheshire, they absolutely insisted on wrapping it with a number of talismans and symbols of Hebrew, Christian and non-Christian origin. Then they wrapped it completely to prevent any of their spells being moved during the car journey and warned Robin never to have it inside the house.

He said, 'They were convinced that this thing was Roman in origin. They said they had a message from spirits to say that this object was a representation of a Roman soldier who had died a horrible death. They had obviously used it in some way in their rituals, but how I don't know.' The puzzled and now somewhat frightened owner of the head arrived home safely and without any mishaps. 'When I got it back I just did not know what to do with it, so it hung around in the house for a couple of years before I decided to take it to a museum to see what they made of it. They said it was rather unusual and didn't fit the standard model for Celtic heads. If it was a Celtic head, it was very different, and if it was not, it could possibly be medieval or ecclesiastical in origin. The general opinion was that it was pretty ancient rather than recent, probably the first few centuries after the Romans rather than the eighteenth century. On receipt of their report, I was asked if I would like to collect it as they did not wish to keep it, but to this date I have been most unwilling to retrieve it! Presumably it still lies somewhere in their basement archives.'

Robin, who has suffered no ill-effects as a result of his ownership of the 'evil' head, concluded, 'As far as I'm concerned, it was a mysterious object that I dug up and everybody who has been involved with it since that time seems to tell some pretty horrendous tales about it. This was without prompting too, because I didn't actually tell any of these people the stories related by others. People's reactions to it seem to have always been spontaneous.'[23]

23 Story adapted from letter to Andy Roberts dated 15 November 1990; notes from interview, 1993

CELTIC WEREWOLF

Unbelievable as Robin's story may seem, it is certainly not unique. Paranormal retribution and 'bad luck' for those who interfere with, move or use sacred ritual objects and certain stones is a well-known motif in folklore, and we have heard similar stories several times in our quest. Stories like these are not confined to the realms of folklore, for there is much recent testimony to suggest that certain ancient cult objects do indeed retain some kind of supernatural power, perhaps invested in their structure by a form of ritual or through generations of belief.

Probably the best-known example of this kind concerns a nightmarish 'werewolf' creature which accompanied two strange stone heads found in the garden of a semi-detached council house in Hexham, Northumberland, not far from the Hadrian's Wall.[24] This tale has since become a classic in the supernatural field, and remains an unsolved mystery to this day.

The first of these heads was originally unearthed in 1972 in the garden of a house on Rede Avenue by an 11-year-old boy, Colin Robson, who called out his younger brother, Les, to make a search, which soon uncovered a second head. Both were smaller than tennis balls and were very heavy for their size; one was skull-like and became known as 'the boy'; the other was female and was called the witch. While the finds were stored *inside* the Robson household, a series of poltergeist phenomena began, with the heads turning around by themselves and various objects smashing for no reason. One night the household was woken by a scream and crash coming from the house next door, where Mrs Ellen Dodd, her husband and their six children lived.

Mrs Dodd later told reporters how that night she had gone into a bedroom to sleep with her ten-year-old son Brian, who was ill. 'He kept telling me something was touching him, but I told him not to be silly,' she said. But as she began to climb into bed with the child she felt something trip over her foot. She looked up. 'Then I saw this shape, a creature very big and black – half sheep, but with a man's head. It came towards me and I definitely felt it touch me on the legs. Then, on all fours, it moved out of the room.' As Mrs Dodd screamed in terror, her husband rushed into the room and appeared to cross paths with the creature – but he could not see it. As it disappeared, she heard it going down the stairs 'with its hoofs clicking'.[25]

An excorcism put at rest the strange presence in the semi-detached house, but by this time the terrified Dodd family had been rehoused because they could no longer bear to live there. The stone heads which appeared to have started their problems were duly sent for examination at a university. Here the story becomes all the more peculiar, because of the independent testimony of Anne Ross, the expert to whom the heads were initially sent for analysis. At the time they arrived at her Southampton home inside a cardboard box in 1972, Dr Ross had no idea about their background or the odd experience of Ellen Dodd.

Speaking in 1994, she recalled her first reaction to seeing them. 'As soon as I opened the box and touched them I was filled with horror, which is very odd because although I have inherited a lot of psychic tendencies, I am very objective

24 For full version of story, see Paul Screeton, *Tales of the Hexham Heads* (Outlaw Press, Hartlepool, n.d.); see also Anne Ross, introduction to *Folklore, Myths and Legends of Britain* (Reader's Digest, 1973)

25 'Eerie Tales of the Two Idol Heads' (*Newcastle Journal*, 3 March 1972); pers. comm., 1994

when I'm working. These two heads were horrible. There was something about them staring balefully out of that box, and they were so small, I couldn't bear them, so I just covered them up quickly. It was obvious from an early stage that there was something attached to them, that they hadn't come alone, as it were.'

Dr Ross planned to have a geologist at Newcastle University examine the heads, but before they could be returned north some very strange events occurred. A night or two after they arrived she woke up suddenly at about 2 a.m., 'deeply frightened and very cold'. Looking towards the door of the bedroom, she saw a strange figure, 'dark like a shadow . . . part animal and part man'. The upper half of the creature was like a wolf, she said, while the lower part was human and covered in thick, dark fur.

Despite her fear, Dr Ross felt an irresistible urge to follow the creature, as if compelled by some invisible force, and heard it going down the stairs and disappearing at the back of the house. She roused her husband, Dick Feachem, and together they searched the house, but nothing was found. Dismissing the bizarre experience as a nightmare, even though it seemed very real, the pair decided to tell no one else about it. But a few days later, when the house was empty, Dr Ross's teenage daughter arrived home from school and saw 'something huge and dark' on the stairs which rushed down towards her, vaulted over the banisters and landed in the corridor with a soft thud, which made her think its feet were padded like those of an animal. The creature had run towards her room and, though terrified, she too felt an urge to follow it, only to see the figure vanish, leaving her alone and in a state of shock.[26]

These experiences were just the first of a long series of frightening encounters with the half-wolf, half-man creature which disrupted the entire Ross household for a number of months. During the time the 'werewolf' was resident, many visitors commented on the 'evil presence' and Dr Ross's archaeological husband, who was not normally sensitive to psychic phenomena, was distinctly aware that something was dreadfully wrong.

'Dick was very level-headed and not given to seeing ghosts but we all saw and heard it, including the two children,' explained Dr Ross. 'The most awful moment was when the cats became terrified, because they would see it on the stairs and their hackles would rise and they would back off absolutely rigid. There was no doubt the haunting was that of a werewolf, but where it came from and why I just don't know. This thing took form very gradually, and when it actually became not just audible and hinted at but tangible and visible, something had to be done, because it was definitely growing.'[27]

By this time Dr Ross had been warned by a number of visitors that the only way she could rid the house of the unwelcome visitor was by getting rid of the two 'evil' heads. If not, she was told there would be terrible consequences, a tragedy which she said nearly occurred on the day after the heads finally departed from the house. Subsequently the Ross home was exorcized, but the strange presence was not completely erased until seven other archaic heads from the collection, which appeared to have been 'triggered' by the influence of the Hexham pair, were themselves removed.

Attempts to solve the mystery took a strange turn when an account of Dr Ross's experiences appeared in a book and were later featured on a TV news

26 Screeton, op. cit.;
Ross, *Folklore, Myths,*
op. cit.

27 Ibid.

Carved stone heads were often used as guardians of houses, shrines and other important boundaries in the Celtic world. The location of this archaic head, built into a wall in the Derbyshire Peak District, is closely protected by its owner, who believes it contains the 'luck' of his fields.

broadcast. It was then that a Hexham truck driver, Desmond Craigie, came forward and announced the two heads were not gruesome Celtic cult idols at all, but merely toys he had made for his daughter Nancy in 1956, when he lived at the house on Rede Avenue where they had been later found. At that time he worked at a firm casting artificial stone, and when his little girl asked what he did, he made the two heads in his lunch break for her to play with. Eventually one got broken, and he had surmised they must have ended up in the garden, where they were eventually found by the Robson children.[28]

However, rather than providing a solution to the mystery, Desmond Craigie's claim failed to answer the crucial questions posed by the Hexham heads saga. If the heads were only 20 years old, why did they independently trigger psychic phenomena in three households? And why was the haunting associated with a hybrid creature which was so in keeping with Celtic legends like those of the brollachan and the Irish fomor – both shape-shifting monstrous forms?

The description of the creature which haunted the Dodd and Ross households also recalls that of the boggart of northern folklore, which often had a symbiotic relationship with a particular house, family or object. On the Continent, there are also traditions of a monstrous wolf-like creature called the Tarasque, a hybrid beast associated with the River Rhône. In one famous carving dating from the fourth or third century BC, the monster is depicted devouring human limbs and grasping severed heads in its claws.[29]

28 'New Twist in Head Puzzle' (*Newcastle Journal*, 20 March 1974)

29 Ian Stead, 'The Linsdorf Monster' (*Antiquity*, 225, March 1985)

Dr Ross, who has much experience of dealing with strange happenings at Celtic sites, continues to believe the place where the heads were buried in Hexham may have transferred some form of baleful guardian to the carvings. Geological experts who examined the heads confirmed Craigie's claim that they were made of artificial stone but were unable to date them precisely, which added fuel to Dr Ross's and the Hexham witnesses' assertions that these two *particular* heads were not the ones which Desmond Craigie remembered making.

With the mystery still unsolved, the heads were passed for examination to an inorganic chemist, Dr Don Robins, who wanted to test a theory that mineral structures have the ability to store an electrical charge and therefore possibly imagery too. Although his experiments were inconclusive, Dr Robins said he also found the presence of the two heads in his home 'disquieting' and blamed the unpleasant 'presence' upon the 'witch' or female head.[30] When last heard of, in 1978, the Hexham heads were in the custody of a dowser and astrologer who was subsequently involved in a serious car accident. What happened to the boy, the witch, and their werewolf companion after this last incident remains a complete and baffling mystery.

HEADS AND TALES

Although the mystery which surrounds the present whereabouts of the heads from Marple and Hexham prevents us from reaching a clear understanding of why they became associated with bizarre psychic phenomena, another head said to be connected with a 'prehistoric curse' currently sits in a cellar in the Calderdale valley, West Yorkshire – deep in the heart of an area associated with a head cult since Celtic times. The owner of the head is one of the writers, Andy Roberts, and in this case we know the complete history of the stone and the origins of the fantastic story which became attached to its 'presence'.

This sandstone boulder, dubbed 'the Druid's Head' by the national Press, came from the grounds of a sixteenth-century house, Ryshworth Hall, at Crossflats near Bingley. In November 1990 the owner, Michael White, found the head in the roots of a giant sycamore tree which he had dug up with a mechanical digger. Following the head's discovery in 1985, the White's luck changed dramatically. Mr White's wife, Alison, was struck down by an unexplained illness which left her weak and debilitated, and her husband's building business later collapsed. In desperation they gave the head to a sceptical friend, only to be dismayed when he went bankrupt shortly afterwards.

Then the Whites' two daughters began to experience ghostly phenomena, and Mrs White encountered a disembodied hand just as she was preparing to switch off an upstairs light. These events led the Whites to try to sell the eight-bedroomed hall in an attempt to change their luck, and it was not long before the story of the haunted head came to the attention of the media. The head was put up for sale by auctioneers, who claimed it 'almost certainly originated in Celtic Britain', but despite the publicity gained by the yarn's exposure in the press, the Whites' failed to sell the hall and their luck remained unchanged.[31]

30 Don Robins, *The Secret Language of Stone* (Rider, 1988)

31 'Cursed Head Goes under the Hammer' (*Yorkshire Evening Post*, 13 November 1990); see also Roberts, *Ghosts and Legends*, op. cit.

But yet again there was an unexpected twist in the tail of this story. Following the appearance of the press stories, a Halifax woman contacted a newspaper and told how the 'Celtic' head had actually been carved in 1978 by her father William Hodgson, a previous occupant of Ryshworth Hall. 'He buried it for a joke to amuse his grandchildren, telling them it would be dug up in hundreds of years. He'll be sitting on his cloud rocking with laughter,' she said.[32] In fact, the actual age of this 'cursed head' and indeed all the others we have investigated has no bearing on the subsequent development of the stories, but tells us a great deal about how strange beliefs and superstitions develop often from mundane beginnings. The crucial factor is not the heads themselves but what people *believe* about their power – as important a factor today as it would have been 2,000 years ago.

The human head has been a magical symbol for thousands of years, from a time long before the Celts, and appears in the earliest written tales, where speaking or oracular heads are found, always in connection with magical or supernatural events. Our examples show how carvings of heads, whether 'Celtic' or modern, still retain an aura of mystery because of their ancient association with the world of the spirit, the Celtic Otherworld. Heads were carved by their creators for a purpose, and in tradition could clearly be instilled with both good and evil intent.

Carved stone heads feature strongly in the folklore of northern England, but rather than bringing bad luck they were usually carved to avert it, and hundreds of examples can be found built into Pennine farmhouses above doorways, on window mouldings and guarding gable ends. In local tradition they are magical charms, like rowan sprigs or horseshoes, placed there to protect the household from evil, and in some areas local belief identifies them with 'the Old Ones' – the shadowy Celtic deities and spirits themselves. The majority of these guardian heads are found in the upper Calder and Aire valleys of West Yorkshire, which historians have identified as the heartland of the last independent Celtic kingdom in England, Elmet. Celtic influence survives here in place-names and tradition, with heads appearing on the first permanent stone houses built by yeoman farmers and weavers during the sixteenth and seventeenth centuries.[33]

The population of the Calder valley seems almost to have had an obsession with the 'severed head' symbol at this time. The town of Halifax was the last place in England to use a guillotine to decapitate criminals, a grisly custom which ended only in the middle of the seventeenth century. However, the head carving and placing tradition has survived in West Yorkshire into modern times, and to this day stonemasons and artists like Hebden Bridge's Craig Chapman are still busily carving and burying fine pieces, following the archaic tradition of the valley. One local mason continues the protective tradition of heads by placing them upon houses always facing towards the town centre, because, he says, 'That's where all the trouble comes from nowadays!'[34]

In the West Yorkshire village of Haworth is the Sun Inn, a coaching house turned pub on the edge of the beautiful moors made famous by the Brontë sisters. Visitors to the eighteenth-century building will see a strangely carved head positioned just above the door. It is not Celtic, but was placed there early in the 1980s by the landlord, Rennie Hollings, to 'lay a ghost' before a planned

32 *Yorkshire Evening Post*, op. cit.

33 See Ross, *Pagan Celtic Britain*, op. cit., Chapter 2; Brears, op. cit.; David Keys, 'Heads of Stone Cast New Light on Celtic Cult' (*Independent*, 30 May 1988)

34 John Billingsley, *Archaic Head Carving in West Yorkshire and beyond* (unpublished MA thesis, Centre for English Cultural Tradition and Language, Sheffield University, 1992)

refurbishment of the premises. The apparition was of an old packhorse carrier who, dressed in a long leather cape, haunted the pub for years. Mr Hollings had learned about the ghost from local people and decided to deal with it by following the local time-honoured tradition. He said afterwards, 'There is a local tradition that these were put on buildings when a workman had been killed on the site before the work was completed, and they are supposed to ward off evil spirits. I feel now that I have quashed any ideas of ghosts for good.'[35]

In the Peak District and Yorkshire stone heads were used for a variety of magical purposes. In Longdendale, carvings could represent guardians, and were often buried at secret places or kept at the entrances to natural shrines, often springs or wells. 'There are places, quiet places very often, beside a stream or at entrances or exits which might be guarded by a stone head,' I was told by a guardian. 'It was an old form of protection. You used the head to keep away evil or absorb evil.'

In some rural areas, these heads have until very recently been used in efforts to cure illness, to encourage fertility and to combat ghosts. When their usefulness came to an end, they would have to be buried for fear of the power they had absorbed. For these reasons, it has been suggested, some heads were buried face-down in subsoil to neutralize any baleful influence with which they were imbued, only to be dug up years later by unsuspecting gardeners.

According to a number of informants, heads are commonly found in parts of the Peak District and Ireland in bogs, fields and bases of walls, where they too have been buried for magical reasons. One expert, K. M. Dickie, wrote, 'These heads had hereditary keepers as the relics of the Celtic saints had. They are still being buried in Ireland and I know of one in County Cavan which was buried between two searching visits of mine in the 1960s. The family had particularly bad luck and decided that the head was the cause. At one place in County Cork where there are two extraordinary heads, I was allowed to see only one, although I went with the priest and asked about the second. I was only allowed to see the other head on the second and third visits. It is built into a wall just above a ditch, but that was only done a few years ago, and the owners are frightened about their powers and would never throw them out.'[36]

While some heads functioned as guardians of the house or hearth or as charms promoting fertility or luck to land and farm, others may have been positioned on bridges, building gables and even mill chimneys. Some seem to have been stone representations of gods or ancestors, carved as a means of communicating with the dead. This points to a belief that heads were objects of power, bringing luck and strength into a house. Some have a distinctive mask-like appearance, which suggests that they may have been intended to be viewed only from a certain angle; others are flat from behind, suggesting that they were made for insertion into niches inside a temple or stood on pillars in a shrine. Often the eyes are outstanding, which in most cases are larger than normal facial proportions allow. In some cases, only one eye is portrayed; in others, one eye is closed, as in a carving from Castleton, Derbyshire, which is perhaps a representation of a one-eyed god like those found in early Irish literature.

Another odd feature is the 'cigarette hole' or soul hole, normally a shallow hole drilled in the corner or centre of the mouth. The purpose of these remains

35 'Heading off a Ghost' (*Yorkshire Evening Post*, 21 October 1971); see also Roberts, op. cit.

36 Undated letter in Sidney Jackson card index file, Yorkshire Archaeological Society, Leeds

This unique Celtic figurine, known locally as 'Robin Hood', was once kept beside a spring on a farm at Mottram Moor, Longdendale. It appears the figure once had horns and carried a bow, suggesting it represented the Celtic horned god of the hunt.

a mystery because we know the Celts did not smoke, but one suggestion is that they originate in a belief that this was an oracular hole through which the spirit inhabiting the head could 'speak'. Some heads have carvings of leaves or leaf crowns, which identify them as Celtic forest deities; while others have hollowed crowns, which may have served as the receptacles for offerings of food and drink, turning the heads into portable wayside shrines or altars.[37]

One way of adding power to the heads was to carve a number of faces on to a lump of stone. A number of cult carvings from north and western England and Ireland are double-faced, and others have three or four faces. Janus or two-headed stones, usually carved back to back, are sometimes paired with an animal, and the tricephalic or three-faced stones are important, as this number was magical in Celtic mythology. Three-faced heads are commonly carved on one stone, the individual faces sometimes sharing features like ears and eyes. In the early Irish stories there are numerous references to three semi-divine beings, and deities are often described as having three faces or occurring in trios, being born at the same time and sometimes meeting the same fate – often decapitation.

One special type of stone head found commonly in northern England displays the remains of stone horns. These appear to represent a Celtic horned god, a popular deity among the northern tribes, who often depicted him with ram's horns rather than antlers. Antlers may have been awkward to carve, but in some cases this problem may have been overcome by drilling sockets into which real animal antlers may have been inserted. The carrying or wearing of antlers or horns is found elsewhere in British folk tradition, where, for example, Herne the Hunter, who is the guardian spirit of Windsor Park, appears as a horned figure on a horse, followed by the Wild Hunt. Herne, and other personifications of the hunting god, seem to represent local variations on this primeval horned deity, who was known in Gaul as Cernunnos.

The cult of horned gods has a pedigree as old as that of the stone heads themselves, and there are early prehistoric references to such a cult in northern Europe as early as the Bronze Age. On the southern border of the Peak District, in the land of the Cornovii or 'horned ones', the well-known Abbots Bromley horn dancers of Staffordshire's Needwood Forest continue the association of the area with the fertility god. At Wall in Staffordshire, archaeologists who excavated the site of a Roman settlement found it covered in the remains of a Celtic shrine which may have been built by the Cornovii. Nine carved stones from the shrine had been reused in the wall of a Roman house, seven of which had been set upside-down and facing inwards to neutralize their power and use it to protect the building's foundations. Five stones contained carvings of human heads, and a number of these were horned.[38]

The 'cursed head' found beside the Peak Forest Canal at Marple could well have been a later medieval carving depicting the Horned One. Similar heads have been found in other areas of north Britain, particularly in the frontier region of the Roman wall, and a horned head is associated with the collection of carved stones found at Mouselow in Glossop, less than 16 kilometres (ten miles) from Marple. Beliefs continue to surround horned deities in the living tradition of this region, and there are rumours that seasonal rites are still practised surrounding their cult.

37 See Keys, op. cit.; *Celtic Stone Heads* (Manchester Museum leaflet, 1988)

38 Ross, 'A Pagan Celtic Shrine at Wall, Staffordshire', op. cit.

SUPERNATURAL SKULLS

'"What's that i'the nook John?" she suddenly cried,
And shaking with terror they clearly espied
The head of Ned Dickson upright on the stone,
As wan and as ghastly as when he was done.

'Many years passed away and the murderers fell,
By just retribution as ancient folk tell;
By a blow from her husband the woman was killed,
By the fall of an oak was Jack Johnson's blood spilled.

'But the head of Ned Dickson still stood in the nook,
Though they tried to remove it by bell and by book;
Though wasted of skin and flesh still the skull,
Will remain at its post till it's weird be full.'

traditional Derbyshire folk-tale

Hidden away from the public on the top shelf of a storeroom in the depths of a museum in Lancashire, is perhaps one of the strangest relics of Britain's rich living Celtic tradition.

The Timberbottoms skulls are uninviting objects at first sight. Just two bits of dark brown polished bone mounted on a plinth and secured firmly on top of a hefty, yellowing family Bible. But the story surrounding these human skulls, like many others in the Celtic tradition, is bizarre and fantastic to say the least.

The Bible, which has been their home for the last 200 years, is there for a good reason; removing them from its protection for whatever reason is sure to bring about hauntings, bangings, thumpings and other manifestations of paranormal fury. At one time the skulls were on display in the Chetham Room at Turton Tower Museum, which was taken over by Lancashire County Council in 1987. Call there today and you will find no mention of their existence in the official guidebook, nor will you be allowed to view these fascinating artefacts of belief – in the opinion of the authors, the most interesting relics in the whole building.

'Consequent to the change in authority, a new guidebook has been produced which does not include the skulls, neither are they on display,' explained Turton Tower's keeper, Martin Dowland. 'Because of their sensitive nature, access to the skulls is limited.'[39]

When we visited Turton Tower in 1994, we were carefully questioned before we were allowed into the storeroom where the relics are kept. The keeper seemed genuinely concerned about our motives for wanting to examine the skulls, around which there continued to be a taboo about moving or disturbing them in any way. He spoke of hauntings in the museum as recently as the 1980s, when the skulls had been temporarily removed from the Bible. Even after reassurances, we were not allowed to touch the skulls or move them from their shelf, and we had to take photos from a far corner of the room. There

39 Pers. comm.,
M. Dowland, 3 May
1993

Skull from the entrance portico of an Iron Age Celtic shrine in Provence.

are no plans to display them in the museum, and questions about traditions or beliefs connected with them are discouraged.

What we could find out about the skulls came largely from local oral tradition. The two pieces of bone – one badly damaged as if from a severe blow – were said to be male and female; some versions speak of three skulls, three being a mystical number in Celtic tradition. The third, they explain, is on display to this day behind the bar of the Pack Horse public house in nearby Affetside (an inn known locally as 'the screaming skull').

Tradition tells how the skulls were originally fished out of the Bradshaw Brook by a farmer from Timberbottoms Farm at some unspecified date in the eighteenth century – a story which continues the ancient association of cult heads with water. The skulls were taken home by the farmer, who placed them upon his mantelpiece. Immediately strange things began to happen, with pots and pans flying around rooms, footsteps and ghostly figures fighting in the moonlight; peace was restored only when the skulls were placed upon a Bible.[40]

On several occasions during the following 200 years, attempts were made to return the skulls to the brook from which they came, but with no success. They were also buried with reverence in Bradshaw churchyard, but to no avail; once again, peace was restored to the household only when they were exhumed and replaced on the Bible in what became known as 'Skull House Farm'. The strange beliefs which surrounded these ancient lucky charms survived the physical demolition of both Timberbottoms Farm and their second home, Bradshaw Hall, earlier this century. Since 1939, the skulls have never been separated and from their arrival at the Turton Tower Museum, all their movements have been under strict supervision.

Historians who refer to legends like these often assume they are unique to their locality, where there is usually some highly improbable story fixed just outside living memory to account for their presence and continuing mystique.

40 Oral traditions, collected 1993 and 1994; Kathleen Eyre, *Lancashire Ghosts* (Dalesman, 1989); Marc Alexander, *Phantom Britain* (Muller, 1975)

Guardian skulls are a little-known aspect of British folklore, but there are dozens of stories which suggest they once played a major role in the traditions of many communities. Significantly, the vast majority of stories about magical skulls come from the very areas of the British Isles where archaic Celtic traditions have survived for longest. In the Peak District, northwest England and the West Country, ancient and mysterious human skulls have been associated with the 'luck of the house' for centuries, a belief which dates back to pagan Celtic religion.

Legend often accounts for them as grisly *memento mori* of periods of violence and upheaval in English history: they become the skulls of priests and soldiers killed during the social unrest of Civil War and Reformation. Historical investigations have rarely found any documentary evidence to support these stories, and often clues lead to the conclusion that the skulls have older and more mysterious origins.

One good example concerns the fourteenth-century Bettiscombe manor house near Lyme Regis in Dorset, where a famous 'screaming skull' refused to be removed or destroyed, according to local legend. In 1874, a local collector of curious stories, Judge J. S. Udal, said the skull had been carefully preserved in the house 'for a time long antecedent to the present tenancy' and, he wrote, 'the peculiar superstition attaching to it is that if it be brought out of the house, the house itself would rock to its foundation, while the person by whom such an act of desecration was committed would certainly die within the year'.[41]

Judge Udal recorded an ingenious theory which suggested the skull belonged to a Negro slave who travelled to Dorset in the service of his exiled master from plantations on the Caribbean island of Nevis during the seventeenth century. On his deathbed he made his master promise to return him for burial to the Caribbean, but the promise was broken and he was buried in the local churchyard. Soon horrible screaming and moaning noises plagued the manor house in Bettiscombe, forcing the owners to dig up the skull and restore it to a place of honour in the house to placate it. This story, widely believed in the area, was dispelled in 1963, when the archaeologist Michael Pinney, then owner of Bettiscombe, had the skull examined by a pathologist. He concluded it belonged not to a Negro male but to a European female aged between 25 and 30.[42]

Experts now believe that the Bettiscombe skull is actually that of a prehistoric woman who died between 3,000 and 4,000 years ago. The skull is fossilized and is believed to have come from the fossilizing well beside the Manor near the foot of Pilsdon Pen, a hill which contains the remains of an Iron Age ritual enclosure. The skull may therefore have come from the Pen itself and its shiny texture suggests that it has absorbed minerals after being immersed in a spring.

It will be recalled how the Timberbottoms skulls too were fished out of a brook, a practice which harks back to ancient offerings to water spirits, and a theory supported by the discovery of severed heads in wells and springs dating to Iron Age and Romano-British times.[43] In folklore the head in the sacred well was imbued with strong powers of healing and there is much folklore, legend and archaeological evidence for a connection between heads, skulls and springs as gateways to the Otherworld. In Wales there were until recently several human skulls preserved as the 'guardians' of holy wells. Once removed

41 John S. Udal, *Notes and Queries* (4th series, 1872)

42 Pers. comm., Michael Pinney, 1991; Ross and Robins, op. cit.

43 Anne Ross, 'Severed Heads in Wells: An Aspect of the Well Cult' (*Scottish Studies*, 6, 1962)

from their shrine or burial place, the skulls refuse to go back, at some point transferring their magical potency to the fabric of the building to which they have become attached.

Although the origins of these traditions in some cases may have been long forgotten, the remaining heads or skulls have often become the focus of strange phenomena if they are disturbed or moved from their specially made niches in old halls, manor houses and farms. One typical story which contains all the elements of this placement tradition was recorded in 1895 by the Rev. Sabine Baring-Gould. He wrote of a Cornish farmhouse on the edge of Bodmin Moor where, he said, there was a human skull preserved in a niche. 'Why it is there, no one knows,' he wrote. 'It has been several times buried, but whenever buried noises ensue which disturb the household, and the skull is disinterred and replaced in its niche. Formerly it occupied the gable end of the farmhouse'.[44] The gable of a household was one of the geomantic entrance points for spirits, and the display of severed heads in this position is a direct link with the beliefs of the Iron Age Celts. Bodmin Moor is another area rich in Celtic traditions, and today visitors to the Witchcraft Museum in nearby Boscastle can see a skull which was until recently purportedly kept in a niche inside a rocky shrine on the slopes of the moor. According to its caption, the last 'guardian' of this shrine died within living memory.

DICKY

According to an informant, in the last century almost every large house or hall in certain parts of the Peak District had preserved somewhere in its walls or structure a human skull or a carved stone head. Often special wall-niches or compartments were fashioned to house these strange relics, and the authors have seen a number of them, often bricked up or covered only in recent times. At Flagg Hall near Buxton a human skull has been kept upon the windowsill positioned at the top of the main staircase – corresponding with the general position of the gable – since at least the seventeenth century, the tradition having been passed down from generation to generation within the family who own the building.[45] Another head, this time carved in stone, which at one time acted as the guardian of a well, is preserved at a house on the outskirts of Glossop. When we spoke to the owner, we were told that the head had been passed down through his father's family. In his own words, the only thing he knew about it was a story that 'it is not to be moved from the house, for if it is ill-tidings will come to pass'.

Disturbance of these talismans would break a strict taboo, and one tale connected with Dunscar Farm below Mam Tor at Castleton suggests that if the resident human skull, preserved on a windowsill, is moved 'the crops will fail'.[46] The link between ancestral skulls and the 'luck' of the household and the

44 Sabine Baring-Gould, *Strange Survivals* (London, 1892)

45 Oral tradition, collected 1991; see also Daniel, *Ghosts of Derbyshire*, op. cit.

46 Sidney Addy, 'A Skull as a Protector of a House' (undated paper in Sheffield City Libraries collection)

This guardian skull is preserved at an isolated farmhouse in the Halkyn Mountains of North Wales. Like others in Celtic tradition, it is dangerous to remove it from the house it protects.

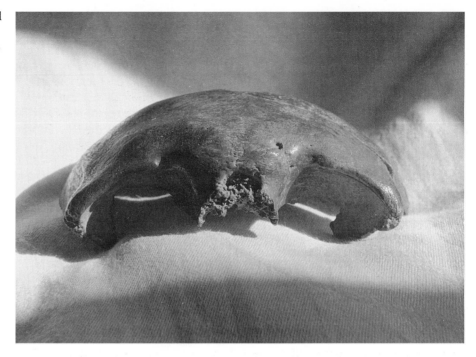

fertility of the land is of very ancient origin, and is such a strong tradition that it has survived in some areas of the Pennines until the end of the twentieth century. This is certainly the case with the most famous Peak District skull, 'Dicky' or 'Dick' of Tunstead, which was for many hundreds of years preserved within the walls of an isolated hill farm between Chapel-en-le-Frith and Whaley Bridge, only a short distance from the Dark Peak valleys, where so many of the Old Ways have survived.

The late Clarence Daniel once said that there were enough stories told about this pile of decaying bones to fill a book. Such was its grip upon local imagination that Dicky became a rallying point for those objecting to progress. The power of this particular *genius loci* was said to have caused a railway company to alter the route of a planned new line between Whaley Bridge and Buxton in 1863 because it threatened to cut through part of Dicky's farm. According to the old and still remembered story, the bridge carrying the road to Tunstead Farm over the new track kept sinking, and eventually a new bridge and road had to be made at a different spot so as not to upset its supernatural guardian.[47]

The best-known story which tries to explain the presence and power of the skull at Tunstead suggests it belonged to a soldier, Ned Dickson, whose family owned the farm for a long period up until the 1940s. Dickson was murdered and buried on the farm by his cousins when he returned unexpectedly from a foreign war to reclaim his lost inheritance. After the foul murder, all kinds of misfortunes and ill-luck fell upon the guilty cousins, including weird and unaccountable noises, illness, death of livestock and crop failure. Driven to distraction, they were forced to take advice from a local witch, who said

47 Daniel, *Ghosts of Derbyshire*, op. cit.

Dickson's skull must be dug up and given a place of honour in a niche inside the farm, for 'he will then feel he has had his fair share'.[48]

Despite its name, an examination of Dicky has indicated that the skull belonged to a woman about 18 years old. This may support a rival theory that tells of two sisters who quarelled over the love of a man. One murdered the other, but the dying woman vowed her bones would never rest and her skull must be kept in the staircase window. Other theories suggest the skull is actually that of a witch, or of a woman sacrificed to provide a foundation offering in prehistoric times. Experts feel it possible that the bones may have originally come from an ancient tumulus or stone circle on the moors above the farm. Perhaps it was brought into the house as a good-luck charm to protect the building in a wild and lonely area, following a long-established tradition. This was certainly the case in a story from the nearby valley of Longdendale, where two skulls were unearthed from a mound earlier this century by a man who was clearing land for a new greenhouse in a village on the edge of the moors. The man's granddaughter remembers how the local advice was to place the bones in the eaves on either end of the new building, 'because that's the place for skulls'. The tradition was observed, and no supernatural disturbances occurred.[49]

When traveller John Hutchinson, author of *A Tour through the High Peak*, inspected 'Dicky' in the year 1807, he was told that it had been in the house for 'near two centuries during all the revolutions of owners and tenants in that time'. The tenant at that time, Adam Fox, told him, 'The skull is looked upon more as a guardian spirit than a terror to the family, never disturbing them but in cases of an approaching death of a relation or neighbour, and showing its resentment only when spoken of with disrespect or when its own dreadful mortality is removed.'[50]

This tradition was still strong in 1938, when folklorist Christina Hole visited Tunstead Farm and spoke with the owner, one of the last of the Dixon line. She was told the family still carefully preserved the skull, which continued to act as a guardian spirit of the house, and even then warned the family whenever there was anything amiss in farm or field. The Dixon family has now left, and the farmhouse has since passed to new owners, who have buried the skull – now in three pieces – in a secret place in a bid to bring an end to the story and the ceaseless stream of visitors who ask to see the decaying bones.

Today, one of the few local people who had preserved stories about Dicky's skull speaks of the tradition very much in the past tense. Historian Margaret Bellhouse, who has lived in the hamlet of Coombs, in the valley below the farm, all her life, has strong memories of the stories from her childhood. 'It was very difficult to get to know much about it firsthand, as the old country people would not open their mouths on the subject, because they believed it was bad luck to talk about Dicky,' she explained. 'I think I must be the only one left of the old people who really did think there was something in it, that there was a curse on the skull. I have known about it from being a child, and my mother used to be very afraid of it.'

Dicky's skull, if moved, always brought bad luck to the farm. 'I know of the animals dying, the farm roof falling in and different accidents to the men if

48 H. J. Rose, 'Two Derbyshire Folktales' (*Folklore*, vol. 41, 1930)

49 Oral tradition, collected 1993

50 William Bunting, *Chapel-en-le-Frith: Its History and People* (Manchester, 1940); Llewelyn Jewitt, *Derbyshire Ballads* (London, 1867)

it was disturbed. I myself have known of happenings when the skull was moved and which righted when it was replaced. Some of these things happened in my childhood, but many of them have not been written about,' she said. 'One of the last farmers here, he did something wrong and got his hand caught in the turnip chopper, and they all said it was Dicky. I don't know what he did, but it was something he shouldn't do. The Dixon who lived there when I was young was very superstitious. He used to say, if you were good to Dicky, believed in him and didn't say stupid things about him, he was good to you. He used to find that when he was going up the drive with a horse and trap, which meant him having to stop and open every gate, he would often find them swinging open themselves!'

Mrs Bellhouse heard of one attempt to bury the skull in the churchyard at Chapel-en-le-Frith, but this did not lay the spirit. Neither did casting the skull into the nearby reservoir, for an old account tells how it was quickly retrieved when all the fish suddenly died: 'There was no peace, no rest, it had to be replaced.' The niche made for the skull 'just seemed to be in the right place', said Mrs Bellhouse, and there was a peculiar silence in the room where the guardian skull gazed out upon the farmland – Dicky's land, the locals called it. 'People were very superstitious in those days and the main superstition was Dicky,' she said. 'People wouldn't dare walk across Dicky's land after dark, and there was a strange black dog which used to follow people down from the main road and then vanish into the hill. The tradition was that this was Dicky's spirit seeing them off his land. I've seen that too.'[51]

Several years ago the authors interviewed a gentleman named Neville Slack, whose family had been Peak District hill farmers for many generations. His great-grandfather, who died in 1945 aged 93, often spoke of the legend of the skull, he said. 'Legend has it that it was uncovered during renovations to the ancient farmhouse,' he explained. 'It was encased in the thick rubble wall directly beneath a window-ledge. The skull was placed on a windowsill and if it remained there, all was apparently quite peaceful. If, however, it was moved from this location there was apparently considerable noise and disturbance in and around the house, including moving furniture and ornaments. At these times the skull was also said to weep and moan loudly. My grandfather, who was a very tough, level-headed hill farmer, not given to wild imaginings, claimed to have witnessed such occurrences. According to the old gentleman, one resident of the house actually threw the skull out on to the midden at which all hell is supposed to have broken out. The skull was said to have screamed out, while pandemonium reigned all around through one night. The skull is said to have rolled itself back to the house door, where it tapped to be let in.'[52]

Mr Slack was also of the opinion that the skull was the head of some Celtic tribal chieftain, or perhaps the remains of a foundation sacrifice in some far distant time. Similar stories are told in other areas where skulls have taken up residence. One, kept in a niche at the Catholic bishop of Manchester's residence at Wardley Hall, is protected by a clause in the deeds, which stipulates that it must be kept in the house if it is sold. At another 'Skull House' in Lancashire, not far from Turton Tower, legend says the house will collapse if the skull is ever taken away from the building.

51 Oral tradition, collected 1993

52 Letter from Neville Slack, 27 April 1990

DEATH HOUNDS

'Oft have I heard my honoured mother say.
How she has listened to the Gabriel hounds –
Those strange unearthly and mysterious sounds,
Which on the ear through murkiest darkness fell;
Of death premonished, some sick neighbour's knell.
I too remember once at midnight dark,
How these sky-yelpers startled me, and stirred
My fancy so, I could have averred
A mimic pack of beagles how did bark
Nor wondered I that rustic fear should trace
A spectral huntsman doomed to that long moonless chase.'[53]

There is an eerie, wooded valley tucked away in the folds of the Pennine hills where the phantom huntsman and his pack of ghostly black dogs still pursue their timeless chase across the night sky. Many local people have encountered them here, including the local parson and a writer who clearly heard the sound of a hunting horn while walking on the secluded moor earlier this century. It was only later that she was told of the legend of the death hound, a story which today clings strongly to the imagination of those born and brought up in the Old Ways.

Elsewhere in the Peak, Doug Pickford writes of an area of woodland between Dieulacres Abbey and Swythamley where people have experienced a phenomenon known as the Rush, which is 'a weird gust of wind or dispersal of air as invisible forces rush, moving grass, branches and clothing in its wake'.[54] Locally, it was said to be caused by a pack of demon dogs rushing to claim the soul of the abbey's founder, the Earl of Chester, as he lay on his deathbed at Swythamley Hall. Doug writes, 'I personally know of people who say they have felt, seen and heard the Rush, one being knocked to the floor by its ferocity. I have also met a person who is convinced he heard the hounds one cold winter's morn as he walked the field skirting the ancient woodland'.

Belief in the spectral hound of death – sometimes alone and at other times part of a spectral pack led by Odin or Herne – is of very ancient origin. Elsewhere in folk tradition the Wisht Hounds hunted unbaptized souls across the lonely wilds of Dartmoor, while in Yorkshire the spectral pack were known as the Gabriel Hounds or Gabble Ratchets – ominous harbingers of death.

In both the Celtic and other traditions, dogs were able to sense the approach of death and acted as guardians of the threshold and the route taken by the coffin. Ghostly black dogs are ubiquitous throughout the British Isles, guarding the twilight and liminal places – gates, crossroads and bridges – and following time-worn routes along ancient trackways.

It was the long-standing tradition of the ghostly black dog that haunted the moorland tracks of Dartmoor which is said to have inspired Arthur Conan Doyle's classic book *The Hound of the Baskervilles*. One of the earliest accounts of it dates from 1889, just before the opening of the railway between Okehampton

53 From a verse by Sheffield poet John Holland, written in 1861 and quoted in William Henderson, *The Folklore of the Northern Counties* (Folklore Society, 1879)

54 Pickford, *Magic, Myth and Memories*, op. cit.

and Lydford when a coach was carrying passengers across the moor: 'The driver cried out, "There, there, do you see that?" and running alongside the coach, and keeping pace with it without apparent effort, was a large, sinister-looking black hound. "That's the thing that haunts Dartmoor," the driver went on excitedly, and he lashed his horses to a gallop.'[55]

In the Peak District the death hounds are usually only ever heard. The ghastly yelping of the animal precedes death, and tradition tells how the noise would begin at dusk and slowly increase in volume until life finally ebbed away from the sick person. Local author David Bell writes about how belief in the hounds continues to this day, even in the age of TV and computers. He tells how a Peak Forest woman heard the howling of the phantom hound as recently as January 1987, on the night her brother passed away. She sat up with him on his final night and listened as the noise ceased at 2 a.m., the time of his death. 'We both heard it and Arthur knew that his time had come,' she said.[56]

Dogs figure prominently in both Celtic mythology and folk tradition, symbolizing death, hunting and healing. In the ancient Welsh stories the Hounds of Annwn (the underworld) appear, and images of dogs are associated with both the Mother Goddess and Epona, the horse goddess. Archaeologists have found evidence for the worship of a mysterious dog god, Nodens, at a pagan shrine beside the River Severn in Gloucestershire, and there is much evidence of dog sacrifices in pits and wells, perhaps as offerings to the chancy chthonic powers.

Folklorist Ruth Tongue wrote of her own knowledge of dog sacrifices practised by a clan of church sextons in rural Somerset, where she grew up in the 1950s. Tongue was a 'chimes child' – one born after midnight on a Friday and before cockcrow on a Saturday – who had powers to see spirits and heal. She described how, because of her gift, she was freely admitted to the confidence of the sextons and listened to many 'gruesome and frankly heathen rites practised by various members of this far-flung family'.

Prominent in their tradition was the belief that a black dog must always be buried first when a new churchyard was consecrated – 'to keep the Old Un out'. There were always problems when a new cemetery was opened, because no one wanted a member of his or her family to be the first to be buried there, and to become the 'Churchyard Walker'. In order to avoid this taboo, the sexton was often appealed to by local people, behind the back of the parson.

She wrote:

> I knew of a knowledgeable clergyman who expected trouble of this kind on one
> occasion, and was correspondingly pleased to find that the first funeral in the
> new ground went off decorously and smoothly . . . But I also knew that a large
> black dog belonging to a local farmer had mysteriously disappeared shortly
> before the burial. 'He runned back to his whoame out-over,' declared the villagers
> as one man. The sexton had known what to do.[57]

55 Brown, op. cit.

56 Bell, op. cit.

57 Tongue, *Somerset Folklore*, op. cit.

BLACK HORSEMEN

The supernatural world of British folk tradition is filled with a variety of shape-shifting anthropomorphic creatures – black demon dogs, ghostly horses and hybrids between human and animal forms. Such beings often provided a link or gateway to the Otherworld, and a vision of them was seen as a premonition of death. Ancient carvings from Britain often depict supernatural creatures with three or more heads, horns or ram-horned serpents, and from Gaul there are the terrifying carvings of the Taraque of Noves and the Linsdorf monster – half-wolf, half-reptile, devouring humans and clutching heads or skulls in their claws. The frightening half-man, half-sheep-like creature encountered by the family of scholar Anne Ross in association with a pair of mysterious stone heads was perhaps a manifestation of one of these *genii loci* or baleful guardians.

From the viewpoint of the early stories, there were few rigid boundaries between human and animal forms, and the gods and goddesses in that tradition were shape-shifters. This belief was perpetuated in local tales describing supernatural creatures who haunted boundaries between parishes, over water, and between this world and the next. In 1900 Yorkshire historian Edmund Bogg described an evil spirit or 'water kelpie' which haunted a stretch of the Lower Wharfe between Bardsey and East Keswick: 'This water fiend generally presented itself to the belated traveller in the shape of an old, shaggy-haired pony near to some well-known crossing place on the banks of the river, and if the unwary traveller mounted the horse it instantly sprang with a wild shriek of laughter into the deepest whirlpool.'[58] Bogg's description fits that of a creature known in Scotland as a *each uisge* ('water horse') and the late Guy Ragland Phillips believed the Yorkshire dialect term for these creatures was dobbin, which may have used the Celtic *dhu* ('black') as its first element.

Dobbin or dobbie was not just a name applied to the shape-shifting spirit of river crossings, but was also associated with the magical holed stones which can be found at a number of farmhouses across this region. 'Dobbie stones' are just one local variation of luck or charm stones used for magical purposes in Britain and Northern Ireland, and are commonly known as witch stones. They are large natural pebbles with a hole through the centre, by which they are sometimes suspended.

Holed or witch stones are still widely used as house guardians, especially those with a hole formed naturally by the action of running water. The practice of using such stones was first mentioned in 1696 by John Aubrey, in his *Miscellanies*, and presumably dates from long before his time. They come in all sizes, from small pebbles hung in stables or in windows, to large holed pieces of limestone forming part of a garden wall or door decoration.

In the eastern parts of Yorkshire, where they are known as 'witch steans', they continue their guardian function by being attached to door keys or hung behind the door – as one countryman put it, 'to keep the witches out'. Sometimes whole strings of these holed stones were hung in window recesses, such as those discovered at Catterick in North Yorkshire in the nineteenth century by Margaret Gatty, wife of the Vicar of Ecclesfield. When she questioned

58 Bogg, *Lower Wharfedale*, op. cit.

the inhabitant of the house, she was at first met with reticence as to the stones' purpose, but eventually the old woman disclosed that they were there for protective purposes. When asked if she still believed in witches, she replied, 'No! I don't say' at I do, but certainly i' former times there was wizards and them sort o'things. I do believe in the yevil [evil] eye.'[59]

Around Sedbergh in the Yorkshire Dales special stones are used to protect vulnerable places against the dobbie, boggart and other supernatural terrors. Several old houses have their own dobbie stones, and Phillips said that in one snap survey in the eastern part of Settle he found eight houses all with walls decorated with the charm stones cemented into a gate or door. In Brontë land, one property has a dozen built into drystone walls around the farm. The farmer explained they were 'cat-troughs', where milk was put for local cats. But when a local writer pointed out their true function, the old farmer said, 'Well, it don't seem to have done me any harm, lad, an' the cat's aren't complaining, are they?'[60]

Like the archaic carved heads in other parts of Brigantia, some of these stones – often large, water-worn limestone blocks – are known to have been in their present locations for over a century. Phillips, who was familiar with a number of archaic traditions in the Dales region around Settle, where he grew up, was convinced there was 'a surviving dobbie cult' in this upland region. But, as elsewhere, he found secrecy was an inherent part of the tradition too.[61]

Phillips believed this 'dobbie cult' was focused upon a mysterious, but natural, image known as the Black Horse of Bush Howe ('Busha' in local dialect). This 'horse' can sometimes be seen – if the weather and mood are right – on a hillside in a remote valley hidden in the Howgill Fells north of Sedbergh. This chain of rounded mountains lies on the border region between the Yorkshire Dales and the higher, more forbidding peaks of the Lake District. It is another area, like those we have encountered elsewhere in our quest for Britain's Celtic inheritance, where ancient beliefs have survived primarily because of remoteness.

Writing of the Black Horse, Phillips said, 'Clouds and their shadows often fall on these hills. When they lift, they reveal for a moment a strange shape high on the flank of Bush Howe: the dark outline of a huge black stallion that looks like the horses painted by ancient man in French and Spanish caves. It dominates the entire valley.'[62] Despite its apparent prominence, this strange image is at the same time nebulous. Sometimes it is there and at other times it appears to dissolve and change shape, just like the *each uisge* or dobbin of folk tradition. Only this is a huge figure, 130 metres (140 yards) long and 110 metres (120 yards) high – made up entirely of natural shale.

Until recently, the Black Horse was completely unrecorded except in the oral tradition of this close-knit upland region. It is not marked on detailed Ordnance Survey maps and few local guidebooks give it a mention. In his writings, Phillips expresses puzzlement at the attitude of local people, some of whom refused to accept the existence of the figure, even when they were looking directly at it. 'You knew they were not at ease when talking about it,' he wrote.

A local tradition suggests that long ago the children at Sedburgh School would groom or 'clean up' the outlines of the horse once every year, a custom associated with other ancient hill figures, including the White Horse of

59 Phillips, op. cit.

60 Gerald Dodd, *Ghosts of Brontëland* (Bobtail Press, Haworth, 1986)

61 Guy Ragland Phillips, 'The Black Horse of Busha' (*Ley Hunter*, 72, 1976)

62 Guy Ragland Phillips, 'Black Horse of the Howgills' (*Dalesman*, February 1972)

The Black Horse of Bush Howe, a shape-shifting landscape figure on the Howgill Fells, high up in the Pennine hills, said by many to represent a Celtic deity.

Uffington and the virile Cerne Giant in Dorset. Elsewhere we have heard of various attempts to photograph Celtic carvings and artefacts which have ended in failure, often resulting in a belief that some malign influence is at work. Phillips and other local residents are said to have experienced difficulty when they attempted to photograph this strange Black Horse.

Along with various colleagues, we have also encountered similar photographic problems, grappling with light and shadow, when we approach the horse along the ancient track across Long Rigg Beck, which ends at a beck crossing below White Fell, opposite the horse. The constantly moving sunlight and clouds give the observer the impression that the figure, rather than being a horse in the conventional sense, is actually some hybrid creature half horse, half dobbie.

How old is the Black Horse? Local people have in the past suggested a Norse or Roman origin for the image but it is strange they should avoid giving due credit to native inhabitants, who are far more likely to be associated with this natural image. During the so-called Dark Ages, this region remained in the hands of the native British or Welsh kingdom of Rheged, until the defeat of their leader, Urien, at the battle of Catraeth (Catterick) early in the seventh century AD. A few fragments of poetry about the battle is all the evidence we have of this tribe, who inhabited an area stretching from North Wales to Cumbria and Strathclyde. It is interesting that reference is made in one verse to a war leader named Arthur, whose symbol some scholars believe to be a black horse. Other poetry from this time refers to the Three Horses of Britain, of which one was Dhu y Moroedd, or 'the Black One of the Sea', a magical steed which carried seven warriors on an invasion of Anglesey from 'the north'.

Later folk traditions suggest the Black Horse of Busha was used as a landmark for smugglers at Morecambe Bay, 32 kilometres (20 miles) to the east, and it is curious that the 'horse' lies at the head of a large notch in the hills formed by the valley of Long Rigg Beck. In fact, the Black Horse is not the only mysterious hill figure in northern England whose existence has been associated with some long-surviving pagan Celtic cult. Miles to the east, across the high Pennines, a similar tradition in another remote valley suggests the existence of an enormous image of a Celtic harvest god on the slopes of a hillside in Wensleydale, North Yorkshire.

The giant of Penhill seems to be remembered both in the legend of a ogre who once lived on the hill and terrorized the population, and in the strange ritual which takes place in the foothill village of West Witton every year in August. The ritual centres on a grotesque effigy, resembling a Bonfire Night guy, known as 'Owd Bartle' who is paraded through the streets of the village and then destroyed by fire in a special ceremony.[63] Bartle may have originally represented a pagan god associated with the end of the harvest, perhaps a Pennine equivalent of Crom Dubh, 'the Dark Bent One', a harvest god who figures strongly in Irish folk tradition. There are many parallels between Irish deities and those found in Brigantia, suggesting a common religious and cultural milieu dating back to pagan Celtic times.

63 Ian Taylor, 'The Burning of Bartle' (*Northern Earth*, 30, spring 1986); Julia Smith, *Fairs, Feasts and Frolics* (Smith Settle, 1989)

GODS OF MOUNTAIN AND STORM

The Celtic tribes perceived their gods in the landscape itself. Divinity, as we have seen, was manifest in the natural world and place-names often provide evidence of this link. The spirits were everywhere, but especially immanent at certain numinous places, like the sources of streams and rivers, at wells and springs, special trees, fairy mounds and mountains.

High hills, cliffs and rocky escarpments like Alderley Edge were always perceived as forbidding boundaries, places where the curtain between this world and the Otherworld was permanently thin. On the Continent, there is substantial evidence that Celtic peoples worshipped a number of gods connected with high places. In the Pyrenees a number of Romano-Celtic altars were dedicated simply 'to the mountain', while others in simple mountain shrines were decorated with symbols of the sky god – the wheel and the swastika. In Gaul, there were a number of gods associated with different mountains, including the great sanctuary at Le Donon in the Vosges, which was dedicated to the Celtic form of Mercury.[64]

The fearsome Linsdorf monster from Alsace, in Gaul, a powerful Celtic carving of third- or second-century-BC date.

64 Craig Chapman, 'Moons, Saddles and Mountains' (*Northern Earth*, 60, winter 1994); for Celtic mountain deities, see Miranda Green, *A Dictionary of Celtic Myth and Legend* (Thames & Hudson, 1992)

Gods of mountain summits were associated with the weather and storms. In Europe there is some archaeological evidence for a Celtic cult surrounding the god Taranis, 'the Thunderer'. Linked with the Roman Jupiter, he was the equivalent of the sky god Thor, worshipped by the Germanic tribes. Tribal weather gods could also be female, like the Cailleach in the Scottish Highlands. Earlier we learned how in the Highlands the hag or Cailleach was associated with the winter months. When a particularly heavy storm was brewing, the Highlanders of old would say, 'The Cailleach is going to tramp her blankets tonight.'

Many dozens of Scottish mountains had their personal hag as a guardian. Ben Cruachan had the Cailliche nan Cruachan, who lived on the summit and, whenever upset, 'gathers a handful of whirlwinds and descends in a tempest, steps across Loch Etive at a stride, and lashing it into fury, prevents all passage at Connel Ferry'.[65]

Elsewhere in Britain this perception of sanctity clings to many hills and mountains. Brigantia/Bride of the northern tribes was a deity clearly associated with hilltops and high places. Many of these locations – meeting places between the earth and sky gods – were later sanctified by Christians, who often built chapels dedicated to the archangel St Michael on hilltops associated with earlier forms of worship. A classic example is the ruined medieval chapel of St Michael which stands upon the holy hill Glastonbury Tor, a well-known entrance to the Celtic Otherworld in the folk tradition of Somerset. Elsewhere there are hilltop chapels like Brentor in Devon, where the old gods have become associated with the Devil, or Th'Owd Lad in Pennine tradition.

In the western Peak District, there are a number of hilltops which have associations both with pagan and with later Christian worship. The most prominent is the stark medieval church of St Michael and All Angels at Mottram-in-Longdendale, where we began our story. Known as the Cathedral of east Cheshire, the church was built upon a hilltop with long pagan associations. Mottram comes from an Anglo-Saxon word meaning 'meeting place' or crossroads, and official histories suggest the first church built was actually a memorial to the dead from a great battle fought here between warring barons during the twelfth century.

There are indications that the Romans used the hilltop as a signal station, and there have been a number of finds to suggest it was special long before the church was founded. Local stories make the hilltop an entrance to the Otherworld, for there was a tradition about 'St Michael below as well as above the ground'. There was also an association of the hill with witchcraft and body-snatching, and one local resident used the phrase 'God's house? More like the Devil's!' when the church was mentioned. Elsewhere in the High Peak region, the same feeling of magic is attached to a number of hilltops and mountains – Werneth Low, near Mottram, Mouselow in Old Glossop, Shutlingslowe in Cheshire, and the moorland crags of Kinder Scout and Bleaklow.

This feeling or perception still continues today in the twentieth century. Mountains in particular have a special feeling of otherness, and stories of strange experiences connected with them are legion. Tales concerning ghosts, giants and 'presences' stalking mountains in Britain are common. In Wales, the

65 McNeil, op. cit.

Gwynedd mountain of Cader Idris has a very strange reputation. A rock seat on the summit is said to be the residence of the giant who gave his name to the mountain, and folk tradition says that anyone who stays the night there will either find death or madness, or become a genius. Folk-tales also tell how strange lights appear on the summit on the first night after the new year.[66]

Should anyone suggest these tales are merely apocryphal, it is not difficult to find climbers and outdoor people who have experienced firsthand the terror of an encounter with the Otherworld. For instance, I know of one group of experienced climbers and members of a mountain rescue team who had a terrifying night-time encounter with the unknown as they descended a rocky ridge out of eerie Glencoe in the Highlands of Scotland. They were in a party carrying equipment down the King William Ridge, and the narrator admitted they had been a touch foolhardy setting off along the Ridge that day, because they didn't have a chance of getting back before darkness fell.

Consequently, they decided to take a short cut down the ridge, using ropes to descend one at a time. The first member of the party went down and was supposed to tug the rope when he reached the ledge. But minutes passed and no tug came – the man had just disappeared into the darkness. A second member went down on another rope and the same thing happened. Soon afterwards, the others followed a route down to investigate what had happened, and upon reaching the ledge found the two men comforting each other in a state of terror. One was stammering, 'It was right bloody next to me. I could have touched him.'

'It turned out, the first one stepped off ridge and saw this great shadowy figure standing next to him,' said a colleague of the climbers. 'It disappeared and he was so upset he just sat there in a huddle. The others just couldn't get any sense out of him. He was absolutely and totally in a state of shock. The man who told this story was a very sensible down-to-earth type, and he said anyone who has spent time in the mountains can tell you tales like this.'[67]

Giants, of course, play a prominent part in Celtic mythology, and were originally weather gods or deities of mountain ranges, hills and skies. They seem to reappear later, after Christianization, in folk-tales and legends. A giant phantom known as 'the falm' is said to haunt a mountain pass in Glen Aven in southern Banffshire, Scotland. Poet James Hogg wrote of him, 'He appears to be no native of this world, but an occasional visitant, whose attentions are evil and dangerous. He is only seen about the break of day, and on the highest verge of the mountain . . . and if any living creature cross the track over which he has passed before the sun shine on it, certain death is the consequence.'[68]

By far the greatest number of these stories of spirits or *genii loci* are associated with the Scottish mountains. The most famous is the mysterious spectre known in the Gaelic as *Am Fear Liath Mhor*, in English, the Big Grey Man. The name is an apt description of the presence which haunts Ben McDhui, the highest mountain in the Cairngorms, with its desolate summit rising to 1,322 metres (4,296 feet). Although it seems that contemporary accounts of this strange phenomenon go back only to the end of the nineteenth century, the mountains were very rarely visited and written about before this time. Marc Alexander, in his account of the haunted mountain, makes the point

66 See Janet and Colin Bord, *The Secret Country* (Paul Elek, 1976)

67 Notes from conversation with friend of eyewitness, 1995

68 Spence, op. cit.

that mountaineering is actually quite a new sport and even the famous Matterhorn was not scaled until 1865.[69]

The 'Ben McDhui Ghost' was first described by a professor of organic chemistry, Norman Collie, in a talk to the Cairngorm Club during 1925. He told how, over 30 years earlier, he had been returning from the cairn on the desolate summit of the mountain in a mist when he began to hear crunching footsteps, seemingly three or four times the length of his own. As he tried to make sense of the phenomenon in a logical fashion, he was suddenly 'seized with terror' and rushed blindly through the boulder field into the Rothiemurchus Forest, stopping only when he realized the mysterious footsteps were no longer following him.[70]

His tale was supported by Henry Kellas, the brother of a famous mountaineer, Dr A. M. Kellas, who died on an expedition to Mount Everest in the 1920s. Kellas described how the two men, on a geological trip to the mountain, were together on the slope of a hill late in the afternoon when 'suddenly they became aware of a giant figure coming down towards them from the cairn', which was shrouded in mist. They watched in amazement as the figure passed out of sight behind a dip on a slope, and soon they too were gripped with the same kind of fear which possessed Professor Collie. Fearing the figure was following them, the two tore away in the direction of Corrie Etchachan to escape it. Afterwards, the Kellas brothers refused to believe the figure was the product of an optical illusion, and it was said of Henry, 'No one who knew him or heard him relate his story could doubt his complete faith in his experience.'[71]

These stories, published in 1925, brought forth a flood of accounts from other outdoor and local people who had experienced inexplicable phenomena, not just on the summit of the mountain but in surrounding regions, including the high Lairig Ghru Pass and Rothiemurchus Forest. Although a few of the accounts do indeed describe a giant grey figure, the majority involve psychic phenomena and eerie feelings of an intangible 'presence' on the deserted mountain.

This was the case in the experiences of Richard Frere, an author and mountaineer with over a decade's experience of climbing in the Cairngorms. One of Frere's walking friends, Peter Densham, described how once the two held a conversation with some invisible being during an expedition to find a lost aircraft on the slopes of Ben MacDhuie. Densham was sat beside the cairn upon the summit of the mountain when he heard Frere apparently talking to himself on the other side, and when he walked around the stones he found himself joining in with the conversation: 'It seemed we had carried on with this conversation for some little time when we suddenly realized there was no one there but ourselves [but] afterwards neither of us, strangely, could recall the purport of this extraordinary conversation.'[72]

On another occasion while walking in the Lairig Ghru Pass, Frere had another uncanny experience. It began with a feeling that he was not alone and then a feeling of 'presence . . . utterly abstract but intensely real' and a high, almost inaudible note or whine almost like ethereal music, which, 'it seemed, was coming from the very soil of the mountains'.

69 Ibid.; Marc Alexander, *Phantom Britain* (Frederick Muller, 1975) op. cit.; Peter Underwood, *This Haunted Isle* (Javelin, 1986)

70 Alexander, op. cit.

71 Underwood, ibid.

72 Alexander, op. cit.

Then there is the story told by the well-known Scottish Nationalist Wendy Wood, in her book *The Secret of the Spey*, concerning 'an attack of panic' she experienced while walking in the same high pass. This took the form of a loud voice shouting in Gaelic, the noise echoing around her feet. Thinking at first someone was lost or buried in the snow, she desperately searched for them, but without success. Suddenly gripped by the same fear experienced by others in the area, she stumbled desperately down the pass, feeling that some kind of huge and invisible presence was following her, taking giant footsteps. Her account ended: 'Are such things the concretion of the imaginings of the race, clinging to a particular place, discernible only to those whose racial sensitiveness is open to receive the primal impression and fears of a bygone day? Or is the day not bygone?'[73]

Spirits of place, or *genii loci*, were a fundamental feature of the Celtic perception of the supernatural and their legacy has become one of the strongest features of the surviving traditions in many parts of the British Isles. The nature spirits of rivers, trees, hills and mountains have survived the passing generations in the form of fairies, hobgoblins and other supernatural creatures who populate the rich folklore of Britain. In the Highlands, the Cailleach or Blue Hag of Winter is the protector of herds on mountains, a function also associated with Biddy or Bride in the Pennines. In the Cheviots, the Brown Man of the Moors was seen as the guardian of all the wild game in his territory, which covered the Elsdon Moors in County Durham.

Traditions of elementals and nature spirits have evolved and often became enshrined in literature, a tradition established in the sixteenth century by Shakespeare, who makes reference to magic, moonlight and fairies throughout *A Midsummer Night's Dream*. Even Emily Brontë's character Heathcliff, in the *Wuthering Heights*, has been interpreted by some from clues within the text as actually being the personification of the 'spirit' of the beautiful Haworth Moors in West Yorkshire, where the novel is set.[74]

The Brontë children are said to have found the inspiration for many of their stories as they sat upon a large boulder at the base of waterfalls near the village on the footpath up to Top Withens, a ruined farmhouse. The ghost of a young woman, head bowed, has been seen trudging along this old packhorse track for many centuries, and recently it has become accepted as the ghost of Emily Brontë herself. But it is more probable that the female spirit of the moors provided the inspiration for the ghost of Cathy, who in the novel wanders over the purple heather calling her lover Heathcliff, whom she finally joins in spirit.[75]

This male/female mapping of features of the natural world occurs frequently in the Celtic tradition and is especially strong in the wild, remote moorland and mountains of northern England. In lore and legend, the god appears as a giant or under a multitude of local names, from Odin, Herne the Hunter and Robin Hood to innumerable hobs and boggarts, while the goddess has become Brigid or Bride, Helen or Joan. Their life and death are often used to explain the presence, shape or form of landscape features, most commonly large stone boulders, standing stones and the source of springs and rivers.

At the gateway to the Saddleworth Moors, on the Pennine foothills in Lancashire, the legend of two giants and a water goddess is still remembered.

73 Peter Underwood, *A Gazeteer of Scottish Ghosts* (Fontana/Collins, 1973)

74 Mike Haigh, '*Genius loci*', text from Calderdale Earth Mysteries pamphlet, n.d.; see also Kenneth Muir, 'Folklore and Shakespeare' (*Folklore*, vol. 92, 1981)

75 Dodd, ibid.

Towering on either side of the valley watered by the Chew Brook are the twin rocky heights known as Alderman Hill and Alphin Pike. Folk tradition tells how two giants once lived happily on these mountains, until they quarrelled over the heart of a water nympth, Rimmon, who lived beside the sparkling waters of the Chew below. Alphin won the favours of the nymph and, in a fit of rage, his rival flung huge boulders across the valley. This sparked a seven-day battle which left Alphin mortally wounded, but as Alder was about to take his spoils, the heartbroken nymph drowned herself in a deep pool and was buried with her lover beneath the peak which bears his name. The goddess may still be seen as 'the brook rider', a wild white horse which gallops down the stream from the hills at certain times of the year.[76]

Writer and broadcaster Mike Harding was struck by the similarity of this story to one he had heard while climbing in the remote Dingle peninsula, on the west coast of Ireland's County Kerry. Here the same tale was told of a tumulus and a loch which are named after a god and goddess who perished in a similar manner. A broadly similar story is connected with three other Pennine valleys, with the motif of a mountain giant turned to stone following an abortive attempt to mate with the female spirit of the waters. Comparing the two folk-tales, Harding writes, 'Go back in time and the common heritage of these two tales in Celtic mythology is obvious, and I think it's nice that a version of the legend should have remained up here in this, at one time, remote Pennine valley.'[77]

TH'OWD LAD

A doctor was called out one dark night to visit a patient living on a farm high on the rugged moors of the High Peak. On his way home he felt that he was being followed; turning his head, he saw a tall dark figure dressed entirely in black – the Devil, or Th'Owd Lad himself. The doctor put his horse to the gallop, remembering that he had to cross a stream of clear running water, which he knew evil spirits were unable to abide. The Devil, however, reached the stream almost as soon as the doctor and, by stretching out his hand, just managed to grasp the horse's tail, which withered at his touch. The doctor and his horse, with the exception of the tail, passed over the water in safety.

Thereafter, so the story goes, a stretch of the paved Roman road across Bleaklow became known as Doctor's Gate and the deep groove of earth further north became the Devil's Dyke, scratched from the earth in fury by the horned one.[78]

This version of the traditional Tam O'Shanter is just one of a rich tapestry of stories and legends associated with the haunted Peakland mountain of Bleaklow – a dark, high desert covered by a thick layer of peat and heather. At its bleak 634-metre (2,060-foot) summit Bleaklow is known as England's only true desert; empty, chilling, harsh and hostile, it is a place where the weather and elements are still very much in control and where man is vulnerable. The only breaks in

76 *The Saddleworth Story* (Manchester, 1964); see also *Notes and Queries* (4th series IV, 1869); oral tradition, collected 1993

77 Mike Harding, *Walking the Peak and Pennines* (Michael Joseph, 1992)

78 Rose, op. cit.; see also Bellamy, op. cit.

The scowling, ram-horned head of a Celtic warrior god, from Netherby Roman fort in Cumbria. It has been described as one of the most expressive pieces of Celtic sculpture found in Britain.

the acres of loneliness are occasional walkers on the Pennine Way and the sheep, mountain hares, curlew and grouse that live there. Despite the desolation, an elemental presence has made its home on these moors for as long as the memory of man can stretch.

Strange happenings have become associated with this mysterious mountain for many centuries – tales about dark, malevolent figures, strange burning lights and the ghosts of Roman soldiers tramping the old route from Brough to Melandra. The story associated with the naming of the Devil's Dyke is just one of many traditions associating landmarks with the *genius loci* of the moors. Elsewhere there is Devil's Bridge and also the Devil's Elbow, a sharp hairpin bend in the minor road from Old Glossop to Woodhead which runs along the flanks of the mountain.

In local tradition the Devil's Elbow, a boundary between the inhabited valley and the moor, was a frightening place haunted by burning lights and Th'Owd Lad, or Dark Lad – the Horned One. It was here, one night during the 1950s, that a veteran railwayman, John Davies, had a bizarre encounter as the full moon lit up the moors. Mr Davies, in his eighties when he shared his memories with us, has lived in an old cottage in this part of Longdendale all his life. On the night in question he was riding a motorbike home to Woodhead when something 'told' him to stop, he said, and as he pulled up he saw an object like 'a huge black slug sliding across t'road and up t'moor'.

He went on, 'as it came slowly across the road in front of me, I could see it was completely black and really peculiar, like a whale. It had a head like a whale and a white eye, with a black pupil going round and round. It disappeared and I got off and had a look but it had gone. I've been over there thousands of times but never seen anything like it before.'[79]

He is not alone in sensing a baleful presence at the Devil's Elbow. Another local man, returning home from Manchester late at night, felt something huge and black was following behind him, hauling itself along the path up the moor.

79 Oral tradition, collected 1992; see also ibid.

Mr Davies knows of the weird reputation of the area. 'I've heard many stories about ghosts of Roman soldiers being seen on the moors too,' he admitted. 'They are supposed to appear on the night of the first full moon in spring. I'd believe anything about this valley. It's a weird place at night.'

From the Devil's Elbow, Ogden Clough leads vertically upwards into Torside Clough and the high moors, towards the rocky heights of Shining Clough, where an oddly shaped mound known as Torside Castle is encountered. Archaeologists are divided as to whether the castle is a prehistoric burial mound or purely a natural hillock. In fact, Bleaklow may actually take its name from the mound, for the word low or *hlaw* in Old English refers to a barrow, and bleak/black can also mean 'shining' or 'burning', hence 'shining barrow'.

Whatever the explanation, the moors around Torside Castle are the haunt of sinister moving lights, known locally as the Devil's Bonfires. These unexplained phenomena were a well-known mystery to Longdendale folk earlier this century, but were accepted as just another aspect of the 'otherness' of the valley. This was long before the 1970s, when staff at the new Youth Hostel built in the valley bottom first reported seeing what they thought were searchlight beams on the rocky crags on the remote western face of Bleaklow above Shining Clough and Bramah Edge. Other reports described a string of moving lights which have been mistaken for the torches of walkers lost on the moors. So persistent and convincing have these reports become that the local Mountain Rescue Team have turned out from their Glossop base to search for people stranded on the desolate moors, only to find the elusive Devil's Bonfires fade from sight as they approach.[80]

On one occasion Barbara Drabble, a trainee teacher, was driving home past the Youth Hostel late at night when she saw what she described as 'a brilliant blue light' lighting up 'all the bottom half of the mountain, all the railway, the reservoirs and about a two-mile stretch of the road'. The eerie light, which lasted several minutes, was not like daylight, she said, but 'brighter, clearer and harsher', and as she drove into it she felt very cold and the hair on the back of her neck was standing on end.

The next day local farmers shuffled uncomfortably when they were asked about what had happened the night before. But two years later, after dozens of people at the hostel spotted the brilliant light on the mountain, leading a rescue team to search the moor in vain, local people reluctantly admitted they were familiar with 'the lights'. 'One of them said they had known it freeze young lambs when it came early in the year,' explained Mrs Drabble. 'Also someone said it had been coming for generations but never so close together as two years and usually about 30 or even 50 years in between. They were still reluctant to discuss it.'[81]

The baffling lights of Longdendale are not the only supernatural horror to make its home in this strange valley. All the moors on the northwest face of Bleaklow are alarming, frightening places in local tradition where one could quite easily meet the Dark Lad or Horned One himself. Another informant, a former resident of the area, explained, 'When I was young, supernatural things were always referred to obliquely, an offside sort of thing, a cross of the fingers;

80 See David Clarke, *Ghosts and Legends of the Peak District* (Jarrold, 1991); 'The Ghostly Legions of the Moors' (*Manchester Evening News*, 31 March 1979); 'The Phantom Light of Bleaklow Moor' (*Sheffield Morning Telegraph*, 27 April 1972)

81 Barbara Drabble, 'Bedtime Story' (*Peak Park News*, spring 1972); letter dated 5 April 1988

T'Owd Lad was a common name, the figure you would come across on the moors. The Dark Lad was another name particularly connected with the moors, the Dark Lad or T'Owd Lad and T'Owd Woman, the same thing.' As was common elsewhere, using the name of the pagan deities directly was taboo. 'People did not want to refer to them directly, so there was always a funny finger-crossing when you did so, sort of crossing your first and second fingers and arcing our thumbs.'[82]

People continue to experience the unknown in Longdendale. New stories and lore have surfaced since the Second World War, when the summit of Bleaklow became the graveyard for a number of ill-fated bomber crews who failed to negotiate the last stretch of their missions and reach airfields on the other side of the hills. John Davies has told of a strange presence which seemed to accompany a fragment taken from one wreck, which was duly returned to the moor and buried with reverence. As in prehistoric times, disrespect for the dead or the disturbance of something offered to the *genius loci* was sure to bring unpleasant consequences.

Despite the arrival of man and his technology, Longdendale's brooding mountains continue to harbour their secrets. The following story was provided by a valued informant whose memories of the valley's past have been explored elsewhere in these pages. This encounter with the Otherworld of the moor deserves reproduction in full; here is the story in his own words:

As kids, the wrecked aircraft on the Bleaklow moors were a great magnet to us. We were all ardent souvenir hunters. I started going up there to these wrecks, with my friends, from about the age of 11. In the autumn half-term holiday, either of 1960 or 1961 – I can't remember which – I arranged with a friend to go up to the wreck of the B29 'Overexposed' that lies just beyond High Shelf Stones.

We had not been so far before, but were to have a guide, a lad who'd already been there. The B29 is the largest and most complete wreck, so it was a prime bag – and since it seemed quite a long way up there – to children – going up there was another rite of passage.

In the event, the guide did not show up on the day, but he had given us a crude sketch map, which proved adequate. We had no OS map. It was a bright, clear day, with an early frost, but pleasantly warm as the day wore on. We did not set off particularly early, but making our way by Doctor's Gate and then up Ashton Clough (taking in the wrecked C47 that lies in that clough), we eventually got up to Higher Shelf Stones some time after one and quickly located the B29 – with much rejoicing. A picnic, perched on one of the bomber's wheels, was then followed by a leisurely inspection of the wreck site.

The wreck is fairly compact, but scattered over several peat groughs. Consequently, as we got engrossed in looking for identifiable bits as souvenirs, we wandered apart and out of sight of one another. Standing in the bottom of a grough, the hags rose higher than our heads – and we were eyes to the ground. However, we kept in touch by desultory calling, and occasionally popping up to see where the other was. I was lost to the world, when I heard my companion cry out in alarm. I looked up. I couldn't see him. I heard him cry again – 'Bloody hell, look!' Real fear!

I scrambled on top of the peat. I saw him a few yards away. He was shouting again – "Bloody hell, what is it!" – and pointing away across the moor towards that awful

82 Oral tradition, collected 1993

wild, lonely depression and swamp called Grains in the Water, at the head of Hern Clough. And I looked and I saw, all in one instant, grouse exploding out of the heather towards us, sheep and hares stampeding towards us and behind them, rolling at a rapid rate towards us from the direction of Hern Clough, a low bank of cloud or fog. It was how high? Thirty feet maybe – certainly higher than a house. That and the fleeing fauna would have been frightening enough. But what was truly terrifying was that, in the leading edge of the cloud bank – in it, but leading it and striding purposefully towards us, was a huge shadow-figure, a man-like silhouette, but far bigger than a man – as high as the cloudbank, as high as a house. And the terror that hit me and was driving the birds and the animals and my friends was utterly overwhelming – like a physical blow – and I have never felt the like since!

We fled. We plunged over the crags above Gathering Hill – and every time I go back and look at those crags, I wonder we didn't break our necks. We fled in mindless terror down that mountainside towards the Shelf Brook and Doctor's Gate – and all the sheep and wildlife that could run or fly went careering down with us in utter panic. And then, about half-way down, we seemed to run out into sunlight – and it was all over! All the panic gone. The sheep stopped, put their heads down, and started to gaze. Everything returned at once to normal. But back up there, on Higher Shelf Stones, wisps of mist were still coiling around.

'I've left me bloody flask and snap tin up there,' says my friend.

'Do you fancy going back for it?' says I.

'Do I buggery! I'll tell me mum I dropped the flask and broke it, and the tin won't matter.'

'What d'you think it were?'

'I dunno. Th'Owd Lad, I reckon. If he'd caught us we'd ha' been done for, I know that.'

So I still believe. I've been back there often. I've been on my own. In Mountain Rescue practice I've been out at night – on Bleaklow Head, at the Wain Stones, at Torside Castle. I can't say I've not been uneasy – but I've never since seen or felt anything untoward. I've even taken my own kids up there. But what I saw then has left a very deep impression – and when I read or hear similar stories in Scotland, in Switzerland, and Nepal and Bhutan, both of which I have visited, I think, 'Yes, I've seen Th'Owd lad too, and I know exactly what it's like.'

Don't ask me to rationalize. Or rationalize it away *– which is what it really amounts to. I've come to the conclusion that that sort of thing amounts to no more than a cop-out, a late twentieth-century defensive mechanism – it's safe if it can be explained. As if 'explaining away' were like defusing a bomb. I do think that every now and then, some of us – maybe all of us – stumble into an encounter with elements deeper and older than we are, and they are not, by their nature, benevolent, though they may be. This certainly wasn't.[83]*

83 Pers. comm. from eyewitness, 1994

CONCLUSION

'You never enjoy the world aright 'til the sea
itself floweth in your veins and you are clothed
with the heavens and crowned with the stars . . .'

Douglas Traherne Harding, Mike Heron, 1968

CELTIC TWILIGHT?

The Hopi Indians were and still are one of the most spiritual peoples on the earth. Their way of life inextricably binds together work, art, religion and the act of living itself. This indivisibility of life also lies at the root of all the traditions recorded in this book and the Hopi give a regrettable but highly suitable example with which to illustrate the twilight nature of belief in the forces we are dealing with.

High above the village of Shungopavi in Arizona, the Hopi tribe once kept four wooden figures or *taalawtumsi*, centuries-old cottonwood root carvings, which were treated as living deities. The figures were three simple representations of the Corn Maiden goddess, her husband and their daughter, central to the Hopi belief system and key elements in their initiation rites. They were specific to a small group of people and of no instrinsic worth in themselves other than for what they represented to those who believed in them. Most of all they were sacred – kept in an isolated location for a particular purpose.

This ancient sanctity was violated one evening in 1978 when two Indian artefact collectors, Jimmy Hinton and Charles Morris, stumbled upon the carvings during a search for ancient Indian pottery relics. Their greed got the better of them and they stole the figures with the intention of selling them to the highest bidder. Initially the pair were unable to sell them to any artefact

Three was a powerful number in Celtic belief and tradition. A number of carvings from Celtic Britain depict three mother goddesses. There are also carvings of three hooded spirits, known as the *genii cucullati*, who seem to be connected with a fertility cult. This carving from a shrine at Housesteads Roman fort, Northumberland, dates from the third century AD.

dealers or tribal art gallery, because they were so sacred that little was known about them outside the Hopi nation itself. Perhaps significantly, during this time the thieves were plagued by misfortunes which almost cost them their lives. Morris suffered near fatal injuries in a car accident, while Hinton developed kidney, liver and gall-bladder failure. When a Chicago gallery owner finally alerted them to the ritual significance of the objects, they drew their own conclusions: they had been cursed!

In blind panic, they quickly sold the artefacts to a collector by the name of Pyle, who, seized by an irrational obsession that he was being trailed by the FBI, destroyed them shortly after he had purchased them from Hinton and Morris. Over the next two years the litany of misfortune continued, with Morris being jailed for an unconnected artefact theft and Hinton too serving time in the state penitentiary.

Following his release from prison in 1981, Hinton foolishly returned to Hopi land at night with friends to once again see if he could make his fortune. The group became separated in the pitch darkness and in Hinton's own words, 'I saw lights and heard all kinds of strange sounds. I was a blubbering idiot by the next morning. When we found each other we discovered we all had the same experience.'

In an effort to find redemption from his actions, he gave himself up to the FBI, who, in an unprecedented decision, told Hinton that he would be immune from all prosecution if he told his story to the Hopi people in Shungovapi, so they could 'achieve spiritual reconciliation', which he did in March 1991. Despite this many Hopi elders still refused to believe that the *taalawtumsi* had actually been destroyed, saying they would still speak to those who longed for their return. Hinton is equally certain of their continuing power and remains haunted by his experiences, unable to free his mind from the pervasive influence of tampering with a tradition several millennia old. He told reporters, 'I fall asleep and at 2 a.m. I hear little wind chimes. Kachinas [Hopi masked gods] appear in my dreams. The *taalawtumsi*, are out there, somewhere.'[1]

The gods *are* out there still in the consciousness of the Hopi, who can come to terms with their power, as well as in the mind of outsiders like Hinton, who clearly cannot. This cautionary tale has many similarities with stories in this book which tell of the retribution visited on people who interfere with sacred shrines or remove ritual objects, like the archaeologist who 'borrowed' a stone from the shrine of the Cailleach in Glen Lyon, Scotland. It also shows the depth of belief and power which people involved in nature-based religion attribute to physical representations of their tradition. It is as though strongly held beliefs can in some way imbue the inanimate with genuine power, that power which believers confer upon their gods and goddesses, their sacred sites and artefacts. And above all else, it sadly demonstrates the lack of respect with which these beliefs and traditions are regarded today in a rapidly changing world; it seems that not only the Celtic gods are in a twilight state.

Of course, it will be easy for some people to dismiss out of hand the central theme of this book: that an oral tradition of which some elements may be as much as 4,000 years old has been kept alive and survives in remote, and some not so remote, areas of the British Isles. From the evidence we have collected, it

1 'Stealing the Hopi Soul' (*Fortean Times*, 76, August–September 1994, quoting *Arizona Republic*, 14 March 1993)

appears that this body of tradition has always been held among families and communities in certain parts of these islands.

It is easy to become jaded and suspicious of such claims in an age when books are published almost weekly by self-styled witches and pagans, all claiming to be part of some ancient tradition and all with an important message for the future. Unfortunately, many of the New Age writings are based upon modern misinterpretations of older works, some of which were products of earlier revivals themselves. Few, if any, have carried out any new research among the living traditions, which is actually not a difficult task. It would have been equally easy for us to perform a similar trick with texts and ideas, to dress this research up with a veneer of fashionable jargon. But instead we have chosen, as folklorists first and foremost, to trace old stories and legends from their origins through to the present day, and as a result have found the past still echoing in the living practices of many ordinary people we have met across the length and breath of the remoter parts of the British Isles.

These contemporary practitioners of the old ways all seem to be putting forward a similar idea and basic underlying tradition, much of which is already known, but their stories contain much material and practice hitherto unknown. This tradition does not have a recognized name and most of the people who have spoken of it are unconnected geographically and socially – even though two informants are distant relatives! So either they are all lying, or engaged in some fantastic confabulation for some unspecified and unfathomable purpose, or it is reasonably safe to assume that genuine ancient traditions, some originating from pre-Christian times, have indeed been handed down and are still alive, albeit with fewer and fewer adherents and locations.

It may also be asked why the information provided by our contemporary informants has come to light only recently, and why it was until recently known to just a few. The simple answer is that it has never been a secret in the true sense of the word. These things have always been open to anyone who wished to know of them, but they have never and are still not just there for show, nor has it ever become necessary to make outsiders aware of them – until now. Timewise, it is only in recent years that there has been any real public interest in Celtic traditions in England itself, and regardless of the modern interest, portions of the tradition have always been around in the vernacular writings and folk and oral tradition of many regions. Our informants have never tried to 'hide' their knowledge, although they have been and are still rightly suspicious of the motivations of those who come and ask questions, fearing delicate and sensitive information might be used wrongly.

As one informant from Derbyshire writes, 'I am against private things ending up as entertainment for know-nothings or being distorted out of all recognition by sensation-seekers. I would prefer to vanish than to end up as such a distortion. It is like the old story of the woman who wanted to repair the damage done by a lie. She was told to take a sack of feathers to the top of the church tower and empty it, then collect the feathers. She said it was impossible. I feel the same. I have been taught that words, once released, cannot be recaptured and that anyone can use them in any distorted form and still attribute them as if truth.'[2]

2 Pers. comm., 1994

This illustrates the dilemma now faced by those who still keep alive the dying embers of the old traditions. Families are becoming smaller and more fragmented; there is less to keep people together in small communities; the two world wars have contributed to the loss of knowledge; children in particular now have so many other distractions to occupy them; and the highly mobile, post-industrial society in which we live today conspires both to take people away from their traditional homes and to bring new people in. Human continuity, which has survived and absorbed centuries of invasion and occupation, is now being eroded at a tremendous rate. These factors, together with the problem that the sort of knowledge we have been recording is so difficult to preserve in its original context, have led to the Old Ways becoming diluted, so they are now in danger of being lost altogether.

It naturally follows that if the people who have specific traditional knowledge – literally, the guardians – do not in some way record or reveal it to outsiders and therefore by default keep it secret, then by the end of this millennium all their tradition and knowledge will have died completely. Either that or it will have become so contaminated that it remains at best just a distinct echo of what it once meant to the people involved. Many of our informants are pessimistic about the future of their traditions, believing they will pass away at the end of this generation. 'Certainly none of us found a way of handing them on as a living tradition as opposed to historical curiosities,' writes one.

One of our central characters, a guardian of the Longdendale tradition, when asked what she believes the future holds, replied, 'I don't know what the future will be, but I presume it will either die out or die down. It will do one or the other. When you get into a situation where a community that has been relatively enclosed, where you have had relatively the same basic stock of people, then all of a sudden you are built up everywhere, and you have masses of people coming in, there isn't any way any community can deal with that and survive.'[3]

In this twilight phase, there are also now a great many people striving to rediscover the Old Ways and traditions and preserve them for future generations. Unfortunately, they often go about it the wrong way, taking their information purely from books which themselves are often fifth-generation copies of earlier works. Few of today's urban pagans have any real practical experience of the countryside and elements they claim to empathize with. It is little wonder then that those who have inherited the old traditions are sceptical of the New Age publishing explosion of the last 30 years. Now anyone can go out and buy a book which will show them 'how to be' a Celtic shaman, a witch or any other adept supposedly at one with the universe, and the enthusiast can go further by joining any number of New Age or pagan groups, all of whom declare commitment to the planet, usually from the warmth of a London flat. To our way of thinking, these modern revivals are largely anachronistic and élitist, harking back to the myth of 'better' past, and to that end are dangerous because they tend to ignore the fact that we are living at the end of one of the most tumultuous and portentous centuries in recorded history. Personal responsibility for oneself and the environment is frequently dressed up with ritualistic trappings which are soon discarded in favour of the next fad.

3 *Chronicle*, op. cit.

The bald facts are that we live and have our being in three dimensions and unrepeatable time. We can't go backwards and nor should we wish to; and go back to what exactly? There never was a 'golden age' as some would have us believe, and in general every era of human existence has been riddled with problems besetting every person, community and the environment. Nor do the ideas expressed in this book seem to be promoting some notion of a great all-embracing Mother Goddess whose only interest is peace, love and understanding – admirable as those ideals may be. The powers of the gods are equally at home with all aspects of life and death, because they *are* life and death. Whether it be at the birth of a child or the moment a pole cat rips a thrush's newly hatched chicks to pieces, the power of the gods is everywhere. Too many so-called pagan and witchcraft groups forget the awesome forces – the gods themselves – which move and animate the natural world, and wish to bend them to their own desires rather than coming to terms with them as they *are*.

Anyone interested in such matters should take the time to study what lies at the bottom of the material we have reviewed in this book and see how it can be applied to the present. We need to address and act upon exactly what lies behind the many strands of genuine belief and tradition found in the British Isles which we have tried to draw together in these pages. At its root, and put simply, this seems to suggest that there is one universal creative power which flows through everything and of which people have been aware throughout time, under many different names, and which has been venerated and personified as being a manifestation of the universe and everything in it – the stars, planets, weather, seasons, landscapes, cycles of life and death, through to the vagaries and moods of man.

These forces were perceived as being the gods, Celtic or otherwise, each manifestations of one all-creating power. As author Ursula Le Guin put it in her book *The Wizard of Earthsea*:

> 'It is no secret. All power is one in source and end. Years and distances, stars and candles, water and wizardry, the craft in a man's hand and the wisdom in a tree's root; they all rise together, My name and yours and the true name of the sun, or a spring of water or an unborn child, all are syllables of the great word that is very slowly spoken by the shining of the stars. There is no other power, no other name.'[4]

This should be explanatory enough, but for those who still think that any belief of this kind must involve the actual worship or veneration of inanimate objects like rocks or trees, a pagan philosopher, the late Guy Ragland Phillips, puts the record straight. Speaking of early man, he writes, 'It is not that he would have made a sky god into a universal spirit; it is that he would have apprehended a universal spirit of which one magnificent aspect was the sky.'[5] And therefore all other phenomenal manifestations can be seen as inextricably linked together. They could all be experienced firsthand or expressed in story, art or ritual. Experience, not rationalization, was and is the key to understanding these matters. This view of the world is better known as pantheism, the doctrine whereby the land, earth or universe itself is seen as god, goddess, or whatever other names are chosen. And this is the view which seems to come through all

4 Ursula Le Guin, *The Wizard of Earthsea* (Penguin Books, 1971)

5 Phillips, *The Unpolluted God*, op. cit.

the voices in this book in one way or another. It is also why our informants have so much difficulty or reluctance expressing what they really believe, as to express it simply and openly can often make it appear strange or credulous. In the words of one, 'I don't think that any medium but the poetic will do.'

The other main advantage this way of seeing the universe provides is that it needs no mediator in the form of a priesthood or hierarchy of any kind. And indeed the nearest we have come to this formalization are the people who act as stewards or guardians of knowledge or sites within the landscape. It doesn't depend upon what books you have read, what coven or New Age group you belong to, or any necessity for crystals, robes or other accessories. This knowledge is accessible to everyone on a one-to-one basis, but it has to be treated carefully and respectfully, for what else can be done with a power that moulds the very people who are aware of it? This is certainly not intended to be a 'how to' book, but we feel it right to point out that the living traditions of those who appear here can at least point us in the right direction, but this is always one step removed from the real thing. Books can take you only so far. We need to reinvent or rather reperceive the old gods if they are to have any relevance whatsoever for a new generation.

The key to this new way of seeing is perception. Remember how our informant in the Yorkshire Dales was taken out by his family members to experience at firsthand the mysteries of nature and the changing seasons. This and all other seasonal practices and customs, like rituals and so forth, are in fact part of the act of dreaming with the land, a way of accessing an alternate perception of the landscape. Then, with the right attitude and approach, it becomes possible for anyone to access the Otherworld. To digress a little, we can speculate, as archaeologists, ethnologists, poets and writers like Alan Garner have done and are doing, that such practices go back even further than the Stone Age to a time when the landscape was seen as a 'field effect', an Aboriginal dreamtime, rather than locations linked by paths and roads.

All this leads us to conclude that while it may be the twilight of the Celtic gods for those people with the ability to learn and change their view of the world and reality, there is at least the possibility of there being a dawn and a new perception of the earth and the powers which flow through it. Musician and storyteller Robin Williamson describes in his unpublished autobiography how he took inspiration from the power of the natural world by, among other techniques, 'drumming upon a hollow log 'til the tide returned against the small shores of the island, singing what the wind sung, horse music to gull music in the language of the earth', and of how he would 'stare at rocks besieged by blinding whiteness of the surf, gaze on until they became the letters of the alphabet and read'.[6] Here Williamson is describing a basic shamanistic trance state which enabled him to see directly into the phenomenal world and return with material which inspired his creative mind. The many ways of accessing this creative power are undeniable and readily unearthed by those with the urge to look for them, and from this personal experience of what lies behind the curtain can be had great knowledge, inspiration and illumination.

Numerous accounts in this book have dealt with events which are at odds with the accepted, rational way of looking at the world, events which can be

6 Robin Williamson, 'Mirrorman Sequences' (chapter from unpublished autobiography printed in *Outlaw Vision* magazine, n.d.)

described only as 'supernatural'. One key question then is whether or not this universal power of which we have spoken is capable of making such events happen. Think back to the many instances in this book of 'strange' phenomena affecting people at certain times of the year, at certain places in the landscape or when certain objects invested with belief are moved from their intended place – like the skulls or standing stones, or the simple sandalwood carvings from the Hopi village. If we accept even a proportion of these events as genuine occurrences – and we believe there is little alternative – then we must accept that strange phenomena are not only possible but indeed probable.

If it is true that the earth is a living organism of some kind and, what is more, one with which we can interact via our own consciousness, as proposed by the Gaia theory and hinted at by tradition and the informants throughout this book, then the impossible becomes possible and people's experiences with the Otherworld can be better understood as being part of a larger *natural* process. This is, of course, speculation, but the weight of evidence demands at least speculation if not a theory. Too many people, besides those whose experiences are noted in this book, have come into contact with this Otherworld for it to be dismissed out of hand.

For example, take the experiences of Whitley Strieber. Strieber was and still is a best-selling fiction author, with many books and several films to his credit. He had experienced contact with Otherworldly creatures over many years of his life. When he eventually went public with his experiences, he was derided by people who simply stated these things didn't exist and therefore couldn't happen. Furthermore, he was misinterpreted by a belief system known as UFOlogy which, on the basis of very little actual evidence, concluded he had been visited by extraterrestrials. Both these perceptions of Strieber's experiences are locked into a small period of history and limited ways of looking at strange happenings. Strieber wisely ignored his detractors and the misguided who tried to turn him into a guru, and after years of encounters with his visitants, concluded:

> We are experiencing a perceptual anomaly that is sufficiently ambiguous and intense that it demands explanation. It is something that human beings have been experiencing for a long time. It is the cause of religion, of mythology, of folklore. Presently it is the cause of the 'alien abduction' belief. What is really behind these experiences? We are. This is a human thing.[7]

If the gods are equally locked into the land and the mind, and most importantly a mixture of the two, then things begin slowly to fall into place. All the alleged contacts between people and the Otherworld, from Celtic tales to the present day, can be understood. For where people once contacted powers, primal nature spirits and gods firsthand, and interpreted them in the same way within a community belief system or tradition, this eventually gave way to experiences with individual fairies and elementals, and latterly it seems the gods now contact us in the most up-to-date way they can.

In the end, the truth is all about how we choose to see and live in this world. We think we have set out the evidence for a system of belief and practice which, although here we have concentrated on the Celtic tradition, is

7 *UFO Brigantia* magazine, 50, November 1991, quoting Whitley Strieber's 'Communion Newsletter', April 1991

fundamental to all people and all areas of the world. We must not lose it at our peril. But the final word must go to our informant from Yorkshire, in whose company we first began our quest.

You ask me to form conclusions. I cannot. This thing is not concluded as long as there are people alive and a world to live in. Even when the people have long since disappeared, there will be no conclusion. Believing or not believing in any of what I have written or experienced is immaterial. At this precise moment we have the privilege to be the eyes of the world. Whether or not we choose to open them, to look and see what is really there is entirely up to us. In the great scheme of things I don't suppose it matters, but the world is an intensely strange and beautiful place and we would be indeed stupid not to.[8]

INVOCATION

You that create the diversity of the forms
open to my words
you that divide and multiply it
hear my sounds
I make yield league to you
ancient associates
and fellow wanderers
you that move the heart
in fur and scale
I join with you
you that sing bright and subtle
making shapes that my throat cannot tell
you that harden the horn
and make quick the eye
you that run the fast fox and the zigzag fly
you sizeless makers of the mole and whale
aid me and I will aid you

I make a blood pact with you
you that lift the blossom and the green branch
you who make symmetries more true
you who consider the angle of your limbs
who dance in slower time
who watch the patterns
you rough-coated who eat water
who stretch deep and high
with your green blood
my red blood let it be mingled
aid me and I will aid you

8 Pers. comm., 1995

I call upon you
you who are unconfined
who have no shape
who are not seen
but not in your action
I call upon you
you who have no depth
but choose direction
who bring what is willed
that you blow love upon the summers of my loved ones
that you blow summers upon those loves of my loves
aid me and I will aid you

I make a pact with you
you who are the liquidness of the waters
and are the spark of the flame
I call upon you
you who make fertile the soft earth
and guard the growth of the growing things
I make peace with you

you who are the blueness of the blue sky
and the wrath of the storm
I take the cup of deepness with you
earthshakers
and with you the sharp and the hollow hills
I make reverence to you
round wakefulness we call the earth
I make wide eyes to you
you who are awake
every created thing both solid and sleepy
or airy light
I weave colours around you
you who will come with me
I will consider it beauty

Robin Williamson, 1970

FURTHER READING

Bord, Janet and Colin, *Mysterious Britain* (Garnstone Press, 1972)
– *Earth Rites* (Granada, 1982)
– *Sacred Waters* (Granada, 1985)
Branston, Brian, *The Lost Gods of England* (Thames & Hudson, 1974)
Briggs, Kathleen, *A Dictionary of Faries* (Penguin Books, 1976)
Clarke, David, *Ghosts and Legends of the Peak District* (Jarrold, 1991)
– *A Guide to Britain's Pagan Heritage* (Robert Hale, 1995)
Dames, Michael, *Archaic Ireland* (Thames & Hudson, 1992)
Devereux, Paul, *Places of Power* (Blandford, 1990)
– *Symbolic Landscapes* (Gothic Image, 1992)
Ellis-Davidson, H. R., *The Lost Beliefs of Northern Europe* (Routledge, 1993)
Evans-Wentz, W. Y. *The Fairy Faith in Celtic Countries* (1911, republished by Colin Smythe, 1977)
Garner, Alan, *The Weirdstone of Brisingamen* (Collins, 1960)
– *The Moon of Gomrath* (Collins, 1963)
Green, Miranda J., *The Gods of the Celts* (Alan Sutton, 1986)
– *Dictionary of Celtic Myth and Legend* (Thames & Hudson,1992)
Hutton, Ronald, *The Pagan Religions of the Ancient British Isles* (Blackwell, 1991)
McCana, Proinsias, *Celtic Mythology* (Hamlyn, 1970)
MacManus, Dermot, *The Middle Kingdom: The Faerie World of Ireland* (Colin Smythe, 1959)
Merrifield, Ralph, *The Archaeology of Ritual and Magic* (Batsford, 1987)
Palmer, Roy, *Britain's Living Folklore* (David & Charles, 1991)
Phillips, Guy Ragland, *Brigantia: A Mysteriography* (Routledge & Kegan Paul, 1976)
– *The Unpolluted God* (Northern Lights, 1987)
Ross, Anne, *Pagan Celtic Britain* (Routledge & Kegan Paul, 1967)
– *The Pagan Celts* (Batsford, 1970)
– *The Folklore of the Scottish Highlands* (Batsford, 1976)
– *A Traveller's Guide to Celtic Britain* (Routledge & Kegan Paul, 1985)

CONTACT ADDRESSES

If you have enjoyed this book and wish to find out more about Celtic belief and tradition, folklore and alternative archaeology, you can write to some of the organizations and magazines in the following list. Some of them specialize in a particular area of the British Isles you might visit using this guidebook:

The Centre for English Cultural Tradition and Language (CECTAL) Sheffield University, 9 Shearwood Road, Sheffield S10 2TD. Began life as the Survey of Language and Folklore in 1964 and is now the principal repository for material on all aspects of English language, folklore and cultural tradition.

Folklore Journal (publication of the Folklore Society) Membership details from University College London, Gower Street, London WC1E 6BT.

Ley Hunter PO Box 92, Penzance, Cornwall TR18 2XL. International journal of Earth Mysteries and Geomancy.

Mercian Mysteries Bob Trubshaw, 2 Cross Hill, Wymeswold, Loughborough LE12 6UJ. Earth Mysteries research in the Midlands.

Meyn Mamvro 51 Carn Bosavern, St Just, Penzance TR19 7QX. Ancient stones and sacred sites in Cornwall.

Northern Earth John Billingsley, 10 Julibee Street, Mytholmroyd, West Yorkshire HX7 5NP. Bi-monthly journal of the Northern Earth Mysteries Group.

INDEX

PICTURE ACKNOWLEDGEMENTS

PHOTOGRAPHS

Alan Chattwood p. 100; David Clarke pp. 26, 54; Derby Museum and Art Gallery p. 96; Richard Holland p. 142; Kendal Museum p. 84; Craig Chapman p. 18; Manchester Museum p. 91; Doug Pickford pp. 47, 48, 79; Andy Roberts p. 112; Sheffield City Libraries p. 13; Dorothy Tate/Dalesman Publishing p. 103; Vanessa Toulmin p. 37; Yorkshire Archaeological Society p. 125.

ILLUSTRATIONS

All line drawings by Craig Chapman, except p. 149 by Melanie Dodd.

MAPS

All maps by Venture Graphics